THE
CHARACTERS
OF LOVE

THE
CHARACTERS
OF LOVE

*A Study in the
Literature of Personality*

JOHN BAYLEY

BASIC BOOKS, INC.
Publishers   New York

© 1960 by John Bayley
Library of Congress Catalog Card Number 61-5551
MANUFACTURED IN THE UNITED STATES OF AMERICA

CONTENTS

ACKNOWLEDGEMENTS

Permission has been granted to the author and to his publishers by John Farquharson Ltd. on behalf of the estate of the late Henry James to quote passages from *The Golden Bowl*. Permission has also been granted by *The New Statesman* to quote the anonymous Clerihew 'The sins of the Prince and Charlotte'. The extract from W. B. Yeats's *Ancestral Houses* is taken from the *Collected Poems* of W. B. Yeats published by Macmillan & Co. Ltd.

CHAPTER ONE

THE
WORLDS OF LOVE

CHAPTER ONE

The Worlds of Love

IT HAS become difficult to imagine literature without love. Since the Middle Ages the two have depended on each other more and more and their interrelation is now as complex as civilization itself. Almost every work of the imagination includes the idea of love, and the phrase 'Art and Love'— like the phrase 'Art and Morals'—would imply a division which has no necessary significance and a contrast which there is usually no point in suggesting. Like the idea of morality, the idea of love is included as naturally in literature as it is in life, and it is apt to seem unreal when it is considered in isolation; we feel it can be intelligently discussed only when it is embedded in the events of a situation or a story. Treatises on love belong to the past, to the ages of *Ars Amatoria* and *De L'Amour*—the time for such formal expositions of the great topic seems to have gone by. Anthropology and psychology have broken it down and subsumed it under their various headings. Where it survives, its own unadorned vocabulary is apt to sound too sententious or too practical, suited only to 'Musings after Plato', or 'The Hindu Love Manual'. Even as a literary kind the love story, as such, has disappeared into that robust and elemental region of fiction where ancient classifications still flourish, and where heart-throbbing romances vie with epics of the war or of the turf.

All the same, the best as well as the worst imaginative

3

writing is still largely about love, for everyone recognizes that—whatever you call it—sexual love is for most people the most interesting and memorable aspect of life. It is this kind of love, *eros* rather than *agape*, with which literature is most concerned, and we shall be considering here the kind of works which are more or less wholly love stories. There is a good deal of love in *Vanity Fair* or *The Brothers Karamazov*, but they are not in any obvious sense *about* love, as are—for example—*Troilus and Criseyde* or *The Tale of Genji*.

Fashions in love tend of course to produce the most whole-hearted literary treatment of it, yet love—like sex—is always with us in some form. And though one could hardly attempt to define love and sex separately, for the best as well as the worst novels are also about sex, the two are in fact fairly clearly differentiated in literature as in life. 'Is it love, or is it just sex?' is the kind of query which illustrates in a simple form our response to the two ideas, and a blurb like—'This is a tale of love and lust in the Welsh valleys'—shows that the average novel makes the same sort of distinction. We may stress the interrelation of the two, pointing out with Havelock Ellis that love may be defined as 'lust plus friendship', etc.—and for various reasons our vocabulary is precise rather than consistent, as is shown by the current upper-class usage of 'lover' and 'to make love'. None the less the dualism remains firmly established in our literary consciousness. Fascinating as it is, the idea of sex is predictable, what is entailed upon us and shared with everyone else: even its vagaries have something mechanical about them, as if pre-destined in the working of the flesh. It is the part of desire which is concerned not with the individual but with the attribute and the gender, while love is preoccupied with the uniqueness of the individual. Besides, sex is ridiculous—lyrically, touchingly, or gruesomely so, but always and in-

escapably ridiculous. Love is not. And love has fewer pre-
conceptions than sex, for the latter is a highly conservative
instinct operating in terms of stock responses. We desire in
obedience to the fixed patterns of our sexual imagination,
but we fall in love because we are really seeing another
person. Love is the potentiality of men and women which
keeps them most interested in each other. Whatever psy-
chologists may say, literature and society agree that it was
love that made Beatrice an object of worship to Dante, that
united the lives of Catherine and Heathcliff in *Wuthering
Heights*, and that led John Betjeman's subaltern to find a
delirious and terrifying magic in everything connected with
Miss Joan Hunter-Dunn. Love is not only more complex
and intriguing than sex but more absorbingly local. And so
it is still invoked and exploited unremittingly in novels and
plays and poems; authors lay down the law about it not less
than men in saloon bars; while the titles on book jackets
continue to offer us love's varieties, its purposes, its prospects,
its progress, its languages, its faces, its wilder shores, and its
worlds.

Indeed, love becomes so universal a theme because of the
remarkable variety of its worlds. Nothing else that unites
human beings so emphatically declares at the same time the
plurality of living; love may sometimes give us a marvellous
degree of mutual consciousness but it also reinforces our
most intractable solipsism. Many things remind us of the
alien worlds that impinge upon our own but the experience
of love does so most forcibly of all: it resembles the artist's
gift of revealing other worlds to us, but it also resembles the
artist's limitation before the actual separateness of things.
For when we say that art can never quite achieve the actuality of life we should also remember that no *one* world—
either in life or in art—can wholly contain the reality of any

other world: art is only in the position that we ourselves are usually in *vis-à-vis* other aspects of living. Anyone who reads a *Times* Leader, an article on golf or gardening, or a manual of diplomacy, childbirth, trench warfare, or sanitary engineering, cannot fail to be struck—and perhaps either depressed or delighted—by the self-sufficiency of these worlds, which excludes any real awareness of what is going on in the totality of things. And yet this sort of obliviousness is only a parody both of our own limited awareness of other worlds and of the almost equally self-sufficient and exclusive worlds which writers present to us. It is a commonplace that the world of Turgenev is quite different from that of Thackeray, and neither is discernible in Stendhal's; the world which Gide wrote about cannot be found in E. M. Forster, and Shelley has no reality in Keats.

No one was more aware of this than Proust, who made a creative principle out of it. But because he made a principle he necessarily ignored the fact that like most truths it is not as true as all that. The opposite, as I have already implied, is also the case. Though life and experience are infinitely segmented they are also a unity, and in this sense Shakespeare and Racine are at one with each other. Art itself has often made use of the paradox involved, and any painter or poet who drew inspiration from neo-platonism, for example, could give it graphic illustration. As W. H. Auden observes, 'the old masters' never forgot that everything takes place on its own, encompassed by other events who ignore it or are unaware of it, and by their successful display of this knowledge they achieve on our behalf a degree of superiority in vision, uniting opposite worlds by artifice on one canvas or in one poem. Piero's *Flagellation* unites the world of a club conversation with the world of the suffering Christ, and the risen figure in his *Resurrection* inhabits a different dimension from that of the huddled sleepers below. Though Botticelli's Venus is unconscious of the twined arms that link the zephyrs, her presence gives their private embrace its meaning. Art has chosen the theme of love both to indicate human separation and to unite humanity again. While a poet like Spenser uses the landscape of love to show how the universe and ourselves are joined by a great divine mythology into an harmonious whole, Proust takes it as the best way of investigating the natural history of human plurality, and of asserting how mutually uncomprehending are the worlds in which we live. But both their attitudes, however capable of being 'true', are essentially doctrinaire. Much more important than any system he may go on to create out of the idea of love is the deep initial sense of human *differentiation* which it offers to the writer. Love need not necessarily unite us, or keep us apart, but it always reveals the differences between us.

In this chapter I shall try to analyse some contrasting approaches to the theme of love. The most important thing I hope to show is that an author's success with this theme is closely linked with his attitude towards his own characters—that author, in fact, is best on love who best loves his own creations. Now this 'love' of an author for his characters is no doubt a pretty ambiguous conception. Obviously he does not feel the more straightforward kinds of *eros* towards the men and women he creates. Nor are we to be concerned with the kind of author whose interest in the subject is ethical or evangelical; who believes that love will save the world and who creates characters in the furtherance of this idea—I certainly do not want to make a plea for love as not only the panacea for human ills but as the universal solvent of the writer's problems. What I understand by an author's love for his characters is a delight in their independent existence as *other people*, an attitude towards them which is analogous to our feelings towards those we love in life; and an intense interest in their personalities combined with a sort of detached solicitude, a respect for their freedom. This might be—indeed should be—a truism, but I suppose it to be one no longer. The writers whom we admire to-day do not appear to love their characters, and the critics who appraise their books show no sign of doing so either. For a writer or critic to show delight in a character would seem to-day rather naive, an old-fashioned response left over from the days of Dickens or Surtees. Characters, it seems, are no longer objects of affection. The literary personality has gone down in the world.

Why has this happened? So much depends on what is meant by character and personality, and how highly it is regarded in life or in literature; and I shall try to analyse in the course of this book some different conceptions of personality and different ways of treating it. My main fields of enquiry will be a poem, a play, and a novel. All have in common the theme of love and all seem to me to be *tours de force* of personality: it is the characters in them who make possible their special sort of success. The importance of personality in relation to the novel and to the subject of love is revealed in *Othello* and in *Troilus and Criseyde* with a singular aptness: its significance can be explored in them more effectively than in most novels, but by much the same methods, and our understanding and appreciation of both poem and play seem to me to gain immensely from a discussion of them in the context of the novel. Their full richness is only revealed against its psychological background, and together with *The Golden Bowl* they offer us a full and complex conception of the characters of love. Moreover all three works seem to me to have been misinterpreted in various ways, or assessed too narrowly, and in addition to using them for the purposes of

8

my main thesis I shall attempt an independent appraisal of each—I am sure that the best way to do this is to emphasize their common theme and discuss them in relation to it. In the concluding chapter I shall offer some reasons for the decay of personality in literature to-day.

Three Approaches. (1) *The Dogmatic Tradition*

Proust provides a good starting-point for a discussion of approaches to the theme of love because his enormous novel is the ultimate development of what might be called the dogmatic tradition. The assumption of authority is very much a part of French literary tradition; their classics bear out the popular assumption that the French take love extremely seriously and have the most decided views about it. It is the destiny of a French author to record not merely a criticism of life but a verdict on it, and Proust is the inheritor of this superb self-assurance, which pronounces on love through the lips of La Rochefoucauld or St Simon, Stendhal or Benjamin Constant, and whose characteristic statement opens: 'When we are in love, we . . .'. Proust is of course well aware of this, and the convention of his intellectual out-look is that he has an exact appreciation of every kind of human assurance, and the reasons for it, but that he himself knows better than to be so self-assured. He collates the despotic perceptions of his literary forebears, and it is not too much to say that his attitude to life—and to love as the most revealing aspect of it—is formed by his feeling for the essential differences between literary worlds, particularly French ones. 'The types of the human mind are so varied, so opposite,' he tells us, 'not only in literature but in society, that Baudelaire and Merimée are not the only people who have the right to despise one another mutually.' The world of the

9

passions in *Carmen*, that is to say, is so different from that of the *Fleurs du Mal* that it is in the nature of things that either author should find the other's vision false because it is so unlike his own, which his whole being tells him to be true. And just as when we read *Carmen* we are carried away for the moment by a truth which quite excludes the one we are offered in the *Fleurs du Mal*, and *vice versa*, so in life we are convinced by the reality of the experiences we habitually have, by the tyranny of the reality that actually confronts us —in the shape of a person or an occurrence—to the exclusion of other possibilities of experience.

So, says Proust, we all share, in varying degrees, the privilege of these authors. The exclusiveness of our responses confers on all of us the right of total incomprehension where other responses are concerned, and thus—by a rigorous and appropriately Gallic logic—the right to despise them. What Proust does not say but leaves to his whole *oeuvre* to proclaim on his behalf is that this contempt is not for him; he is therefore by implication a writer of greater scope and profundity than Merimée or Baudelaire, and he further intimates that if this is so it is because he stands upon their shoulders. 'A fool sees not the same tree that the wise man sees,' said Blake, but it was reserved for Proust to reveal that no two wise men see the same tree either, and if this revelation makes him of necessity wiser than they it is only because he understands the conviction with which each thinks *his* tree the essential one of the universe!

Such, at least, in Proust's ideal stance, his preferred attitude to the world and to his work, and he achieves impressive results by it. But he omits to point out that, whatever their differences, Merimée and Baudelaire share the same tradition of self-assurance—the tradition that nurtures that characteristically imperial opening—'When we are in love...' And

Proust himself shares this tradition. *He* does not invite us to despise his world should we find it not to correspond with our own experiences—his confidence is such that he does not even envisage the possibility of this happening. Having pointed out that no world of love, or of anything else, is comparable or compatible with any other world, he settles down like the great French author that he is to give us, with sublime exhaustiveness, the truth about the whole issue. Like every sensible man, he knows that this business of different worlds does not apply to him. The hopelessly competitive plurality of our experience does not deter him from imposing a rigid system of rule and generalization upon it: he writes as if the plurality were suspended for his own benefit or ceased to matter in practice once its theoretical existence had been pointed out. And it is very proper, we feel, that he should not have been deterred, for the greatly systematic author, like the scientist, achieves results precisely by admitting diversity with one half of his mind while rigorously imposing unity with the other. It is the same paradox with which art and intellect have always been familiar and have always made use of for their various purposes, and his attitude towards it is in a sense a measure of Proust's greatness.

All the same, this confidence in the universality of an approach which the author has already shown to be inevitably limited and exclusive is likely to make his readers feel a trifle dubious, and in fact we frequently find ourselves carried away by the clarity and brilliance of one of Proust's *aperçus* while remaining in deep if incoherent disagreement with it. The penalty of the gap between outlook and method is that it provokes in us a similarly double response: our disagreement is the result of his method rather than his vision. He tells us that 'love, and the suffering that is one with it, have, like drunkenness, the power to make everything seem different to us'—or—'it is desire alone that makes us interested in the existence of another person'—and we feel that it is not truth that confronts us so much as assurance, weighted by so many oracular centuries and yet unaware of the partiality imposed upon it by its form.

While expounding in a different context, Proust himself gives a very good reason for this fatal weakness of the dogmatic tradition. He quotes a remark on love by La Bruyère, and goes on to say that 'those who properly appreciate it' are unable to repeat it without a feeling of immense satisfaction, but that they are 'reduced by their very enjoyment to being part of the enlarged consciousness of another'. It remains simply a thought of La Bruyère, and as such unconnected with those 'negatives' from the reader's own experience which are properly his own, but which only the artist in him can ever 'develop', or alternatively which can only be developed by communion with a very different kind of writer—a Shakespeare or a Montaigne perhaps. The relation between the writer's consciousness and the reader's is complex but highly important, and it is precisely the feeling that everything has been done without us, that our co-operation was not required, and that the words stand there in assured isolation inviting us to take or leave them, that make us distrust the critiques of love not only of Proust but also of a whole tradition of French writers. To perceive and to analyse the workings of love is not to convey to us what it is actually like, and a few paragraphs from *La Princesse de Clèves*, or even from Raymond Radiguet's close imitation of it, *Le Bal du Comte D'Orgel*, may move us more than the whole case history of Charlus and Morel or of the narrator and Albertine. It is not that Madame de Lafayette is more profound than La Rochefoucauld and Proust—her outlook is obviously much more limited and personal—but that she

seems to enlist our response to the truth of her vision: however contrived her muted effects may be they always
appeal directly to our own feelings.

(2) 'The Whole Truth'

Medicine is one of Proust's favourite illustrations of our
chances of discovering truth. Obviously it is not an exact
science, and none of its present theories are true, but we
should not make the mistake of supposing from this that they
never will be. Error is the inspiration both of feeling and of
reason, the mainspring of society, and Proust's massive collation of error is a way of getting at the truth, though the
tradition he works in makes it seem too direct and despotic
a method. What Aldous Huxley has called 'telling the whole
truth'[1] is much more indirect, but as regards the treatment of
love it is often an equally recognizable approach, and equally
deliberate. It is an affair of contrast, not of errors but of tones
and responses, and truth is seen as a kind of Hegelian syn-
thesis arising from the opposition. Huxley's chief example is
from Homer, where the effect may be supposed to be
natural and not sought after. The sailors of Ulysses, after
losing several of their number in the passage between Scylla
and Charybdis, land on an island and prepare their supper
'with their usual skill' before shedding tears at the loss of
their comrades. In the crises of real life, says Huxley, hunger is
more potent than grief and takes precedence over it. But the
deduction is not really justified by the example. Granted that
Homer's account is both moving and true to life, it is quite
possible to imagine an equally moving scene—in Homer or
any other great author—in which events were reversed. What
is true for Homer's sailors or for Dante's Count Ugolino is not

[1] *Tragedy and the Whole Truth* in the essay collection *Music at Night* (Chatto &
Windus).

true for Heathcliff in *Wuthering Heights*, who starves himself to death in his bereavement: and art persuades us of this ultimately because life could indeed take either direction. In detecting 'the whole truth' in an episode of Homer's narration, Aldous Huxley is in fact only coining another despotic formula and recording a preference for a particular possibility in life and a particular effect in art.

And yet romance has always seemed to invite its opposite, and there is logic in the fact that this kind of opposition should be hailed as conveying the whole truth about love. Cleopatra is not only an unfathomable seductress but a vulgar and jealous woman; Tom Jones loves Sophia yet it does not stop him going to bed with Lady Bellaston. But in Shakespeare and Fielding the quality of these contrasts is in their naturalness and their lack of contrived emphasis: they do not have the status of 'a moment of truth', any more than the episode in Homer's narrative. The inevitability of the great author's vision creates its own truth, while the lesser contrives it out of method and convention. Gerhardi makes his lovers in the moonlight suddenly aware of the smell of burning fishbones; Henry Green, and Huxley himself, contrast a human love scene with one among baboons or peacocks; in Nabokov's *Lolita* the hero's exaltation after a night of love is tempered by the fact that he has had no bowel movement that morning. As this last instance shows, tellers of the whole truth can be very precise indeed in their efforts to span the reality of a situation by means of congruity, or incongruity. But the method is too mechanical: it strikes us as a sort of mental compulsion, like the fashion for conceits or for puns.

On the other hand, Matthew Arnold comments on the 'absolute reality'—(a criterion very similar to Huxley's)—of the moment in *Anna Karenina* when Levin cannot find a shirt to get married in. 'The author has not invented and combined it, he has seen it; it has all happened before his inward eye and it was in this wise that it happened'. And indeed Levin's distraction about his shirt, mingled with his exalted state of mind as he contemplates love and marriage, does seem much more real than the previous examples because there is no device of combination or effort of insight involved, but only the calm with which great art displays the fullness of existence.

This is not to say that fullness or inclusiveness for its own sake cannot be as tiresome an approach as contrast, and as disingenuous as the social aim of 'absolute frankness'. The idea that the whole truth can be told now and should be told, down to what contraceptives were used and what was the abortionist's fee, is deeply falsifying, for these matters not only acquire a disproportionate importance in the telling but are also so facile to record. It is easy for Tolstoy to let us know that Anna practised birth control after the doctor had told her she could have no more children, but it is exceedingly difficult for him to intimate—as he does—how this throws light on the nature of her love and jealousy, and at a further remove on the relations of Stiva and Dolly and of Kitty and Levin. The author who sets store by frankness may involuntarily submerge the true relevance of his theme, as Lawrence does in *Lady Chatterley*, and frankness necessarily ignores the idea of decorum, the treatment of a theme in the way most suited to its nature. Kipling, for example, writes about patriotism and family feeling in an indecorous way, and the same effect of indecorum or vulgarity is often produced by an author who appears to attach the same degree of significance to everything he tells us. This is particularly true of the theme of love when the author feels he owes it to us to go into things properly and not to be squeamish. Most novelists to-day would feel it their duty to be quite explicit about the occasion when Anna and Vronsky first made love; how dressed or undressed, on what sofa or in what bed, with what subterfuges as regards maids, valets, chance visitors, etc., and with what degree of physical satisfaction. But Tolstoy gives no impression either of avoiding these things or of being interested in them, for neither do Anna and Vronsky themselves. Where Flaubert would have meticulously described the setting as something quite separate from the lovers' feelings, Tolstoy is only concerned with what really impresses itself at this moment on Anna and Vronsky: how her sense of guilt craves for forgiveness so that she seems —absurdly and movingly—to plead to Vronsky himself for it; and how he sees her as the murderer sees the corpse of his victim, which can never again act of its own accord, a frightful and solitary responsibility. Tolstoy convinces us that in the whirl of these feelings the lovers are completely unaware of the trivia of the seduction, and thus persuades us that his account is the true one. The details will come in later and they will be many and singular, but one of the secrets of Tolstoy's success is that he never allows them to triumph over the response of his characters to a given situation. After the great scene when Vronsky and Karenin weep at Anna's bedside in a passion of mutual forgiveness and love, everything goes back to normal; nothing is settled, and the old resentments and desires prevent a reconciliation; all is gossip and depression; but this aftermath does not invalidate the feelings of the great scene and had no part in them while they were real. For Tolstoy the feelings of his characters come first. But if Thackeray had written the seduction scene all the circumstances would indeed have been essential to the truth as he saw it, and as his characters saw it; he would be genuinely hampered by having to omit them and we should feel they had been omitted.

Matthew Arnold comments that to an English person Anna's passion for Vronsky seems a little too abrupt and un-reflecting, and that she gives way to it with a total disregard for the kind of commonplace caution, and the scruples of duty or mere self-interest, that the reader might expect. He implies that beside every love-affair which takes place there is another which does not, and that Tolstoy makes us in-sufficiently aware of this truth. But however it may have seemed to a Victorian, we are more likely to be struck to-day by the way in which Tolstoy both convinces us of the inevit-ability of Anna's response, and also of the parallel reality of other kinds of love which are as different from it as chalk from cheese; while at the same time he suggests the things that do not happen or happen only in fantasy—the passionate avowals, the acts of forgiveness and renunciation, good Dolly's touching nostalgia for champagne and sin. Both Tolstoy and Chekhov have the power, which seems to us characteristically Russian, of conveying the frequent incom-pleteness of an experience in love, its tendency to start and stop without benefit of intensity and form. Chekhov's story, *The Lady with the Dog*, peters out at the moment when the lovers—had they been Anna and Vronsky—would have been on the point of freeing themselves from their 'intoler-able situation'; and Chekhov's account seems to us no less true and fated than Tolstoy's.

Proust's world, on the other hand, depends on all its denizens knowing their duty to the emotions, and its coherence would collapse if the Baron de Charlus were at any time to decide, on reflection, that his latest passion was not really worth all the trouble and expense. It is necessary to Proust that all his characters absorb themselves passionately in their *milieu*; there must be no inertia, no genial torpidity of habit, no sign of that great body of experience in which indifference prevails, where instead of feeling things we do not feel them, and where we do not even analyse our mistakes and failures. Proust insists that everyone shall join in the game; the smallest inconvenience and the most minor disappointment must be felt with intensity, and the thought of missing a party must throw everyone into despair. Even M. de Cambremer, that dim and delightful country gentleman, is made to *turn pale* when the unexpected departure of the narrator causes some small social arrangement to be upset. The humdrum aspects of social living which Jane Austen understood so well, like the 'comfortable meal, uniting dinner and supper', in *Mansfield Park*, which 'wound up the enjoyments and fatigues of the day'—these are firmly ignored by Proust. Or rather, as in the case of M. de Cambremer, they are not so much ignored as transformed by over-emphasis, denatured by a touch that is too acute. As much as his use of the despotic approach, his insistence on the equation love = suffering = understanding, the weakness of Proust on love is his need to emphasize everything that he touches, a need that is bound up with his whole *raison d'être* as a writer. In his world one only retires from the struggle with love and society to die of a mortal illness or to write a book.

(3) *The Romantic World*

Tolstoy has no world in the sense that Proust has, or in the sense in which Proust himself remarks on the worlds of other writers. But this may be only to say that Tolstoy's world is uncannily like our own, whereas Proust's resembles our observation of the worlds of other people: Tolstoy is like life and Proust is like a vision of it, a vision which we may or may not wish to enter into and share. And this is what we should expect, for with all his skilful collation and his view that the nature of truth is best represented by misunderstanding, Proust is in the end a romantic writer, a writer with a world of his own.

We might expand this conception of the romantic by reference to Coleridge's distinction between the two kinds of creative imagination—that of Shakespeare, which enters into living things and reveals their own life; and that of Milton, which draws them into its own ego and gives out its own unique version of them. Either imagination may of course work through the most elaborate artifice, craftsmanship and style—Milton and Yeats have as much of these as Shakespeare and Chaucer—and the writers, and in particular the novelists, of any period are likely to show something of both faculties. But the Miltonic imagination is essentially the romantic one. The basic contrast involved here has been formulated in a number of ways and remains recognizable in all of them. Keats, who in terms of this dualism had the most unromantic temperament of any poet, echoed the idea of the Shakespearean imagination in his phrase 'negative capability'—the power of creating without having a vision of one's own. Writing about Tolstoy,[1] Isaiah Berlin brilliantly restates the position in terms of the proverb, 'the fox knows many things but the hedgehog one big thing'. Tolstoy was a fox who was always trying to be a hedgehog, a remarkable combination—(to revert to Coleridge's examples)—of Shakespearean novelist and Miltonic sage. And no doubt Tolstoy's greatness, like Keats's great promise, has much to do with the tension between a vivid awareness of things, sensations, people in themselves, and an urge to unite them in one meaningful vision of a world.

[1] Isaiah Berlin, *The Hedgehog and the Fox. An Essay on Tolstoy's Theory of History.*

It is in this sense that the true romantic (if we can agree to call him that), is not 'hovering', as Keats put it, is not divided, but has his own exclusive mood and world. He may not think of it as exclusive; his adoption of it may be quite instinctive, as instinctive as the Shakespearean grasp of, and delight in, difference. His great power is to give us a new way of looking at things; his great danger is predictability. At the best he liberates and at the worst he imprisons. Often he does both, one after the other, and then a further liberation becomes necessary; for romanticism is like ideology, with which it is historically so much identified, always on the move and always appearing in fresh forms. One might say that the most revered aspect of romantic genius has become correct *anticipation*—knowing imaginatively what is likely to happen next. Ezra Pound once called writers—(*all* writers, which shows how romantic were his assumptions about literature)—'the antennae of the race', and the phrase suggests very well a continual groping forward in response to the intimations of Rousseau, Nietzsche, or Stendhal. But it is difficult to see in what sense Shakespeare and Tolstoy are 'antennae'. They do not tell us where we are going and what we are going to be like, except in so far as they imply it by telling us what we are and what is always present to us. Our preoccupation with the romantic flair for prophecy is shown by our critical appraisal of various writers in terms of their special relevance 'in Our Time', a phrase which has come to convey our inability to take an interest in anything that does not immediately concern us, or to look at things for their sake instead of our own.

John Osborne's play, *Epitaph for George Dillon*, provides an instance of this kind of romantic imprisonment which is all the more revealing for being so obviously trivial. The hero is particularly infuriated by a picture of ducks in flight,

which hangs in the living-room of the house where he
lodges—he refers to them as 'those blasted birds'. We need
not concern ourselves with the reasons for his hatred of such
symbolic *petit bourgeois* objects and how this is worked into
effective drama: what is significant is his refusal to see anything except as it affects himself, so that we are trapped inside
his vision of life. The play exists creatively inside this vision;
it cannot show us why the hero should respond like this, or
intimate that there might be pathos and even beauty in the
picture of the ducks, why it hangs there and what it means to
its owners: the play shouts at us with all its force that they are
'blasted birds' and that is an end of the matter. In a grotesque
way this shows how much alive still is the old argument of
Wordsworth and Coleridge about nature. Wordsworth
wanted to think it was outside himself, a real and responsive
presence which interested and comforted him and which he
might love. Coleridge, more rigorous and more perceptive
but as convinced as any romantic that his own experience
was universal, knew that nature and the world were inside
himself.

> *We cannot hope from outward forms to win*
> *The magic and the life, whose fountains are within.*

Coleridge's is by far the more influential attitude, and is still
tacitly taken for granted as a premise of romantic creation.
The ducks have no existence, they cannot possibly impose
themselves upon the hero's consciousness and become something to remember for years with tears. The fountains within
tell him only that they are blasted birds, an attitude which
we may find either oppressive or liberating but which the
strength of the play compels us in any case to share.

This single-mindedness is the obvious thing about
romantic visions of love. Instead of 'the whole truth', or a

demonstration in the despotic manner, the romantics give us a view of the subject whose success depends not on authority or profundity but on their confidence in themselves, and the extent to which they can make us share their view. They have the gift of anticipation, and can hit off to a marvel an aspect of love which preoccupies a particular society and age, or is just going to preoccupy it. When Stendhal portrays the see-saw infatuation of Julien and Mathilde in *Le Rouge et Le Noir*, or Lawrence describes the gruesome relation of the young couple in *St Mawr*, we recognize the force of the thing at once—it strikes the note of the age. And the romantic vision is equally good at getting inside the world of the haunted, obsessed, or self-tormenting person: it presents such a world with complete conviction. We are not the less convinced by Phèdre because no other possibilities enter her terrible world; and we do not feel that Clarissa's preoccupation with Lovelace is too morbid or Jane Eyre's with Rochester too crude. We suffer a willing suspension of our sense of other things and other minds. The only drawback is that the conviction and the imaginative power that makes the vision persuasive ends by making it seem incomplete. After a ten-year interval we have changed but Clarissa and Jane Eyre have not. Their intensity remains, and perhaps their power to move us as we were moved before, but they have not, like the greatest figures of the imagination, gathered 'strength of life with being'.

This is one of the reasons why the romantic vision is always changing, surfacing as it were in some new part of the consciousness in order to repeat its surprise and illumination; and the reason, too, for our idea of the work that speaks to us and that speaks to us in a new way, so that one often hears such a comment as 'I dare say Tolstoy is great but he *says* nothing to me'. Dostoevsky's Myshkin and Stavrogin do indeed

speak to us, while a character like Stiva Oblonsky in *Anna
Karenina* simply *is*. We may delight in his existence but he
tells us nothing. Like Lucio in *Measure for Measure*, whom he
curiously resembles, he has the extreme naturalness of someone who can tell society nothing significant about itself;
criminals, saints and madmen may do so, but not Stiva; he is
emphatically not a man 'of our time'. He seems as involuntary a product of Tolstoy's mind as a boil on the sage's body,
and though there were no doubt deep affections and a half
grudging collusion between Tolstoy and such men as Stiva
—('he both sees through and admires' as Henry James said of
a similar literary relation)—there could be no place for Stiva
in Tolstoy's moral vision, for the mere existence of Stiva
makes it impossible for that vision to achieve its ideal reality.

There is nothing mysterious about the way we receive the
romantic message—we receive it in the head, in the most
conscious and questing part of ourselves. The paradox of the
romantic vision is that though it is often directed towards the
dark and mysterious places of human desire and experience,
its appeal is that of darkness made visible: the pleasure of its
reception is as cerebral as mathematics, and may well lead us
to reflect that it is the artificial that is truly mysterious and
not the visionary. 'Lord Bacon was a poet,' claimed Shelley,
making a significant gesture of solidarity with the great
methodologist. Nothing could be more intellectually
straightforward than Blake's doctrine of his Four Visions,
and how transparent is our reception of Wordsworth's
Prelude or *The Sorrows of Werther*—the story of a poet's
imagination, or of his youthful anguish, turns out to be as
simple as ABC. The figure of Stiva is by contrast as enigmatic as a Ming vase—there seems nothing discoverable
about the art that produces him. Even David Copperfield is
a mystery. And how immediate and mysterious is our

reception of the experience of Hamlet, or even of a single line in the play like—'Since my dear soul was mistress of her choice' . . As many critics have found, romantic insights are to a great extent wasted on Hamlet. For as a character he *exists*; he is supremely natural—nature in this sense, as Dr Johnson pointed out, being the highest effect of art—though of course he is not *clear*.

And one might almost say that romanticism, if it is to make its novel impact successfully on our consciousness, knows that it cannot afford not to be clear. The epiphany, so to speak, of a romantic writer is never a difficult task: nothing is easier than to show why D. H. Lawrence is a great writer but it is exceedingly hard to show why Sir Walter Scott is one. The difficulty of showing it is in fact the reason for the assumption, in circles where a writer like Lawrence's greatness is taken for granted, that Scott is not much good. He has no unity or intensity of intelligence— Bernard Shaw declared in a famous *mot* that his intellect was even less worthy of respect than Shakespeare's—and his creative world is all muffled, obscured and diversified by prudence and worldliness and the deep conflicting fascinations of the past. Unity and intensity of intelligence is what Lawrence supremely has—the way they shine out is indeed 'too divine to be mistook'—but it makes his world of love more strangely and purely abstract than that of any other great author. The more intense and urgent it is the more it is a world inside the head. *Women in Love* and *Lady Chatterley's Lover* offer us, paradoxically, relations between men and women of an almost totally cerebral kind; their sense of themselves and of each other is a nightmare of mental awareness. They are quite lacking in the ordinary acceptances of contiguity. No doubt Lawrence yearned—as what Romantic does not?—for an end to this tormented lucidity and for the state of perfect mere being in which an animal lives; he yearned for men and women to live harmonious, mutually uncritical lives; he detested the highly selfconscious ethos of the Cambridge and Bloomsbury of his day, in which every 'independent little state of consciousness' wished to live as and for itself. But his obsession with the contrast between what he called the 'mental' and the 'phallic' consciousness strikes us as an intellectual prison out of which his imagination cannot break. He cannot leave the ideas alone, and their tyranny increases the mental effect, so that the 'phallic consciousness' seems a hyper-intellectual, hyper-aesthetic affair, making *Lady Chatterley* one of the most inflexibly highbrow novels ever written.

Of course Lawrence had far too much humour and good sense, as well as intelligence, not to realize all this, but he saw too that for him there was no way out: he was fully committed to the romantic rôle, to be the antennae of society as he saw it. 'I do think art has to reveal the palpitating moment or the state of man as it is.' In a letter to Dr Trigant Burrow, the theorist of the 'societal instinct', he shows his sense of the prison of the ego. 'There is no repression of the sexual individual comparable to the repression of the societal man in me, by the individual ego, my own and everybody else's. I am weary of my own individuality, and simply nauseated by other people's.'[1] 'I sit in my crow's nest of a soul,'[2] he had written in an earlier letter, a phrase which strikingly echoes the great romantic egotists who surveyed the world 'from the dread watch-tower of man's absolute self'. His perception of the 'societal' was from the solitude outside, and from this solitude he castigates us for leading our own separate lives. Kipling has a far more natural sense of 'societal' man, and—what is more important—a natural delight in the unselfconsciously tribal

---

[1] *Letters*, p. 685.   [2] Ibid., p. 347.

society. Lawrence was fully aware of the anomaly. In another letter he writes: 'How to regain the naive and innocent soul—how to make it the man within man—your "societal"; and at the same time keep the cognitive mode for defences and adjustments and "work"—*Voila!*' In the face of these penetrating comments Dr Leavis is begging the question when he states that in Lawrence—and almost uniquely in Lawrence—the man and the artist are one. If the idea of the artist is to mean anything in this connection it must surely mean the capacity to fashion a bridge across these gaps, the power of forgetting them in creation or of creating from them so many and varied viewpoints that they no longer matter. Leavis's claim for Lawrence's 'wholeness' is very sensibly denied by Lawrence himself; he knew that the instinctive and societal man was not the 'cognitive' man who produced the 'work', who spoke with such clarity and who beheld with such brilliant insight what he called 'the real fighting line', the battle between separate egos, men and women, in the modern world.

Lawrence's apprehension of the external world, particularly as it appears—'slips idly from him' as it were—in the *Letters*, does indeed strike us as one with the humour and good sense, the shrewdness and stillness, that are so much there, and which themselves lie behind the relevance of judgement about books and people which Leavis so justly claims. His description of a snowscape ('the sun lies bright on the field, like the movement of a sleeper'), followed by a *scène de famille* of magical warmth and ordinariness that reminds us of Tolstoy, ends with the words, 'Well—life itself is life'. Here indeed the artist is the man, but it is not the artist of the novels, 'the man speaking to men'. It is strange that a writer with such a power of rendering life and delight and of delighting us, too, with flashes of grotesque rhetoric like 'Why should one howl when one's grandfather is pushed over a cliff?'—should be so incapable, as an artist, of delighting in the existence of another person. To do so would have been to surrender the dominance of his own intellect and the incorruptible ferocity of his idea. But surely if the realization of love means anything it must mean precisely that: our delight in the existence of another person? It is difficult to see how the reality of love could be conveyed in any other way, but to follow Lawrence here is to follow a blind man. The nature of animals he can intimate to us marvellously (though we may catch a Swiftian note in his contrast between horses and men), and in his poem *Fish* he emphasizes that the fish is quite independent of him and outside him; he can only admire and wonder and not understand it.

I didn't know his God.
Which is perhaps the last admission that life has to ring out of us.

Why is the fish more privileged than the man? The letters will provide many examples of tolerance to individuals and good sense about their differentness, but as 'man speaking to men' Lawrence claims to know what gods human beings have, or should have. Once more Lawrence the human being is removed from Lawrence the seer, for whom Man—like Fish—is one idea. His conception of character, in which he made use of the proclamations of Marinetti, is based on the principle that Man should be Man as Fish is Fish. 'What is non-human [i.e. non-individualized] in humanity is more interesting to me than the old-fashioned human element. ... I don't care so much about what the woman *feels*—in the ordinary usage of the word. That presumes an ego to feel with. I only care about what the woman *is*. ... You mustn't look in my novel for the old stable ego of the character. There is another ego, according to whose action the individual is unrecognizable[1]' It is the same idea as the mental and the phallic consciousness—the mental ego is our individuality, the phallic is our status as man or woman. We see then why Lawrence the author cannot admit, far less delight in, the individuality of a particular person. He is confined to his idea of human beings, and it is this idea which depersonalizes his characters. He implies that the traditional observation of men and women is trivial. 'Life is more interesting in its undercurrents than its obvious, and E. M. [Forster] does see people, people, nothing but people, ad nauseam.'[2] But the dilemma for the artist is hopeless—as Lawrence later tacitly admits—when he is forced to create with his abstract and 'cognitive' intelligence men and women as elemental and societal beings, without the aid of personality—what makes us different instead of what makes us alike—to bridge the gap between himself and them.

Lawrence's view of love corresponds to his view of Man—'the one quality of love is that it universalizes the individual'. Of this all one can say is that it is exactly half true. Love also makes the individual more unique, and it is this property upon which literature has most effectively and successfully seized. Anna may love Vronsky for his maleness, but what makes her passion real to us is that she loves him because he *is* Vronsky, tall, handsome, with very white teeth, bald on the top of his head, etc. How much we learn of Othello and Desdemona, and of their love, when he says,

> *She loved me for the dangers I had passed*
> *And I loved her that she did pity them.*

[1] *Letters*, p. 198.   [2] Ibid., p. 606.

Beside this, Birkett and Ursula are bloodless ghosts. In renouncing human variety and removing individuality Lawrence is left not with human 'wholeness' but with mere mind and will. Like Blake, he moves further and further into his abstract universe. But of course it is quite unhelpful to suggest what Lawrence was not, and imply that he should have been other than what he was. We must take what he gives us, and what he gives us is marvellous; we cannot look at one of his stories without being completely taken by the sureness and authority of his medium. In *Samson and Delilah, Daughters of the Vicar*, and many more, he makes the reality of a generalized male or female feeling, or an inarticulate passion, almost intolerably convincing. He makes us aware of human beings as we might be aware of lions into whose cage we had been suddenly thrust. But it is a hit-or-miss affair; if his successful characters are as vivid as animals his failures are as abstract as ghosts. And he fails when—as in *Women in Love*—he has to stay with a character and conduct it through the actual business of a human being's life. Lawrence sees people's lives much as he saw history, (and his letters reveal him as an ardent historicist), in terms of movements and tendencies, twilights and dawns, deaths and rebirths; and this metaphorical abstraction has no effect of continuity—the continuity of *The Old Wives' Tale* gives much more impression of what people actually feel their lives to be like.

It must however be clear by now that where our subject is concerned there is no peace between the prophet and the artist. The romantic approach to love is not an approach but a manifesto, and Lawrence more than any other romantic tells us that if we are for him with reservations we are really against him. To write about him with attempted neutrality is to be like Chaos in *Paradise Lost* and 'by decision more embroil the fray'. His romantic genius is at its most apparent in this compulsive taking of sides: it is the idea which divides, and the romantic ideas are the most potent of any. We might remember in this connection T. S. Eliot's remark that Henry James 'had a mind so fine that no idea could violate it'. Artistry, the desire to make rather than to say, imposes its own neutrality, and one might add, reciprocally, that James would never have dreamed of violating with an idea the mind of his reader. For him the normal method of romantic communication was not possible. 'Make something fine in the medium most suited to you', was his prescription, and then see what it will say; and one odd consequence of this is that *The Golden Bowl*, for all its obvious artificiality, is yet a far more physical and less abstract novel than *Women in Love*.

It is the artist as neutral, controlling and balancing a romantic ideal of love, that makes *The Great Gatsby* so impressive and memorable an achievement, though FitzGerald has of course not a tithe of Lawrence's creative genius or even his sureness of style. FitzGerald shows us the practical effects of something very like Lawrence's 'impersonal' view of love. Gatsby, we are told, is a 'Son of God'—he has a romantic ideal of himself and his destiny. The narrator, on the other hand, is a Lockwood-like figure, his participation in the romantic dream tempered by a nature indolent and speculative. In contrast to Gatsby's dedicated pursuit of money, he has found himself on the stock exchange because that seemed the thing to do: he adopted passively the rôle expected of him, the very opposite of an ideal of the self. Though he is so caught up in it, there is something unforceful and meticulous about the way he tells Gatsby's story. Moreover nothing escapes his sympathy, which is as fasci-

nated by the sight of Alice and her husband through the
window, brooding over their crisis together with a kind of
absent-minded indivisibility, as it is by Gatsby's answer to
the suggestion that Alice does indeed love her husband—
'Well, it was just personal'. Gatsby conceives of himself and
Alice as united in some absolute way by his ideal, like Lawrence's unions in the blood between Daphne and Count
Dionys, or March and the young soldier. The idea that Alice
is also a girl who lives and loves in conformity with individual habits and attachments has no significance for him,
but it has a great deal for the narrator and author. Gatsby is
'a hero of our time', but like Lermontov's Pechorin his
significance as such is presented to us from different viewpoints which relate it to the enduring background of human
nature. It is this background of unchanging feelings which
Lermontov movingly conveys at the moment when the old
Captain meets Pechorin again after a long separation and
with tears in his eyes tries to embrace him, only to be met
with the cultivated indifference of the contemporary *âme
damnée*. In both cases the balance of viewpoints helps to
make the book a masterpiece.

Such a balance also avoids the impression we often get
from 'one man' treatments of love—it is very noticeable in
Dostoevsky—that the author is surreptitiously excited by a
particular aspect of his theme but not prepared to share this
excitement openly with the reader or admit the part it plays
in the genesis and *raison d'être* of the work. Freud observes
that Dostoevsky's imagination of love only comprehends
lust and sado-masochism, and we certainly feel that he has
something to hide, that he is creating—possibly indeed with
the 'sanity of true genius'—a structure involving ideals like
forgiveness and self-sacrifice in love out of some obsessional
knowledge that he does not want us to see clearly, but which

he cannot help continually suggesting. Other authors dissemble their excitement by means of a kind of romantic frivolity, lingering with humour and ridicule over what attracts them most strongly. The urge to deride where one loves, like the urge to hate, is no doubt always with us, and the humour of Stendhal and Byron is an integral part of their obsession—indeed Byron keeps an ironic eye on the legend which drives him forward, and postures as much in humour as in passion. Without this frivolity, exciting oneself sexually by what one writes about often appears as a kind of pornography, particularly if there is also the intention or the willingness to excite the reader.

But the muse of pornography is blindfolded and cannot tell beforehand what will excite desire. The most unlikely things may do so, the most obvious things may not. Most readers of Elizabethan poetry would agree that *The Faerie Queene* is a much more effectively pornographic poem than Marlowe's *Ovid* or *Venus and Adonis*, though Marlowe and Shakespeare are straining every nerve in their efforts to be curious and wanton. Spenser on the other hand does not seem to distinguish in his imagination between what appeals to his sense of beauty and what appeals to his desire: his lady-haunted landscapes are also prowled by the quite unselfconscious beasts of his sexual imagination. Moreover he does not distinguish between provoking desire in the reader and delighting and instructing him. There is a moral here for the author who wants to convey the idea of love, as well as to transmit sexual excitement. The most unlikely things may do it. Hardy, like Spenser, has an extraordinary knack of creating for us the situation that symbolizes desire—Sergeant Troy showing the sword exercise to Bathsheba, or the moment in *A Laodicean* when the lovers stand by the embrasured railway tunnel—

and he also catches the moment, it is sometimes the same moment, that conveys the knowledge of love. In both cases, though, emotion and symbol are unselfconscious; they are not proclaiming themselves for what they are, but merge—unlike the symbolic set pieces of Lawrence—into the undifferentiated background of human activity and response to living.

Conceptions of Character

This has obviously been a very arbitrary survey of an extremely wide and complex field; the judgements are bound to seem perfunctory and important issues too rapidly glossed over. For any purposes except my present argument my categories and distinctions are probably as unreal as most of the abstract paraphernalia of literary criticism. But I hope that by now it should be becoming clear why I have passed over the three approaches to the theme which I have called 'the dogmatic', 'the whole truth', and 'the romantic', in favour of what might be called 'the neutrality of love'. This implies a mode of creation particularly necessary to love as a theme, because the idea of the artist as holding the balance between opposing forces—however much or little he may be aware of them as such—is one most clearly brought out by this theme. I have suggested that whereas we talk of 'Proust's world', or Richardson's or of Lawrence's, we cannot attach the same idea of exclusiveness to the world of Shakespeare or the world of Tolstoy—these worlds disappear as we enter them and become *the* world, our world. The world, the theme, the meaning, exist and yet do not exist: they are both inside us and outside. And this inside and outside effect is echoed by the characters that are drawn by the great neutral artist. 'Character', one might say, is what other people have, 'consciousness' is ourselves, and—as

Shakespeare's Troilus discovers—the lover is uniquely capable of feeling the difference between the loved person as an extension of his own consciousness and as a separate 'character'. Only occasionally do we appear to ourselves in the light of such a character, for our own consciousness seems free and unbounded and also neutral, aware of and acknowledging our own personal and moral characteristics but made independent of them both by its formlessness and by its isolation. We do not really think of ourselves as fat, kind, irritable, short-sighted, etc.—these are the qualities by which we are known to other people and which we may play upon and cultivate as a conscious *persona*. We do not even think of ourselves as necessarily a separate and special person, for—as Hume implies in his enquiry into Personal Identity—the uniqueness of our personal existence is itself an idea suggested to us from outside.

The great author can make us see his characters both as we see ourselves and as we see other people. Chaucer's Criseyde, for example, is both an unfaithful mistress and an open consciousness in the complexity of which—as we experience it—this description loses its power of definition. The charm, the infidelity, the facile emotion of Tolstoy's Stiva is for the most part seen from the outside, but it is very significant that as the book opens we *are* Stiva, waking up on the uncomfortable couch in the dressing-room, remembering the distressing scene with Dolly, and wondering—with no real apprehension of how our conduct looks to an outside judge —how the devil we are going to get ourselves out of this mess. Art achieves here a freedom of inner and outer vision which we can rarely experience in life, and which is very different from the romantic identification of hero, author, and reader in a common consciousness. The people we know in life may surprise us, like E. M. Forster's 'round' char-

acters, by behaving 'out of character', but we adjust ourselves to this by the same process of critical definition which
led us to form our original estimate of them: we say 'so-and-
so is usually feeble but I have known him to be unexpectedly
strong-minded'. The same process occurs at those moments
(so dear to Proust) when we receive an unexpectedly different view of so-and-so from a third party. But in no case can
we see so-and-so from the standpoint of his own consciousness, as Chaucer shows us Criseyde and Tolstoy shows us Stiva.
And yet these great feats of neutral creation have no appearance of method, the methods of collating character as Proust
does, or of trying to reproduce another consciousness. The
elaborate techniques of Joyce and Faulkner do not really
seem to slip us into the alien consciousness: they rather symbolize or totemize it. Molly Bloom's ruminations are a
symbolic extension of Joyce's own mind; even Gertrude
Stein's *Three Lives* is really a personal monologue. There is
an analogy here with descriptions of perceptual experience—
'on looking at this object we experience the sense-datum
red', etc.—where the philosopher is symbolizing what may
be supposed to take place in our minds. But the successful
creator of characters somewhat resembles the modern
logician in that he starts with the *fact* of consciousness and
personality: he does not attempt to symbolize their appearance or working. The search for techniques to portray consciousness ends with Mollys and Benjys who are as much and
as obviously hypotheses as 'sense-data', or the 'super-ego'
and the 'id'. How little we are concerned with an *idea* of
consciousness, for instance, in Defoe or in Boswell's Journals,
or—to take a modern example—Salinger's novel *The
Catcher in the Rye*. Presentation of the consciousness is
entirely freed here from any idea of its process, though it is
not of course freed from the isolation of a single awareness.

Criticism does not interest itself much to-day in the old idea of character. Where the drama is concerned we have quite stopped asking whether a character is 'convincing' or not, or discussing what he is 'really like'; and we more and more assume that the novelist, too, need not start out by making his characters like 'real life', but will subordinate their individuality to the general atmosphere and purpose of the work. We feel we should estimate them not in themselves but in relation to the kind of achievement the novel aims at. Seen in this way character becomes much less important, much more something for the author to manipulate to secure his main effect, and the author appears, so to speak, as a dictator rather than as a constitutional monarch holding the balance of power between the conflict of individuals in his work. The new view does not envisage a Falstaff, an Oblomov, or a Mrs Proudie getting *out of hand*, engrossing the dimension of the novel and having to be cut down to size. Even in Dickens, modern criticism emphasizes not the proliferation of character but the purposefulness of atmosphere—fog, prison, the streets of London, etc.— and the way in which the characters contribute to this atmosphere. On the new view of character a man with a wooden leg, say, is given it by the author not to individualize him but to reinforce a controlling theme—the impotence of modern society or something of the sort.

Criticism often takes for granted this subordination of character to the author's will and temperament. By implication it accepts the authority of the romantic imagination and the decline of the individual character to a shadowy and subordinate status. 'The real elements, of course, of any work of fiction,' says Edmund Wilson in *Axel's Castle*, 'are the elements of the author's personality ... his personages are personifications of the author's various impulses and emotions: and the relations between them in his stories are really the relations between these.' In the last chapter I shall try to analyse some of the implications of this pronouncement and relate it to our ideas about psychology and society, but for the moment it is enough to notice the fact: many forces are at work helping to dissolve the uniqueness of the personal existence, and 'the old stable ego of the character'. What unites us seems more significant than what distinguishes us: the distinguished man appears as a kind of Arnold Bennett dummy, with a set of eccentricities and a gold watch chain across his waistcoat. The novel becomes as subject as play or poem to the critical requirement of the work of literature as a single organism, a living entity, almost a living *person*.

The metaphor of something alive shows how the older idea of personalities inside a novel has been replaced by that of the personality of the novel itself. The life of a Lawrence novel, says Dr Leavis, 'is all significant life; not a scene, episode, image or touch but forwards the organized development of the themes'.[1] True no doubt, and admirable, but by describing the novels as 'dramatic poems' Dr Leavis implies a comparison with Shakespeare, and though what is true here about Lawrence would indeed be equally true of Shakespeare it would at the same time be misleading. From this description of Lawrence we correctly infer a self-absorbed world, a closed shop, a work of art with a life on its own; but if we say of a Shakespearean masterpiece that not a scene, etc., 'but forwards the organized development of the themes', it would be a limited truth which would need immediate qualification. We should need to go on to say that not an episode or touch or character but does not have its own separate existence and justification, its own

---

[1] *D. H. Lawrence, Novelist*, p. 151.

unmanipulated freedom. Shakespeare has it both ways and Lawrence only one. This is obvious enough, but it is worth emphasizing because the life of a Shakespeare play is so emphatically not, in Dr Leavis's sense, 'significant life'. It is clear that he understands here by 'life' the very reverse of a neutral and comprehensive vitality: by life he means what he thinks life should be like, what will fit in with the moral organization of living that he prefers.[1] 'Lawrence,' he says, 'stood for life, and shows ... a sure sense for the difference between what makes for life and that which makes against it.'[2] 'Life' is referred to here as a supporter might refer to 'The Church' or 'The Party'; the life of a novel, as opposed to the liveliness of its characters, would be a more acceptable criterion if life had not acquired in this context such a combative sense and such a censorious flavour.

But may not this moralistic mystique of 'life' be more than justified by the degradation of the old-fashioned idea of character? From the intense and curious apprehension of a separate being—('it was by loving them that he knew them,' said Henry James of Balzac's men and women, 'not by knowing them that he loved')[3]—it has sunk into the vast middle deeps of fiction, where it survives in a diminished and mechanical form and where the conventional character is observed rather than loved. In what indisputable masterpiece of to-day could we expect to find a character of such vitality that he established his right to existence—even to domination of his *milieu*—in the very teeth of his author's purpose? For the author to see a character with the vision of

[1] Another of the senses which criticism gives to the word 'life' is agreeably illustrated by Dr Leavis's treatment of Professor Elton's comment that 'George Eliot, while exhaustively describing life, is apt to miss the spirit of life itself'. 'For anyone whose critical education has begun,' says Leavis, 'this should be breathtaking in its absurdity.'

[2] *The Common Pursuit*, p. 284.

[3] *The House of Fiction*, Essays on the Novel, p. 77.

love is rare indeed; more often he is in love with his own vision and with his characters as projections of it; and the novel, Narcissus-like, comes to love only itself. But the great conventional character can only be created by love, by our delight in the existence of another person; and conversely, as I have been trying to suggest, the reality of love can only be conveyed through the medium of such characters. For in the hands of a master their existence enables us both to see them from outside and to feel what they are feeling, both to be aware of love as a phenomenon and to experience it vicariously in ourselves.

And this is particularly true of the three masterpieces which we shall be examining. I have brought them together because they seem to me supremely effective and moving love stories whose quality can best be brought out in relation to each other and to the theme of love. I hope it will be illuminating to discuss them in terms of the conventional characterization of the novel, for although one is a play and one a narrative poem their *genre* is less important than their theme, and in the case of *Othello* in particular it has distracted our attention from the real significance of the theme. Their achievement becomes more impressive and their status more clear if we realize, too, how decisive in all of them is the idea of a conflict of sympathies, the kind of conflict which can only be set up by an opposition of characters of the old kind. In each of them we are led to take sides, and by doing so we experience that inner and outer effect—the effect both of emotion and dispassion, of surveying and also experiencing —which I have suggested is the highest achievement of the neutral artist. And though all three are intensely localized in their varying ways they also have the quality of timelessness. Even in *Anna Karenina* we are more aware of the part played by historical and social circumstances in the larger issue of the story than we are in *Troilus and Criseyde*; although Chaucer is writing both of Courtly Love and of Christian belief he seems less involved in either than is Tolstoy in the implications of his tragedy—no doubt because Chaucer does not have a *personal* attitude towards the conditions of his time. I hasten to say that I do not for this reason consider Chaucer's poem better than Tolstoy's novel, any more than I would consider it better than *The Tale of Genji*, which seems to me wholly absorbed in its own convention: in bringing together my three works for comparison I am not claiming any absolute superiority for them over all other love stories.

None the less my interweaving of comparisons between them might seem at the moment as desperate as Fluellen's discovery that Monmouth and Macedonia are alike in that each has a river and that there are salmons in both. Henry James and Chaucer are not after all very obviously akin. But I can only hope that my purpose in relating the three will justify itself when we come to consider each in turn. The only other generalization that I shall make about them now is that in all three the strictest of forms contrasts with the broadest of implications. All three begin in a close artistic confinement and expand into the widest possible range of effect, a range which may again give us reason to reflect on the mysterious nature of great artifice. For artifice is their most obvious common principle. *Troilus and Criseyde* and *Othello* are cunning adaptations, or rather transformations, of existing stories, and *The Golden Bowl* is fashioned with equal skill from the implications of a fragment of anecdote. These beginnings imply that it was not the original aim of the authors to lay down the law about love or to go deep into the human heart: the origins of their works secure them from pretension. We must also note that each is far more

controlled than most novels by a given precision and strict-
ness of form, for while *Othello* may have the subject matter
of a novel *The Golden Bowl* deliberately incurs many of the
formal limitations of a play.

W. P. Ker, who knew so much about many literatures of
many periods, long ago observed that the characters in
Troilus and Criseyde resemble those we meet in fiction, and
he has been echoed by other Chaucerian critics. But so far
as I am aware this resemblance has not been explored much
further. What precise qualities that we connect with the
novel are to be found in the poem, and with what particular
novels might a comparison be made? That the poem is a
great masterpiece is not self-evident to the modern reader
and can best be demonstrated by appeal to the kind of effect
with which he is more at home: and though any close study
of *Troilus* cannot fail to be indebted to C. S. Lewis's
masterly account of it in *The Allegory of Love*, he is chiefly
concerned to relate it to mediaeval literary development and
tradition, whereas our object will be to see it in the unlocal-
ized perspective of theme and novel.

To approach *Othello* in terms of the novel may seem to be
asking for trouble. Not only is it usually taken to be the
most simply and obviously dramatic of Shakespeare's
tragedies but the whole idea of discussing the tragedies and
their characters in terms of fiction is now very much
frowned upon. It is an approach associated with Bradley's
classic on Shakespearean tragedy, and though Bradley's perceptions are still respected his critical premises are not. They
are held to lead to the kind of query which Maurice
Morgann had raised a hundred years before in his essay suggesting that Falstaff was not *really* a coward at all—the kind
of query which L. C. Knights satirized as *How many Children*

had Lady Macbeth? But perhaps the time has come to ask ourselves whether this sort of query is really quite so absurd as it sounds. Its great virtue, as I shall try to show in more detail in the section on *Othello*, is that it takes for granted the scope and completeness of Shakespeare's tragic setting, and also his success in conveying the wider consciousness of his major figures as well as their dramatic and functional personality. There is a sense in which the highest compliment we can pay to Shakespeare is to discuss his great plays as if they were also great novels. Can one, in fact, ask an irrelevant question about the completely successful 'inside and outside' character? Of either the Ancients or the Moderns, observed Dryden, Shakespeare had the largest and most *comprehensive* mind, and one can be sure that somewhere in that mind the problem of Lady Macbeth's children would find its appropriate resolution.

It is quite true that a good performance of *Macbeth* does not need to suggest this kind of question overtly, and probably should not do so. The home life of the Macbeths is not an immediate concern of the actors and audience at any particular dramatic representation—they have other and more urgent matters to engross them—but it is certainly something that has its place in the totality of the work of art, and *Macbeth* would be a less great play if such queries about it were really not worth making. In *Othello* on the other hand, the same kind of query—for example, what was the real nature of the hero and heroine's love for each other?—has not only the same general relevance, the relevance that it would have in a great novel, but it has an immediate dramatic relevance as well. In *Othello* the domestic and the dramatic are one: the material of the novel is also, so to speak, the material of the play. And in spite of its speed and deceptive simplicity it thus becomes necessary to ask more, and more varied, questions about it than we need to do about the other plays.

For in the case of *Othello* it is particularly worth bearing in mind the probable relevance of four basic critical approaches to character in Shakespeare, all of which can complement each other. Iago, that much debated personality, will provide a simple example of what I mean. Our first approach to Shakespeare's scene and characters is like our approach to real life, or—by a slight extension of sophistication—to the novel. Seen in this way Iago appears as a malignant, envious, perhaps intelligent man, with a certain sardonic amiability it might seem, and a reputation for speaking his mind. We might wonder how much more there is to him, how old he is, whether he has succeeded in doing anyone down before— we might even speculate that he is consumed with jealousy, has an inferiority complex, or that he has homosexual tendencies. As in real life, these queries have an obvious fascination, and it may be that about Iago they are the most important kind to ask. Secondly, however, we can look at him from the standpoint of Elizabethan dramatic and ethical convention. Is he just the Elizabethan fashion of the Machiavel, coupled with those of the braggart soldier and the satiric clown? His soliloquies certainly show him in this formalized role. Thirdly, we can see him in terms of his dramatic function, and from this point of view his motives and character are unimportant; he exists in order to deceive Othello, and the actor must show him doing this both efficiently and realistically, for the plot depends on his slander being convincing enough to be believed. Finally we may see him in a metaphysical light, as an embodiment of the evil side of Othello's own nature, or as an emissary of the devil himself. These four approaches apply of course to the whole play as well as to the characters in it, and here the final one has a particular importance, for it takes note of the unique metaphysical personality of the play—the Othello-ness of *Othello* so to speak, or the Macbethness of *Macbeth*—their special atmosphere of poetry and meaning which is like nothing except itself.

Such approaches are, as I have said, complementary: with varying relevance and in varying proportions they apply throughout the whole Shakespearean theatre, rarely in conflict with each other and supplying us with a valuable index and reminder of its immense scope. It is a reminder that will prevent us, too, from making genuinely inadequate judgements about the plays, for the boundless charity of Shakespeare's imagination makes inadequate judgements more misleading than absurd ones—the plays thrive on eccentric interpretations but inadequacy shrinks them without giving any benefits in return. We shall not, for instance, be disposed to remark that *Measure for Measure* is weakened by the Duke striking us as 'a frivolous monster', because we shall remember that he is not only the controlling agent of plot and comedy but also that he presides over a play with a vein of the Morality in it, almost as a symbol of God's omniscience, as well as being a very human figure whose image of himself does not go undetected by at least one of his subjects and is impishly teased for our amusement. In *Othello* and *Measure for Measure*, more markedly in the latter, it is particularly worth bearing the four approaches in mind, because the articulation between the four *personae* of the main characters may seem a little disjointed and not, for various dramatic reasons, smoothly intermingling. Perceiving the claims of the four, and the possible gaps between them, will give us the clue to the full riches of these plays; whereas elsewhere in Shakespeare, most notably in the early comedies, one of the four may so dominate and simplify the dramatic world that it becomes unnecessary to weigh the claims of the others.

But the first is of course the master approach. Always in Shakespeare—it is the simplest measure of his greatness—we can fall back on the conventional or naturalistic idea of character, the character whose freedom and absoluteness of existence is displayed by the fact that we can say what we like about him and there is always something else to say. Such characters have a richness of selfhood which is both inexhaustible and immediately recognizable. What struck the admiring Stendhal so strongly about Shakespeare, in contrast to the great French dramatists, is the way in which his most minor figures have only to speak a few lines for us to know so much about them, far more than their dramatic status seems to require. It is something which English critics of Shakespeare have lately taken for granted to the point of forgetting altogether.

And the 'inside and outside' effect, which I have suggested shows the greatest art of character drawing, is continually used by Shakespeare to present the subtlest kind of dramatic conflict—the conflict between the indefinable interior man and the *persona* that is required of him by society, or imposed on him by his own will. In the history plays the conflict is often an external one: the anarchic, richly individual world of Richard II or Falstaff confronts the world of public necessities, the world of Bolingbroke and the Lord Chief Justice. And although in their heroic function Shakespeare's heroes are trapped to abide our question, they escape and are free in themselves. We see Henry V as person and as king, Hamlet and Antony as Prince and Emperor and as men who reveal to us all the strangeness of the individual's existence. But a word like 'conflict' is too facile to convey the inimitable space and ease with which Shakespeare secures this effect. Often it has no dramatic scale but is a quite uncovenanted minor revelation, as when the unfortunate recruit Feeble in *Henry IV*—seemingly only a type figure in a gaily satiric sketch of military corruption—discloses that he has it in him to wish to do his bit for king and country.

> *By my troth, I care not. A man can die but once: we owe God a death: I'll ne'er bear a base mind: an't be my destiny, so; an't be not, so: no man's too good to serve's prince; and let it go which way it will, he that dies this year is quit for the next.*

The 'inside' of Feeble is suddenly revealed as like the 'outside' of Henry V; and it moves us more, because it is the uncalculating and unapplauded inner man that speaks, making a sudden free space in the limits of the scene.

We are back to our starting-point here—the plurality of worlds that cannot be ignored by the eye of love. And in Shakespeare we are consummately aware not only of human differentiation but of the different worlds which are brought into co-existence in the play. There is a sense in which for Shakespeare poetry itself is an aspect of character. Consider Lear's vision of his kingdom at the opening of the play:

> *Of all these bounds, even from this line to this,*
> *With shadowy forests and with champains rich'd,*
> *With plenteous rivers and wide-skirted meads,*
> *We make thee lady ...*

This is The King's England, the gracious landscape of country life where retired majors in deer-stalkers are pottering with trout-flies. It is England seen through Lear's eyes. And it is a real world, not just a deluded vision: its undoubted reality gives all the more real presence to the figure of Lear himself.

It is also a delightful world—our imagination dwells with fondness on the denizens of those shadowy forests and wide-skirted meads. But it is one world only, and Lear is soon to discover the others that are superimposed upon it, and which will force their equal reality upon him—the England of 'poor pelting villages, sheep-cotes, and mills', the fields of 'rank fumiter and furrow-weeds'. We have the sense not only of two different places but of two different awarenesses, and the gap between the two: the relation between world and character is perfectly expressed.

What strikes us most strongly about this interrelation is the *expansion* that takes place, the quantity and quality of natural effects that are conjured out of the artificialities of dramatic form. And here we touch on the supreme pre-occupation of Henry James. A devotee of the theatre and its necessary economies, he is said to have once been introduced to a puppet show, which he watched with deep concentration and pleasure. 'What an economy of means,' he pronounced eventually, 'and'—with a deep sigh—'what an economy of ends.' So he might have murmured of Sardou or Sue, even of Racine himself. His ideal of a work of art was the closest compression of form with the widest expansion of meaning, and in the third section I shall try to show how *The Golden Bowl* attains this ideal.

LOVE
AND THE CODE:

Troilus and Criseyde

CHAPTER TWO

Love and the Code:

TROILUS AND CRISEYDE

A GREAT DEAL has been written about the origins of the
Code of Courtly Love. How much did it come from what
has been called 'Ovid misunderstood'—the earnestness with
which the Middle Ages perused and took to heart the elaborate but not wholly serious instructions of the classics? Did
the Saracen love poets carry into Spain and Provence the
literary image of a worshipped and idealized mistress? One
scholar assures us that only in Petrarch do we find a worthy
successor to their greatest poet, Ibn Zaydun, whose Laura
was a Princess of Cordova. On the other hand the Christian
cult of the Virgin is obviously connected with Courtly Love,
but in what way, and which came first? Is the whole movement really a religious aberration, a heresy like that of the
Cathars and Albigenses, one of the many sorts of other-
worldly mediaeval enthusiasm which became too literary
and too little localized to be persecuted and stamped out? Is
there a link with the Platonic ideas held by the poets and
philosophers of the School of Chartres before the Aristotelian revival of the 12th century? Or, to adopt a more
material hypothesis, was it simply due to the peculiar conditions of mediaeval society, especially in Provence, where
numbers of landless and unemployed knights, susceptible to

poetry and courtly usage as their northern counterparts were not, lived for months together in a stronghold presided over by a lady who became for all of them the focus of interest and emulation?

Probably all these explanations are true in part. The history of ideas abounds in marshlights which can be pursued to any distance and in every direction, and it is no more unreal to claim that love was invented in 11th century Provence than to say that a certain period saw the Dawn of the Renaissance or the Rise of the Middle Classes. But to call it an 'invention' is of course misleading: love was not invented in the Middle Ages so much as granted full recognition and honours, and we continue to honour a phenomenon which was thought of before—when it was thought of at all —as an illness or a divine affliction. The appearance of Courtly Love was singularly abrupt and local, but it has left an immense legacy of received ideas about sex and society— the idea of love at first sight, of fidelity and secrecy in love, of the lady being seldom or never at fault, most of all the superior status of the lover. Just as our day-to-day manners are the honourable detritus of all sorts of cults and affectations, jumbled and confused beyond any possibility of sorting out, so our behaviour in love has its more methodical and conscious counterpart in mediaeval practice.

Class fashions are sometimes extraordinarily persistent, particularly when they modify an instinct into a social form. Courtly Love made a gallant attempt to convert the more uncontrollable kinds of sexual feeling into the civilities of fashion and habit, and one consequence of this—as La Rochefoucauld noted—is that such feelings become more common; people have heard of love and therefore experience it, and by a social arrangement both its bliss and its anguish is brought within the compass of all persons of education and refinement. What has been a rare and often impressive visitation, setting the sufferer apart from his fellows, now becomes common, and there is a rush to expose oneself to the infection that used to be shunned.

Where literature is concerned this involves both loss and gain. As a subject to write about, love becomes much more interesting but also much less tragic. When pursued in this way instead of being the pursuer, love forfeits much of its legendary terror and awe but none of its fascination; once in its social cage the beast can be examined with comparative impunity and the curious may absorb themselves in every stripe on its flank and every variation of its growl. Its presence gives an interest and often a meaning to the business of civilized living, to social ramifications, customs and events, even to triviality and boredom. It becomes a sport, an aspect of culture, a means of passing the time; and it can be used to portray and give life to a social setting that without it would be merely dull. It creates the novel, and the novel in turn gives it new intricacies and new dimensions, of which the most significant is also the most fatal to tragedy; for tragedy depends on the existence and nature of the beast being universally recognized: in it there can be no question of what love is, what forms it takes, and who has really got it and who has not. The status of the lover in tragedy is never in doubt: he merely *is*, but since the 12th century made love into a social accomplishment, writers have become more and more interested in what he appears to be. In making the lover its most interesting citizen society destroys his tragic isolation and surrounds his predicament with possibility and query. From being the awe-inspiring exception he becomes the ambiguous and infinitely various rule.

In *Othello* the tragic idea of love is in conflict with the social idea. The hero's tragedy in love is connected with the primitive violence and simplicity with which Shakespeare invests him, and his lack of contact with love as a part of the social mechanism. Like Dido and Phèdre, Othello suffers his fate in isolation; none of them can be brought into the world of Courtly Love. But the tragic ladies whom Chaucer celebrates in *The Legend of Good Women* have become mere negative illustrations of failure and success in observing the Code. Under its terms unrequited love is an honourable estate, and Dido and Ariadne are not tragic victims of love's power but martyrs to a way of life which they embraced freely, knowing the rules and accepting the risks. They are dignified, respectable, and pathetic, and their faithless lovers are by contrast cads who have let the side down.

Moreover, as De Rougemont has pointed out, there is an interesting sense in which the heroes and heroines of Courtly Love are deliberately 'accident-prone', because the more crises and divisions that part them the more they will be able to glory in the strength and fidelity of their love, and the more love itself will increase by the absence of habit and consummation. When nothing else keeps them apart Tristan and Iseult sleep with a drawn sword between them, and their only true rest is the *liebestod*, in which fulfilment cannot be followed by anti-climax. But what makes this passion touching rather than tragic is its essential conformity. Like the young men of Rousseau, Goethe, and the coffee-bars, perhaps even like the churchgoing gentry of the 18th century, Courtly Lovers were paying tribute to a spiritual convention of communal life, a fashion which might be mechanical but which might also be fruitful enough to breed and transform itself in the individual imagination. Out of this very tradition of civilized love the Romantic movement is able to recreate the old tragic darkness. Heathcliff and Catherine in *Wuthering Heights* in many ways resemble Tristan and Iseult; they cannot live together and do not want to, but they are a part of each other and must be united in death. Yet what was approved and conventional in the 12th century has become splendidly isolated and rebellious in the 19th: the solitude of tragedy has again asserted itself.

This solitude none the less helps to make *Wuthering Heights* more limited in scope than *Tristan*; compared to the medieval legend the novel is a *cul-de-sac*. For the great strength of Courtly Love is its ability to absorb into its given topic any number of contrasting personal and social attitudes—the topic goes through social and literary history like a snowball, enlarging itself constantly with the changing idioms of civilization. Courtly Love is never in the least out of this world; its tendency is always to humanize and anthropomorphize, and allegory—as Professor C. S. Lewis has so superbly and comprehensively demonstrated—is its natural mode of expression, a way of feeling that merges into a method of describing the feeling. First love—the first interchange of eyes, the first sound of the loved one's voice—is represented as a shot from Cupid's bow, on the receipt of which the hero of *The Romance of the Rose* swears fealty to the God of Love. Palamon, the Courtly Lover of Chaucer's *Knight's Tale*, becomes a casualty in exactly the proper manner.

> *And therewithal he bleynte and cried 'A!'*
> *As though he stongen were unto the herte.*

Oddly enough it is precisely this irrepressible tendency to allegory which gives the literature inspired by Courtly Love its complexity and ambivalence of tone. The tone of Chaucer's couplet already conveys a hint of the fact that nothing is more natural for the allegorist than to combine the moving and lyrical vision of Cupid's arrow in *The Romance* with the delighted and comic vision of Dan Cupid thumping the sufferer with his bird-bolt under the left pap. This gift for responding to the same moment and the same emotion in such different pictures helps to fertilize our whole descriptive tradition of the feelings. And it is of great importance that the pictures can be set side by side to enrich each other—indeed the first seems actually to be ennobled by the comparison and the second to gain greater piquancy; the allegorist's art seems to ensure that there is nothing mechanical in the contrast, no merely negative juxtaposition for effect of the full moon with the stink of fish. And the art requires a fuller and gentler human understanding than can be registered, in the tragic compass, by an abrupt change of mood. The famous metaphysical alternation of levity and seriousness is usually a much cruder thing. Donne could write a line which conveys the electricity of love at first sight with a swifter shock than any number of Cupids and arrows.

By our first strange and fatal interview ...

But when he wants to relax, change the tune, and generally stand his emotions on their heads, he can only be ribald or heartlessly clever. Donne's response to love is like a knife where Chaucer's is as blandly absorbent as a sponge. And Donne's tragic outlook results in significantly the same contrast that we find in the ancient world—the awed magic of *Qualis nox fuit illa ...*, or the cheerful animalism of Ovid and *The Golden Ass*. For the real interest in the subject which results in subtlety and sympathy we must go to the literary tradition which began with Courtly Love.

Just as the novel of manners depends on a complex social set-up, so the literature of Courtly Love draws its variety and sophistication from the elaboration of the Code. The difference is, no doubt, that the novel makes use of manners which are current and widely observed, whereas—although we have no exact means of knowing—the literature of Courtly Love celebrates an idealized state of affairs, helping to make it more actual by assuming that it already exists. Nature's tendency to imitate art was strong in the Middle Ages, but it seems likely that the imitation was always limited and imperfect and that only a very few people really lived by the Code. But this very discrepancy helped to bring out an aspect of literature which again looks forward to the novel—the enjoyment of perceiving the difference between an ideal state of affairs and a down-to-earth one, and in presenting two separate versions of reality. *The Parlement of Foules* is a simple instance of this kind of sophistication. Chaucer uses the common convention of the love-debate, held by birds and presided over by the Goddess Nature, who together with her omniscience has a personality shrewdly suggested by her response to the avian *lumpenproletariat*.

> *Nature, which that alwey had an ere*
> *To murmur of the lewednesse behynde,*
> *With facound voys seyde, 'Hold youre tonges*   [eloquent
>   *there!'*

When they settle down to discuss the problem, the goose earns the contempt of the courtly birds by opining that if his lady won't respond the lover should look elsewhere. The turtle dove appropriately urges the duty of fidelity, 'though that his lady everemore be straunge'. The duck retorts that unrequited love is a contradiction in terms—'daunseth he murye that is myrtheles?' 'Out of the donghil cam that word!' exclaims the indignant falcon, classing all these down-to-earth birds with the owl who cannot see in the heavenly light of love. The aristocratic basis of the Code is obvious here (just as it will be, *mutatis mutandis*, in Proust and Henry James), but none of the 'estates' is satirized: as C. S. Lewis has pointed out, the treatment is only in the most delicate sense ironical. It rather conveys a full and genial acceptance of differentiation, and a gratitude for the earthy commonsense of the world as much as for its noble and poetic ideals.

Just as Chaucer fully subscribes to the doctrine that the true height and sublimity of love is found in adherence to the Code, so he assumes that the greatness of literature stems from the due observance of rules and regulations and from the mastery of that mediaeval art of rhetoric whose requirements were as complex and exacting as those of Courtly Love itself. 'The lyf so short, the craft so long to lerne.' The famous line refers directly to love as well as indirectly to literature, and Chaucer's extraordinary sophistication and his no less extraordinary originality can only be understood in relation to these twin poles on which they turn. His 'perpetual fountain of good sense' flows from his agile but reverential attitude towards precepts and ordinances which often strike us as singularly lacking in freshness, intelligence or vigour. He is like one of those dolphins of which one reads in accounts of the great salt-water aquaria, disporting itself among an apparatus of tunnels and bars, a mechanical structure which is none the less essential to the brilliant and lively display. The game depends on sticking to the rules, and by their very indifference and rigidity, their unshakeable self-confidence so to speak, the rules encourage exhibitions of freedom and feeling. Indeed, as in a picture by Crivelli, these qualities seem to be conjured out of the very density of formal elaboration. *Expolitio*, for example, the use of repetitive illustration or decoration—*varius sis et tamen idem*—can be a deadly device, but when Chaucer uses it, as at the moment of the lovers' awakening in *Troilus and Criseyde* after their first night together, its very cumulative thoroughness gives the stanza an endearing and peculiar beauty; as if a divine resignation were mixed with the sense of many different lives, unknowing and indifferent towards each other.

> *But whan the cok, commune astrologer,*
> *Gan on his brest to bete and after crowe,*
> *And Lucyfer, the dayes messager,*
> *Gan for to rise, and out hire bemes throwe,*
> *And estward roos, to hym that coude it knowe,*
> Fortuna Major, *that anoon Criseyde,*
> *With herte soor, to Troilus thus seyde ...*

It is not only that here are three different ways of knowing that dawn is near, but that to one of them the sense of impending fate is also revealed—the terrible insecurity of human happiness that hangs over the whole poem. We do not know what *Fortuna Major* (which comes from Dante), exactly is: it may be Jupiter, or the sun itself, or some constellation whose significance only the learned could guess, but with it the suggestion of men's fates in their diurnal round comes before us with a great strangeness. The rhetorical parallelism helps to bring us back, as nothing else could, from the happy isolation of the lovers to a sense of the indifferent and multifarious world. And the advantage of skilful rhetoric is that its impersonal artifice gives no impression of a deliberate striving for such effects, a point well known to Yeats, who was a rhetorician as accomplished in his own very different manner as Chaucer himself. In *Ancestral Houses* there is an equally Crivellian splendour in the *Expolitio* (though Yeats would hardly have used the term):

> *Mere dreams, mere dreams! Yet Homer had not sung*
> *Had he not found it certain beyond dreams*
> *That out of life's own self-delight had sprung*
> *The abounding glittering jet; though now it seems*
> *As if some marvellous empty sea-shell flung*
> *Out of the obscure dark of the rich streams,*
> *And not a fountain, were the symbol which*
> *Shadows the inherited glory of the rich.*

A fountain or a sea-shell are two ways of viewing the riches from the past, but Yeats adds his own twist by preferring one to the other. A fountain is vigorous and alive: the shell, however beautiful, is hollow and lifeless. The two romantic images are not only as full of meaning as Chaucer's, but their Swinburnian *brio* contrasts with the vigorous simplicity of the syntax and is supported by it.

Even more important is the interrelation of rhetoric with the theme of love. With the famous 'Sin I fro love escaped am so fat', Chaucer adopts for the moment a duck or goose-like attitude towards the mysteries of love by the simple method of shunning the artful mysteries of rhetoric. And when he tells us,

> *Nas never pyk walwed in galauntyne*
> *As I in love am walwed and ywounde,*

he uses rhetoric in a deliberately 'misunderstanding' sense to give a special effect of naive fervour. He is an artful person

simulating the dazzled enthusiasm of an artless one. Rhetoric, in fact, cannot only be used to render many kinds of
feeling but many types of personality as well. We are so
accustomed to the portrayal of personality in fictions of all
kinds that we tend to take it for granted and to ignore the
technique involved; we ask ourselves whether a character
has come off or not, but in a naturalistic medium like the
novel we need not concern ourselves with the means
whereby one character is distinguished from another: description and dialogue are self-evident techniques which
work in the novel as they do in life. But in this sense Chaucer
is not in the least 'like life'; he is a poet of the greatest possible artificiality, and it is easy to overlook the amazing skill
with which he makes use of this very artificiality to create
human beings. It is the most striking aspect of his originality
and the least noticed. He implies that in conversation no one
is 'natural': that everyone, on the contrary, has his own
mode of artificiality. The process is strikingly similar to
Shakespeare's creation of personality in the idioms of
dramatic verse; and we might reflect that in our age, when
an idea of naturalness prevails, and when the modes of
personal artificiality have been reduced to the minimum in
social intercourse, it is not surprising that a play in verse
sounds hopelessly stilted. Speaking in verse reduces all the
characters of a modern play to uniformity, whereas for
Chaucer and Shakespeare it was a way of differentiating
them. In a modern verse play all the characters seem engaged
in trying to *overcome* the verse, not in making use of it.

The main principle of mediaeval rhetoric was decorum,
the fitting of the style to the subject; and its chief contrast
was between the High Style, 'as when men to kinges write',
with all tropes and figures appropriate to such high and
courtly matters as love and war, and the Low Style, plain

and unadorned for the racy tale or *fabliau*. Elaborate description was naturally confined to higher matters, and in his earliest poem, *The Book of the Duchess*, Chaucer describes Duchess Blanche, wife of John of Gaunt, strictly in the manner which convention dictated. In fact he arranges that not the poet but her husband shall describe her, in order to avoid any suggestion of indecorum, and the catalogue of her charms is carried through with somewhat spiritless deliberation. Professor Coghill compares this description with that of Alisoun, the carpenter's wife of *The Miller's Tale*, and points out how vastly more vivid and seductive a picture of a woman is the latter. The reason, though, is not because he is writing in artificial bonds in the first instance, and 'freshly and freely', as if he were Dickens or D. H. Lawrence, in the second. Both descriptions are highly rhetorical, but in describing Blanche he uses rhetoric with obedient literalness, and in describing Alisoun he stands it on its head and makes it perform a series of wholly unexpected turns and flourishes. Instead of using straight *descriptio* he creates her in a series of comparisons that make her as redolent and vivid as a farmyard. And this use of rhetoric really comes into its own when Chaucer uses it to fashion a character in terms of what he says and how he says it. Chauntecleer, the Franklin, and The Wife of Bath are as acoustically alive as Micawber or the Baron de Charlus. The regal dignity of a cock has occurred to everyone, but the particular quality of it can only be seized by a poet who has at his command an official idiom for relaying kingly manners and conversation. The point about Chauntecleer is that he is *like* a king, but yet is so absolutely a cock, and the absurd wonder of this is rendered to a hair by Chaucer's rhetorical transposition.

When the Franklin comes to tell his tale he specifically disclaims any knowledge of the art of literary expression.

I lerned nevere rethorik, certeyn;
Thyng that I speke, it moot be bare and pleyn ...
Colours ne knowe I noon, withouten drede,
But swiche colours as growen in the mede ...

Yet his tale is in fact full of rhetorical 'colours', transposed
into the world of estates and feastings with a kind of coarse
confident energy that exactly hits off his nature and makes
him appear before us as vividly as Mr Hastings, that archetypal squire described by the Earl of Shaftesbury. He
blandly takes over the literary deities, Phoebus and Janus,
and turns them into a likeness of himself, for he—like they
—is all-powerful in his own sphere:

The bittre frostes, with the sleet and reyn,
Destroyed hath the grene in every yerd.
Janus sit by the fyr, with double berd,
And drynketh of his bugle horn the wyn;
Biforn hym stant brawen of the tusked swyn,
And 'Nowel!' crieth every lusty man.

The inwardness of the joke is that the Franklin, though
ignorant and untrained, has a natural skill and vigour that
makes his use of literary manners far more forceful and
meaningful than is that of the Squire who preceded him.
The Squire, carefully nurtured in all the 'gentillesse' of the
narrator's art, is conscientious but uninspired, and his plod-
ding use of artifice is so much by the book that the Franklin
is at last moved to interrupt him, significantly in the middle
of one of those seasonal tropes which the Franklin himself
employs with such spirit. The disarming innocence of the
Squire and his simple belief in all the legends and supersti-
tions of the Courtly Code, is summed up in the formal

occupatio with which he disclaims his ability to describe the
oeillades and whisperings and sophisticated goings-on of
Court life.

> *Who koude telle yow the forme of daunces,*
> *So unkouthe, and so fresshe contenaunces,*
> *Swich subtil lookyng and dissimulynges*
> *For drede of jalouse mennes apercevynges?*
> *No man but Lancelot, and he is deed.*

Many of Chaucer's narrators would have produced that last
line with a flicker of deadpan humour, but we know that the
Squire means it in all devotion. Though Chaucer's creation
of personality is so economical and unobtrusive, it is also so
dexterously based on an agreed code that it gives us, as it
were, the confidence to interpret it. Rhetoric creates for us
the paradigms of personality.

We might try to sum up an extremely complicated
matter by saying that rhetoric, or style, when it is used as
Chaucer (or Shakespeare) use it, is a way of artificializing
and depersonalizing the author's play of intelligence, so that
it conveys to us the reality and the personality of different
kinds of world. Depersonalizing is the important point; for
in Donne and the Metaphysicals, for instance, we have the
play of intelligence all right, but proceeding undisguisedly
from one source, one vision, one personality. In Milton on
the other hand, whose virtuosity with formal styles can on
occasion be as great as that of Chaucer or Shakespeare, we
are sometimes unexpectedly aware of the departure of the
poet, the disappearance of his personality in the splendour of
an artificial transition. A famous and moving example occurs
in *Lycidas*, when after abusing the Laudian clergy in his own
voice he returns to the mood of elegy.

Return Alpheus, the dread voice is past,
That shrunk thy streams; Return Sicilian muse,
And call the vales, and bid them hither cast
Their Bels and Flourets of a thousand hues ...

This is the device called *Epanorthosis*, by which the rhetorician changes gear abruptly and yet smoothly from one tone
to another, and Chaucer is a past master at it, though we cannot be sure he would have called it by this particular name.
But that is the great strength of a poet who works hand in
glove with an accepted rhetorical idiom—he can employ all
the artificialities of style as unselfconsciously as we use the
artificiality of grammar. He covers a wide range of dramatic
feeling almost without thinking about it, even if—like
Milton—his native tone is rigid and single-minded, and
Chaucer's is far from being that.

Rhetoric of this kind cannot be imitated in an age
which no longer takes its premises for granted—the per-
sonalized rhetoric of the Masks and dramatic attitudes
which Yeats employs is a very different thing. Selfconscious dramatic variety, like that of Yeats in his Masks and
Browning in his Monologues, does not really strike us as
true variety at all: it is the same man trying on different suits
of clothes. If we compare a Browning monologue with any
of the Canterbury Tales we realize at once how great is the
difference between the conscientious putting-on of a personality and Chaucer's rhetorical creation of one. Browning
feels his way brilliantly into the claustrophobic aspect of the
individual ego: he imprisons us with a series of bores, which
is why the longer monologues are so hard to read. But
Chaucer's pilgrims are never boring, because they are not
only created by rhetoric but make use of it themselves to
diversify the tale and to get in touch with their fellows, and

hence with us. For them and for Chaucer, rhetoric and artifice are methods of intelligent and lively communication,
supremely suited to 'a man speaking to men'.

Moreover, for all his simplicity, the Squire's account of a
deceitful lover is both graphic and perceptive; his lore 'in all
that souneth unto gentillesse' is not to be despised, and
though the conventions which he accepts so readily give him
his comic side they also enable him to talk about love with
real point. Rather like Troilus himself—(and who could
imagine Troilus being satirical about anything?)—his native
simplicity is seasoned with the readiness for sophisticated
experience for which his education has conditioned him. His
intelligence may be quiescent but his sensibility is always on
the *qui vive*. To paraphrase E. M. Forster's desideratum of a
'developed heart', the Squire and Troilus have well-trained
hearts; their innocence acquires a special quality from their
theoretical *savoir-faire* in emotional matters. Significantly—
in view of the close but uneasy kinship between the servants
of Courtly Love and the servants of religion—they have
here something in common with young priests.

Nothing is more apt to produce an effect of pretension
than expertise in matters of the heart. We have all suffered
under the sensitive hero of fiction, and under the personal
intrusions of his even more sensitive creator. Chaucer's hero
and narrator do not make any show of perspicacity; they
are simply well-informed, as is Chaucer himself. For all its
length and formality, its air of a deeply-considered and
written *chef d'oeuvre*, his greatest poem has an air of unpre-
tentiousness which is quite incorrigible. It so clearly is not
'one of the few really significant works that have appeared
in Our Time'. A mediaeval reviewer would have praised it
warmly, no doubt, but even if such eulogies had been current he would hardly have used them, though he might have

referred to that 'right happy and copious industry' for which Webster was afterwards to praise Shakespeare.

Like so many works that suggest comparison with the novel, Chaucer's poem is no obvious triumph of form. He himself calls it a tragedy, and it conforms to the mediaeval definition of the *genre* as a story of one who first rises high on Fortune's wheel and is then cast down. But like all Courtly Love stories it is quite lacking in the qualities which we usually associate with tragedy. It is notoriously difficult to say just what these are, and probably there is no one characteristic of the poem—its humour, its helpless and unheroic protagonists, its homely detail, protracted catastrophe, or abruptly Christian palinode—which couldn't be found in some indisputably tragic work. Hardy's Tess is for most readers a tragic figure, but she is as confused and as unaware of the dimensions of her plight as are Troilus and Criseyde, and as little able to give it shape and standing in her imagination; the relations of Antony and Cleopatra are as detailed and as undignified as those of Chaucer's lovers; Langland and Dante are as orthodox in their conclusions. And yet Tess is, we feel, a 'natural' woman: her fate is herself in some sense, whereas the 'selves' of Troilus and Criseyde have been accepted by them from society. It is its artificiality which makes the poem so fundamentally untragic, and it is also its absence of discovery. No one concerned with the poem— neither characters nor author nor reader—finds anything out in the blinding tragic manner: there is no *peripeteia*. Possessing the tragic form, a great writer involuntarily begets on it some discovery which will bear the marks of his own mind, his own depth and quality of insight. And such individual tragic insight is all of a piece, or else crystallizes at points in the manner required by Matthew Arnold for his touchstones of 'High Seriousness'. Chaucer evades this requirement, and in Arnold's view was not up to it, but we will not necessarily agree that such tragic summings-up are self-evidently top of the literary class.

That Chaucer does not *discover* for us, that he does not concentrate the human condition in scenes or in moments which seem uniquely true and moving, has certainly nothing to do with religious conformity, or 'the child-like obedience' of the Middle Ages. Dante conformed. He put his old friend Brunetto Latini in hell, where by the precepts of the Church he belonged, but he made him more movingly and impressively a man than any figure in the *Paradiso*. Such moments do not occur in Chaucer, perhaps for the reason that his conformity—easy, discreet, and enigmatic as it is—already seems perfect freedom where Dante's does not. In Dante the struggle between the proud man and the great belief is obvious; in Chaucer there is no hint of it, and no hint of the revelation that might proceed from such a struggle. Whoever felt when reading him that sudden flood of awed comprehension that overwhelms us in so many great—and not so great—writers, the awareness of a truth about life which is suddenly supremely clear and important? He is one of the comparatively rare artists who seem to extend our consciousness, to increase its powers of observation and sharpen its capacity for delight, without revealing anything new to us and without even making us look at things in a new way.

More dependable and less apt to miss its target than revelation, this mode of extension also satisfies a more persistent need—to *live* in art as if we were living in ourselves. With Chaucer pictorial analogies are always tempting. In *Troilus* and *The Knight's Tale* we are as much at home as when our eyes wander round the Gozzoli chapel, dwelling on the great and lesser figures of the pilgrimage—Paleologus with his great plumed crown of golden wire, the liveried servants leaning on their spears, the background of folded crops and olive trees—in all the copious and meaningful presentation there is no element of strain, and it seems to issue from an acceptance of human legends, beliefs and institutions that is as complete and comfortable as Chaucer's own.

Not only is the revelation of tragic art absent in Chaucer but also the appearance of moral exploration, which in the literature of modern humanism has become a kind of substitute for it. This is an obvious enough point, only worth making because of the 'psychological novel' label which has been conveniently fixed to the poem in default of calling it a tragedy. The label implies the deliberate investigation of human conduct by an author who will share his discoveries with the reader and assess them in terms of moral value. No matter how imaginatively it is done, this sort of psychological novel can never wholly escape that air of *demonstration* which we discussed earlier, and which is so marked in Constant, Goethe, or Proust. The moral *trouvaille* may be announced earnestly, as by George Eliot, with Proust's special kind of wry and yet portentous elaboration, or with the spare clinical impassivity of Laclos or De Montherlant. In all of them pretension is a necessary and even a noble quality, setting out as they do on a solitary voyage with fame depending on their own nerve and assurance. Chaucer has no need of this pretension because he does not propose to do any exploring on his own account. His poem is a psychological study only in the sense that his characters' 'adventures and history are determined by their feelings and the nature of their minds'. He follows his source, and the convention in which he conceived and wrote completely absolves him from appearing to discover anything for himself. 'And I seyde his opinioun was good.' His famous dryness and his poker-faced comments are a clear indication of how much

he finds himself in harmony with the pretensions of others—
Dante, Boccaccio, or the ancients. 'I rede it naught, therefore
I late it goon', is a typical comment, and though we soon
learn that a reference to his source usually means that he is
saying something of his own, his reticence and modesty are
such that we hardly realize what a new world is coming into
existence. Sophisticated fiction often employs every device
of impersonality to conceal the analytic zest and ability of
the author: Chaucer's relation to his sources means that he
has no problem of being—or of concealing—himself.

How is one to reconcile the claim that Chaucer is as
sophisticated and highbrow as Proust and George Eliot with
the admission that he neither analyses nor moralizes? I shall
try to prove it by a detailed study of *Troilus*, but before we
embark on the poem a word of comment is called for on the
stumbling-block which mediaeval English seems to impose
on the intellectual enjoyment of persons who are prepared
to trudge through Dante with the aid of a dictionary, and
even to spell out Pushkin. The language of Chaucer is for
them a sufficient reason for not taking him very seriously. He
is remarkably fresh and vivid, of course, in his simple way,
but with an obviousness that succeeds only at school certifi-
cate level, where the dull grind of the class room is enlivened
by laborious explanations of the kind of jokes at which—as
has been unkindly said of certain Stratford productions—the
actors roar with laughter but not the audience. The sophisticated of to-day are apt to assume that his sentiments must
be as irredeemably simple-minded as anything uttered in
those minor European tongues in which *sprog* is the word for
literature or *spuk* for ghost, and certainly it takes time for
our natural sense of incongruity to wear off. Chaucer
resembles modern English as a chimpanzee resembles a man;
it is not easy to realize that his words are not absurd and im-

perfect in so far as they are different from ours, but that they have their own quite separate perfections. He himself shows his usual sophisticated awareness of the problem:

> *Ye know ek that in forme of speche is chaunge*
> *Withinne a thousand yeer, and wordes tho*
> *That hadden pris, now wonder nyce and straunge*
> *Us thinketh hem, and yet thei spake hem so,*
> *And spedde as wel in love as men now do.*

For the intellectual who cannot take Chaucer seriously, language spreads also to personality, and makes the hero and heroine seem boring, sententious, or at the least deeply uninteresting, because they express themselves in a mediaeval idiom and often declaim against fate or call legendary and proverbial wisdom to their aid. Though not exactly mean, they are not fine enough *consciences*, as James would say, to make their story really important and absorbing. One might point out in reply that feeling and response to love have not only their own local expression in every epoch, but their own *raison d'être*: the particular interest of the lover's feelings will always depend on what he feels himself to be in love *for*. The play of intelligence, whether of the hero or his creator, is always more parochial than we suppose, and Proust only seems to us less localized than Chaucer because our intelligence shares many definitions and objectives with his. We are, for example, closer in some ways to the idea of love as a means to enlightenment than we are to the ideas of the Code, so that when Proust's hero reflects that nothing in the love of his mistress is as precious as the truths she reveals to him by making him suffer, we are far less surprised by this view than Chaucer and his contemporaries would have been. It would never have occurred to Troilus to solace himself with the following observation:

> Falsehoods pain us, coming from a person whom we love, and thereby enable us to penetrate a little deeper in our knowledge of human nature instead of being content to play upon the surface. Grief penetrates into us and forces us out of painful curiosity to penetrate other people. Whence emerge truths which we feel we have no right to keep hidden.

Although the Courtly Lover may have been eager to fall in love and enjoy the blissful pangs described by poets and men of fashion, it was at least love itself that he coveted and not the sagacity which he hoped to get from it. Chaucer is fortunate in having a system of love to write about which is artificial but which devotes all its artificiality to the emotion itself: the transparent pathos of Troilus and Criseyde comes from the fact that they do not see beyond love. For them it is an absolute thing, like God, to be betrayed, evaded, ignored, or devoutly worshipped, but not to be used as a means of edifying and enriching the soul. For Proust and his narrator it is an unrivalled method of mapping the moral universe, whereas for Chaucer it is a state with its own advantages and disadvantages which can be seen steadily and whole in the light of that related but none the less infinitely separated and superior dimension—the love of God. Chaucer's conclusion is dogmatic, but then so is Proust's, and it is the measure of our automatic acceptance of the latter's intelligence that we should take his findings so much more for granted, and even (in some cases) assume that Chaucer's intelligence must be voluntarily suspended in the conclusion of his poem. Whether we share Chaucer's Christian conformity or not, we should recognize what an admirable source of detachment it is to him. Just as we feel that Troilus and Criseyde are not in it 'for the experience', so we feel that their author is not compensating for his emotional resentments and humiliations by writing about them.

Troilus and Criseyde and *The Knight's Tale*, Chaucer's longest and most ambitious poems, are both based on originals by Boccaccio, and though *The Knight's Tale* was incorporated in the Canterbury series and may have been touched up to make it better suited to its narrator, it almost certainly had an earlier independent existence, possibly in the same seven-line *rime royal* stanzas as *Troilus*. To the literary historian and Chaucerian scholar the relation of Chaucer to Boccaccio is an absorbing and still controversial topic: Italian authorities imply that the English poems are comparatively slight imitations which reveal a provincial misunderstanding of the spirit and purpose of Boccaccio; while English speaking critics maintain that Chaucer greatly improved and humanized his originals. What is certain, however, and of chief importance for our study, is the way in which Chaucer subtly declassifies the poems which he is adapting (or, in straightforward mediaeval parlance, translating). The *Teseide*, on which *The Knight's Tale* is based, is a very selfconscious epic in twelve books, and filled with all the conventional heroic machinery, accounts of combat, lists of warriors, and so forth. Chaucer reduces it drastically in length and deprives it of its hard shell of form. What else he does is a matter for controversy. Just as *Troilus* is variously catalogued by the critics as a tragedy or a 'psychological novel', so *The Knight's Tale* has been classed as a pocket epic, a perfect romance, an astrological treatise, and a philosophical poem. Looking round for sterling native talent to

73

bolster his own epic-conscious age, Dryden professed to find it England's answer to the *Iliad* and *Aeneid*, while W. P. Ker, more disinterested and a far more erudite scholar, has pointed out the extent to which Chaucer has in fact transformed an epic into a romance. Other critics have put Chaucer's interest in planetary lore or Boethian philosophy into the foreground of the poem. Probably everyone is right. With his amazing and serene eclecticism, his skill in having both 'the wolf ful and the wether whole', Chaucer has brought all these elements together and manipulated them into a poem of a rich and idiosyncratic kind. Significantly, another great mediaeval poem, *Sir Gawain and the Green Knight*, also defies classification, and exhibits the same kind of equable sophistication in taking common mediaeval themes and situations—the quest, the uncanny marvel, the enchanted landscape, the love test and debate, the divided duty—and assembling them with clerkly nostalgia and penetrating affection. Like *The Knight's Tale* and *Troilus*, *Sir Gawain* fully accepts its materials and yet stands back from them.

The feeling for decorum with which these mixtures were compounded, and the resulting sensitivity to mood and atmosphere, is shown by Chaucer's transposition of an important episode from his sources. In the *Teseide* the dead co-hero, Arcite, slain by a divine ruse at the moment of his victory in the tournament, is transported to the ninth sphere of heaven, from which he looks down at the scene of his worldly triumphs and preoccupations and laughs to think how important they once seemed. Such a superlunary emancipation is one of the orthodox comforts of mediaeval philosophy as taught by Boethius, but it is lamentably out of keeping for the hero of an epic whose funeral rites are being celebrated as were Hector's in the *Iliad*. And this is

74

one of the moments in the poem where Chaucer replaces the epic shell of Boccaccio with a truer heroic spirit of his own discerning. Chaucer knew that in the heroic world death was a fearful thing which made the love and bravery of life glow more brightly in contrast.

> *Now with his love, now in his colde grave*
> *Allone, withouten any compaignye.*

His intuition of the ancient sense of death here, expressed in these dying words of Arcite, is very different from his more orthodox presentations of it in Boethian terms. Arcite might have echoed the words of the spirit of Achilles to Odysseus:

> *... think not death a theme*
> *Of consolation; I had rather live*
> *A common slave for hire and eat the bread*
> *Of some man scantily himself sustained*
> *Than reign as sovereign over all the shades.*

When the spirit of Arcite 'chaunged hous', the author cannot tell where it went; it has no confident journey to an established heaven but, like the dead king in Beowulf, goes out into the unknown. Moreover there is another change to be rung on the due appropriateness of feeling and mood which is so much a part of Chaucer s literary decorum, a change not connected with the poem of Palamon and Arcite but with *The Knight's Tale* as it is fitted dramatically into the Canterbury series. The famous line *Allone, withouten any compaignye*, which expresses so movingly the loneliness of the heroic soul in death, is taken up by the Miller in the next tale and employed in a wholly ribald context. The Miller, a truculent and drunken humorist, a churl who fittingly tells 'a cherles tale', describes the Oxford lodgings of his young hero,

> *A chambre hadde he in that hostelrye*
> *Allone, withouten any compaignye ...*

Both the Knight and the Miller use the word in its normal mediaeval sense of sexual companionship, but one uses it with a high meaning and the other with a low one. It is the kind of sophisticated assembly of different worlds in one phrase that appeals to Chaucer's sense of life and style. What is epically appropriate to Arcite is made rhetorically appropriate both to the Knight in a chivalric tale and the Miller in a *fabliau*.

And so the mediaeval idea of death as a release and a call to higher things, which Chaucer finds inappropriate for his tale of *Palamon and Arcite*, is transferred to *Troilus*, where it aptly echoes the contrast between the uncertainties of earthly love and the sureness of the divine. Troilus is not like Arcite; he typifies Boethian man, not heroic man, and his sense of love and death is deeply and conventionally mediaeval, fittingly represented by the journey of his spirit to the ninth sphere. He has none of the tragic simplicity of Arcite, which takes its proper place in a poem which emphasizes the patriarchal spirit, the 'three ages', of the ancient world; for Chaucer has clearly taken pains to individualize and give a more vivid existence than his source to the Nestorian or Anchises-like figure of Egeus, the aged father of Theseus, and to the kingly maturity of Theseus himself. After the death of Arcite they all wait on the words of the old man, who alone can act as a gloss or chorus to interpret the meaningless huddle of events by reference to other calamities.

> *No man mighte gladen Theseus,*
> *Savynge his olde fader Egeus,*
> *That knew this worlde's transmutacioun,*
> *As he had seyn it chaungen up and doun,*
> *Joye after woe, and woe after gladnesse:*
> *And shewed hem ensamples and lyknesse ...*
> *'This world nys but a thurghfare ful of woe,*
> *And we ben pilgrimes, passinge to and fro;*
> *Deeth is an ende of every worldly sore.'*
> *And over al this yet seyde he muchel more ...*

At first sight the last line seems just another example of Chaucer's celebrated humour—the sly dig at 'elde' and its tedious ramblings. But Chaucer's continual play of comic anti-climax is no more just done for laughs than is Shakespeare's play of punning: both have their narrative and dramatic function. The quality of tragic resignation which is so much a part of *The Knight's Tale* depends on this quality of platitude as well as truth, a 'twice-told' tale as well as a moving reality. In the same spirit Theseus insists that in spite of the terrible accident which has snatched victory from Arcite the show must go on.

> *Al be it that this aventure was falle,*
> *He nolde nought disconforten hem alle.*

Chaucer's sense of this timeless tragic equanimity gives a unity to the poem which controls and absorbs the extraordinary mixture of themes he deploys in it.

And his mastery over the incongruous or bathetic elements in a story, the freedom he allows them, and the skill with which he makes use of them, are much in evidence in

77

Troilus and Criseyde. If we compare it with Boccaccio's poem, as we conveniently can in Rossetti's interleaved edition, nothing is more striking than the attitudes which Chaucer takes towards Boccaccio's *topoi*, the conventional moments which outline the progress and proportions of *Il Filostrato*. The strength of the Italian poem lies, as it were, in its standardization; it is a regular model for all love tableaux. There is the first meeting, the encouraging sympathizer, the dream of love—('would I were with her for one winter's night')—the conventional advice to the girl—('lose no time: reflect that age or death will take away thy beauty')—the exchange of vows, the consummation, and the archetypal betrayal. All these Chaucer modifies in some way, throwing round them a haze of the atypical and the individual. Whereas everything in Boccaccio is hard, elegant, and general, in Chaucer it is muted, peculiar, full of objects that are unexpected and yet oddly characteristic. Boccaccio's poem is like a Roman café, and Chaucer's like the spare bedroom in an English country house. The Italian lovers have at their command all the appropriate moods, utterances, and gestures, but the situation of the English couple—though theoretically the same—somehow seems idiosyncratic, a trifle absurd, almost respectable. No stock response seems to fit; no preconception turns out to help us much, and no ultimate verdict will quite hit the mark. Boccaccio's story has the truth of geometry and saloon bar wisdom,

> *Es ist eine alte Geschickte*
> *Doch endlich wird's immer neu ...*

We know as well as he does what is going to happen; anyone could see it was going to turn out like that—the lovers almost knew it themselves. The relish in inevitability conceals a personal animus, for Boccaccio has a grievance against his Fiammetta and needs to feel that with women it is always the same old story.

It is a point of view that has its authority, even its charm, certainly its truth. Chaucer's has the different truth of plurality, of Bishop Butler's 'everything is what it is and not another thing'. For all his formal emphasis on Fortune's wheel, on fate and predestination, Chaucer makes us feel —and indeed the two things are perfectly compatible—that his story might have turned out quite differently. Fate is, as it were, unpredictable. And the pathos of his ending is all the more terrible because it has been hidden behind the random complications of love and living that crowd the body of the poem. Dominated as we are by fiction, we are more used to-day to this kind of truth, and to this extent Chaucer's poem and the 'psychological novel' certainly have much in common.

Chaucer has various ways of altering and giving a different meaning to the conventions of his source, and by a characteristic paradox his most effective method is to make them far more locally and specifically conventional! C. S. Lewis has said that Chaucer 'mediaevalizes' *Il Filostrato*. The word is ambiguous but does not imply, I think, that Boccaccio's poem is 'for the ages' while Chaucer's requires a specialized knowledge and appreciation of his own values and his own time. It means rather that Chaucer places the subject of the poem both more locally and more rigorously: he drives home with a sober and pervasive logic the implications of the mediaeval code of love. In fact he takes love seriously, and he is able to do this because he makes full use of his contemporaries' absorption in the business, while Boccaccio already has something of the much more 'timeless' attitudes to love of the Renaissance: he is no devout and serious scholar of its lore. Boccaccio's Troilo is a young man with plenty of sexual experience: Troilus has avoided it completely and is now smitten for the first time. He is 'sely', that is, *naif* or innocent. *On n'aime qu'une fois* ... the rest are less involuntary—and the idea of first love is moving in any age, but the change is also in keeping with the strict precepts of the Code. Chaucer follows the mediaeval ideal in making his Troilus much more obviously what Usk in *The Testament of Love* called 'a lion in the field and a lamb in the chamber'.

He even makes us feel that the actual *facts* of the tale suit his vision better than Boccaccio's. They were famous lovers, but they separated and she was unfaithful; how did it come about? Both Boccaccio and Shakespeare give us their versions in a no-nonsense way which emphasizes, selectively and ruthlessly, the more obvious aspects of the business. But by confining himself within the elaborate ritual of the Code, Chaucer is able to make the same story cover an infinitely wider field of emotion and feeling. He tells us more about love than they do. And his achievement seems all the more remarkable when we reflect that other celebrated love stories which are also tied to a local intensity—*Tristan and Iseult* or *Clarissa*—can show nothing of this scope.

Boccaccio never quite convinces us that the separation of the lovers is such a mortal blow to them as the story seems to require. He pretends that it is, out of good manners and deference to the love legend, but the thousands of lines he has already written are against him. If love passes and women are false and the emotions are resilient and life goes on, then why this prodigy of despair? Are his lovers perhaps —(shades of La Rochefoucauld!)—chiefly doing what the love legend requires of them? Troilo casts round madly for some way of evading the separation; Griseida assures him that she will keep faith and get back as soon as she can. She genuinely believes that she will, and he is equally anxious to find some way of keeping her, but somewhere in the background we are aware of a shrugging of shoulders, and in his concluding stanzas Boccaccio even discreetly indicates that when Troilus is at length persuaded to go to a party he feels a faint revival of interest in the pretty women there. He has the resilience of the perpetual average man. The helplessness of Boccaccio's lovers does not seem entirely due to force of circumstances but rather to the average man's acceptance of change and chance, and his willingness to let them decide the issue.

Through his far more vulnerable couple Chaucer discreetly and continually emphasizes that love does not grow and flower in a vacuum but is almost ludicrously subject to every kind of misunderstanding and accident, and the more honourably rigid the Code becomes the more subject it is to this haphazard violence. He loses no opportunity of showing how helpless the Courtly Lover is in face of the inflexible requirements of love. Those requirements may be admirable in themselves, they may even have a kind of sublimity about them, and Chaucer implies that he thinks they have.

> This is no litel thing of for to seye,
> This passeth every wit for to devyse;
> For eche of hem gan otheres lust obeye;
> Felicitee, which that thise clerkes wyse
> Commenden so, ne may not here suffyse.
> This joye may not writen been with inke,
> This passeth al that herte may bithinke.

But the Code is a code, not just a vague ideal, and 'the lineaments of gratified desire' are entirely bound up in it. It is all of a piece, and if it fails at one point the status and splendour

81

of love will disappear like the air out of a balloon. This threat Chaucer keeps so constantly and rigorously before us that he makes the dilemma of the lovers, when the news comes that Criseyde is to be sent out of Troy, seem almost unbearably cruel. It is the moral climax and pivot of the tale, far more than Criseyde's subsequent infidelity. Keeping to the rules virtually kills Troilus, but he does keep to them; while the heat of the crisis engenders a moral collapse in Criseyde from which she never recovers.

At this climax Chaucer both leans most heavily on the Code and also most deliberately (except for the final palinode), steps outside it. It is the tragedy of the lovers that they are bound to the Code at this moment, but Troilus remains inactive for the right reasons and Criseyde for the wrong ones. He sacrifices himself to the Code while she merely takes refuge in it. Absolute secrecy and obedience was, of course, enjoined on love's servant; the lady's good name must be kept and her commands obeyed. And if she admits her love for him she must in return neither 'false' him nor give him up. So although they have been lovers in secrecy for three years, when the news of the separation arrives Troilus cannot go to his friends and peers and implore them in confidence to prevent it. The secret would then be out, and the lady's name compromised within the Code, and as Troilus says in all earnestness, 'me were levere ded than hire diffame'. Nor can he carry her off by force; the idea of such a thing is abhorrent to a gentle lover, and besides she might get hurt.

There remains only one way out. He can beg her to run away with him in secret. He does this, and it is the real moment of test for Criseyde. It is her bad luck to be mistress of the situation, because he will have to do what she wants. Although it is a technical violation of the Code she could honourably agree to this solution, but her moral imagination is not fine enough to span the gap between love as they have it now, and as love it might be in an unknown future. Her very real love for Troilus is the absolute prisoner of the circumstances in which it has grown. In another age she would have had to take the plunge because she could hardly refuse and yet maintain her love for him, but in another age she might have had her mind made up for her: the Code laid a burden of moral decision upon the lady which in the case of Criseyde is ironically unfair. To-day she wouldn't have a leg to stand on, and the parting and betrayal would seem correspondingly harsher and simpler. As it is she can fall back on the Code, and she passes a heavy judgement both on it and on herself when she tells Troilus he is making a great fuss about nothing, for of course she will be true to him and return as soon as she can. This he has to accept, but the damage is done, and after this great scene has kept us on tenterhooks we know that all is over. From now on, though Troilus is almost painfully present to our feelings, Criseyde is cut off from them and far away.

The failure, rather than the faithlessness, of Criseyde is the chief example of how Chaucer achieves the 'timeless' effect by the most rigid adherence to the local and the conventional. But though his situation is so effectively orthodox his characters are highly individual. Boccaccio's Pandarus, for instance, is exactly the type that the eponym implies, no more and no less, an economical character with a supply of chilly and professional love dogma which reminds us more of Goethe and Stendhal than of Dante and the Code. 'I think for certain that every woman in wish lives amorous', he remarks confidently to Troilo as they discuss the possible yielding of Griseida. 'My cousin is a widow, and she desires, and were she to deny it I would not believe her. Since every congenial relationship does not come to fulfilment', he adds with a sententiousness worthy of the *Wahlverwandshaften*, 'steps ought to be taken to see that it does so if possible.' At any stage in the history of our conventions about feeling these comments could only have been made by a tiresomely cocksure and opinionated young man, and even the fact that Troilo—after several affairs—is now embarked on a *grande passion*, cannot disguise the predatory pattern of two comrades in a mutual enterprise. Chaucer transforms this relation by the simple method of making Pandarus Criseyde's uncle instead of her cousin. As an older man, his relation to the lovers is much more unusual and subtle; his avuncular susceptibilities are complex and extend to them both; while towards Troilus, the Prince, he also displays a worldly and rather quizzical subservience that may have been characteristic—one cannot help feeling—of Chaucer's own relations with the great, and perhaps of Shakespeare's too.

Equally drastic and effective is Chaucer's transformation of Pandaro's characteristic tone; his sententiousness is exaggerated until he becomes an individual 'humour', which gives him the manner and appearance of one of the great comic persons of Shakespeare or Dickens—but only the appearance, for we soon find that he is far from being, as most comics are, what E. M. Forster calls a 'flat character'. His sententiousness is too highly individualized to leave on us the calculating impression of Pandaro's. Where Pandaro reminded his cousin that 'everyone has a chance in life but not a second chance', Pandarus tells his niece to go on being standoffish until the crows are walking under her eyes. When he upsets her by pretending that Troilus is jealous, and she wants to know what caused it, he protests that it is better to put out the fire than to ask how the candle fell in the straw. 'It is nat god a slepyng hound to wake', he warns her, when she wishes to rouse her women just as his schemes are on the verge of success, and the phrase brings before us, like a line from *St Agnes Eve*, the expectant hush of the night and the impersonal menace of fear and desire. Most potent of all is his aside when Troilus stands anxiously on the walls of Troy, watching with renewed hope day after day for a Criseyde who never comes.

> *From hasel-wode ther Joly Robin pleyde,*
> *Shal come al that that thou abydest here—*
> *Yea, farewel al the snow of ferne yeer!*   [*former*

It is almost like the plain speaking of the fool in *Lear*, that both corrects and enhances a dramatic sorrow. Pandarus makes his aside 'ful sobrely', a phrase often used of the pair when they discuss matters together, and indeed there is a touching earnestness in the way they go about things which reminds us of those actors who run the whole gamut of comic misfortune when they address themselves to mend a puncture or paper a wall. There is something deeply congenial and reassuring in the spectacle of elaborate effort and ludicrous result. The purposefulness and cold strength of will that haunts an intrigue of seduction, and which pervades Boccaccio's poem, is quite neutralized in Chaucer by this continual irruption of the ridiculous, an atmosphere that also makes the very real damage incurred seem far more painful and pathetic.

But though Pandarus has for a moment a touch of the fool in *Lear* this does not mean that the poem is a tragic one. The element of the ridiculous in *Lear*, powerful though it is, is set in motion by—and in fact requires for its function —the real majesty of the king and the goodness of Cordelia. For every comic person or episode in tragedy there exists also an evil or sublime one. But in *Troilus and Criseyde* there is no evil, sublime, or majestic character; everyone is more than human in their hopes and fears, their cowardice and amiability.

This is not to say that they are incapable of reflecting on their plight. Like most lovers, Troilus and Criseyde are fascinated by their feelings for one another, and at every crisis they turn matters over, singly or together, with that inconsequential endlessness which is so absorbing to the sufferer and—in life if not in art—usually so boring for the outsider. Just as our sense of a real person is increased, and as it were domesticated, when he knows us well enough to bore us with his troubles, so our intimacy with the lovers is enlarged by these preoccupied monologues, which in most cases have been added to the story by Chaucer. Pandarus—who also has to listen to them—shares in the leisurely development of our intimacy. It is part of his nature as a stock figure to have no success in love himself, but Chaucer brings out, too, how he uses this fact to reassure his niece. He draws attention to his *débâcles* in love to show what a harmless jolly sport it all is, and to distract her attention from the net that is closing round her.

> *'By God,' quod he, 'I hoppe alwey behynde!'*
> *And she to laughe, it thoughte hire herte brest.*
> *Quod Pandarus, 'Loke alwey that ye fynde*
> *Game in myn hood ...'*

'Let me always be a source of amusement to you.' He positively urges her to find his activities comical. In another creation by another author this could be a sinister trait—the calculating buffoon is a disagreeable figure—but Pandarus has no difficulty in eluding such an impeachment. Although he is driving his poor niece nearly distracted by his intrigues on Troilus's behalf, he feels for the predicament of women, and we do not doubt his good faith when he deplores, in Troilus's presence, their inevitably hard bargain in life.

> *No wonder is, so God me sende hele,*
> *Though women dreden with us men to dele.*

He accepts the fact that all men, himself included, behave badly to women, and he honours them all the more because they are victimized. Through him Chaucer implies, with his usual subtlety, that even at its most admirably civilized the courtly Code is also a way of exploiting the female sex. Worship may be another aspect of oppression. Pandarus indeed positively reveres women for putting on 'the destined livery', and Chaucer emphasizes this by conveying Criseyde's forgiveness of him in a religious metaphor.

> *—God foryaf his deeth and she also*
> *Foryaf, and with here uncle gan to pleye,*
> *For other cause was ther noon than so.*

In spite of the link between religion and the Code there is nothing uniquely mediaeval about this mixture of reverence and shrewd calculation in the dealings of the sexes: it is a profound tragicomic fact, whether in Chaucer or in Thurber. Yet the pursuit of Criseyde—(one of Pandarus's most graphic similes is of his niece as a deer driven towards the bowmen)—is shown by Chaucer to be not less a threat to the civility of love because it conforms to the Code. Her hunting 'to Dulcarnoun, right at my wittes ende' is revenged when she evades every attempt of Troilus and Pandarus to get her to adopt some other course than return to her father in the Greek camp. One kind of 'maistrye' calls up another, and this hard fact underlies the happy idyll of their three years together. Though in some ways the Code makes it easier for men and women to love each other freely, the old troubles remain, and the new ability of women to command in love does not always offset but may merely repeat the trials of male domination. It is in some ways an honourable ending to the pursuit that Troilus should become his lady's servant.

> *she fond him so discreet in al,*
> *So secret, and of swich obeisaunce*
> *That wel she felte he was to hir a wal*
> *Of steel, and sheld from every displeasaunce.*

But the reversal creates as many problems as it resolves.

Sometimes Chaucer sidesteps an explicit fact in Boccaccio with a translator's licence to be vague which also adds something of the uncertainty of real life, in which it is as rare to know all the facts about someone as it is to be entirely right about their character. Sometimes he derives a different and more subtle implication from the same point as his source. Pandaro observes that Griseida is the most virtuous of women (*piu che altre donne onesta*), and that this may be a snag, though he will try to overcome it with sugared words. Chaucer's Pandarus, on the other hand, observes that she is indeed virtuous, but that this may well turn out to their advantage, since among her other virtues will surely be *pité*. The two points of view seem centuries apart, and a whole world of gentleness and civilization seems to have come into being between the first and the second. But in fact the smoking-room and the drawing-room lie side by side, as it were, and Chaucer knows this as well as anyone. For now and again he seems deliberately to leave a fragment of untransmuted Troilo or Pandaro in his own text, with the result that we apprehend with a sudden shock the ugly side of what is on the whole such a scrupulous intrigue, and feel what Criseyde felt when she first saw what her uncle might be getting at.

> What? Is this al the joye and al the feste?
> Is this your reed, is this my blisful cas? [advice
> Is this the verray mede of youre beheste?
> Is al this peynted proces seyd, allas!
> Right for this fyn? [purpose

She sees herself turned into an instrument of 'casuel pleasaunce', and though her fears are set at rest, the passage brings home to us the ambiguity of the idea of sexual love, an idea which has to cover the whole range of feeling, from animal desire to louche or elegant social ideals and up to the loftiest aspirations. Chaucer keeps this perspective before us throughout and never lets us lose sight of any part of it. It is appropriate in Boccaccio that Pandaro should try to cheer Troilo up by pointing out that at least he has had his fun. Chaucer's Pandarus repeats the same arguments,

> Sin thy desir al hooly hastow had,
> So that, by right, it ought ynow suffyse ...
> For sin it is but casuel pleasaunce,
> Som cas shal putte it out of remembraunce.

But now they have a forlorn ring. 'Try to look at love in this way', he urges, 'for after all a lot of people do'. He tries to make it part of the humour, 'betwixen game and earnest', which he has kept up throughout—a kind of trench humour of love's war. But he knows as well as Troilus that their business cannot be taken at this level. The passions and the Code are at one here, as Troilus forcibly points out.

> *Thou biddest me I sholde love another*
> *Al freshly newe, and lat Criseyde go!*
> *It lyth not in my power, leve brother.*   [*dear*
> *And though I mighte, I wolde not do so.*

We realize, too, from these passages that Chaucer leaves unchanged, the dangerous forces at work in a passion which can make two such essentially nice creatures as Troilus and Pandarus engage in such disreputable shifts, and appear at moments so pathetically ignoble. It seemed quite natural that young Troilo should strike a comradely bargain with young Pandaro to procure for him one of his sisters—Polyxena or Cassandra—if Pandaro could only win Griseida for him. But there is a horrid pathos about the innocent and unworldly Troilus making the same offer to Criseyde's *uncle*! Such a touch produces a momentary equivalent of the true dark tragic degradation—the obsession that drives Troilus makes us glimpse the terrible presence of *Venus toute entière*. Nor is this darkness much lightened by the fact that in both poems the two friends assure each other than they mean all in honour, and would not breathe a word that might harm the lady's reputation, even though Pandarus is much more cumbrously in earnest about this than his predecessor.

> *I pose, a womman graunte me*
> *Hir love, and seye that other wol she non,*
> *And I am sworn to holden it secree,*
> *And after I go telle it two or three;*
> *Ywis, I am avantour at the leste,*
> *And lyere, for I breke my biheste.*

One of the most striking results of Chaucer's prolixity, and his lengthening and elaboration of the love-intrigue, is the way it puts us in constant touch during the first part of the poem with Criseyde's awareness. Chaucer sets himself to make a 'mirour of hir minde' in which we see 'al hoolly hir figure'. And this 'register of her consciousness', in Henry James's phrase, is closely and consecutively kept until the moment of climax, when she evades the issue of flight with Troilus. For the rest of the poem it is his feelings with which we are continuously concerned. There is indeed an odd parallel here with *The Golden Bowl*, where, as James tells us, his deliberate plan was for the first part of the action to be seen through the Prince's consciousness, and the second through that of the Princess. In Chaucer it seems to happen naturally, and in accordance with what might be called the laws of literary fair play, that it should be the victim—the person acted on—with whom we should be in close *rapport*, though we shall see later that James's Charlotte Stant does not receive the benefit of this law.

When Criseyde first hears from Pandarus, with a wealth of graphic detail, how Troilus has fallen for her and what a miserable state he is in, her first reaction is one of vexation and alarm. She makes no secret of her dismay that her uncle, on whose advice and support she has come to rely, should suddenly produce this bothersome proposition. His chief function in her eyes is to protect her from difficulties, and now he is actually pushing her into them. (2. 412.) At once Pandarus pretends to drop the subject: if that's how she feels, and if she doesn't mind the young man's cutting his throat because of her, there's obviously no more to be said. Even more alarmed by this she 'catches him by the lappe', seeing that there is nothing for it but 'ful sleighly for to pleye', and her guarded exasperation is beautifully rendered by Chaucer.

She listens in silence to a further description of Troilus's sufferings, and only breaks out again when her uncle blandly assumes that the time is not far off when she will be his as he is hers.

> *'Nay, therof spak I not, a, ha!' quod she,*
> *As help me God, ye shenden every deel!'* [spoil everything

When he has gone she sits down 'as stil as a stone' and reflects on these perturbing developments. She is slightly cheered by the thought that she is a free agent, and it won't be her fault even if he does do himself an injury. (2. 605–609.) There is no need to panic. At this moment she hears a shouting outside. Troilus and his men are riding back from the battlefield, and she runs to the window. She sees an embarrassed Troilus, distinctly out of his element among the cheers of the bystanders.

> *For which he wex a litel reed for shame,*
> *Whan he the peple upon him herde cryen,*
> *That to biholde it was a noble game,*
> *How sobreliche he caste doun his eyen.*
> *Criseyda gan al his chere aspyen,*
> *And leet so softe it in hir herte sinke,*
> *That to hirself she seyde: 'Who yaf me drynke?'*

> *For of hir owene thought she wex al reed,*
> *Remembringe hir right thus, 'Lo, this is he*
> *Which that myn uncle swerith he moot be deed,*
> *But I on him have mercy and pitee.'*

Both 'change their hue'—the sign of the stricken lover—but for a different cause which in neither case is the direct onset

92

of love. Criseyde's rhetorical question to herself—'who yaf me drynke?'—shows how she makes use of the Code's mystique and terminology while retaining a wary sense of self-preservation, an ability which contrasts with Troilus's commitment of himself 'with ful devout corage' to the last demands of the Code. The most famous of love potions was drunk involuntarily by Tristan and Iseult, who were for ever after powerless to escape its effects. Criseyde does not want to be responsible for the coming storm, and her invocation of the lover's state is engagingly modified by her next thought: this is the young man who is so much in love with me that he has threatened to kill himself. She exclaims that she has fallen in love, but the real point is that Troilus has fallen in love with her. Chaucer has it both ways as usual. He gives their first encounter the dramatic properties that the Code demanded, but out of this stock situation he contrives to suggest much more complex and informal emotional processes; and this happens all the more simply and accurately because the relation in life between convention and spontaneous desire is as complex and interwoven as that between Chaucer the poet of mediaeval convention and Chaucer the 'realist'. All this becomes explicit in Chaucer's own comment on the scene.

> For I sey nought that she so sodeynly
> Yaf hym hire love, but that she gan enclyne
> To like hym first, and I have told yow whi ...

Self-interest and natural kindness of heart make Criseyde now feel that she ought to be as nice to him as possible, 'for my estat and also for his heele'. After all, he is the king's son, and an influential man whom it would be as well to keep on the right side of. And vanity adds itself to the promptings of snobbishness and prudence. She reflects that the young man at her feet is one of the most eligible in Troy and that she herself is admitted to be one of the most attractive women, and moreover one who has now no need of a husband.

> *I am myn owene womman, wel at ese,*
> *I thank it God, as after myn estat,*
> *Right yong, and stand unteyd in lusty leese,*
> *Withouten jalousie or swich debat:*
> *Shal noon housbonde seyn to me 'chek mat!'*

It must be emphasized that at no point is there the slightest question of her *marrying* Troilus. So completely does the world of the poem exclude this that we take it as much for granted as we do the Russian social world which contributes so much to the fate of Anna. Marriage was an economic arrangement procured by family representatives, and, as Criseyde implies, it was for a woman a condition as disadvantageous as a liaison in Courtly Love was privileged. Criseyde is comfortably off, and her father has gone over to the Greeks: there is no one to order her about. She reflects on this with a certain complacency.

> '*What shal I doon? To what fyn lyve I thus?*
> *Shal I nat love, in cas if that me leste?*
> *What, par dieux! I am naught religious.*
> *And though that I myn herte set at reste*
> *Upon this knyght, that is the worthieste,*
> *And kepe alwey myn honour and my name,*
> *By alle right, it may me do no shame.*'

If she can keep it dark why shouldn't she have an affair? But this sanguine mood soon passes.

A cloudy thought gan thorough hire soule pace,
That overspradde hire brighte thoughtes alle,
So that for feere almost she gan to falle.

That thought was this: Allas, syn I am free
Sholde I now love and put in jupartie
My sikernesse, and thrallen libertie? ...
For love is yet the mooste stormy lyf
Right of hymself, that ever was bigonne ...

Love is its own torment, 'right of hymself', quite apart from
any allied considerations; she shrinks at the thought of all its
unavoidable intensity and fuss. Moreover (1. 787–88) she has
no illusions about the tendency for the whole apparatus of
romance to vanish away as soon as male desire is appeased.
What is she to do? Her mood varies between optimism and
despair, and at last she abandons the problem and goes out
into the garden, where she strolls with her niece Antigone.

This yerd was large and rayled alle th'aleyes
And shadewed wel with blosmy bowes grene
And benched newe, and sonded alle the weyes,
In which she walketh arm in arm betwene,
Til at the laste Antigone the shene
Gan on a Troian song to singen cleere,   [*bright*
That it an heven was hire vois to here.

Antigone's song is of course about love, and in answer to
Criseyde's query she explains, with an enthusiasm which
indicates her age and temperament, how few people know
what love is really about and what a rare and delectable
thing it is. But she does not claim to have experienced its
bliss herself, and with the cheerful insensitivity of youth she

assumes that her widowed aunt will not have done so either. Criseyde hastens to change the subject.

> Criseyde unto that purpos naught answerde,
> But seyde, 'Ywis, it wol be night as faste'.
> But every worde which she of hire herde,
> She gan to prenten in hire herte faste,
> And aye gan love hire lasse for t'agaste
> Than it dide erst, and sinken in hire herte ...

They go in and Criseyde goes up to bed. The long passage, faithfully recording her consciousness but as far removed from mere exhibition and statement as a scene in a great novel, ends with two beautiful stanzas.

> A nyghtingale, upon a cedir grene,
> Under the chambre wal ther as she lay,
> Ful loude sang ayein the moone shene,
> Peraunter, in his briddes wise, a lay
> Of love, that made hire herte fressh and gay.
> That herkned she so long in good entente,
> Til at the laste the dede slep hire hente.

> And as she slep, anonright tho hire mette   [dreamed
> How that an egle, fethered whit as bon,
> Under hire brest his longe clawes sette,
> And out hire herte he rente, and that anon,
> And dide his herte into hire brest to gon,
> Of which she nought agroos, ne nothyng smerte; [feared
> And forth he fleigh, with herte left for herte.

> Now lat hire slepe ...

The garden, the song, the nightingale, and the dream, are all conventional mediaeval properties of love allegory, but Chaucer mingles them without effort in an atmosphere that seems as we read it as naturalistic as Chekhov's.

Meanwhile Pandarus continues the offensive, urging Troilus to write her a love letter and giving advice about its composition.

> *'Biblotte it with thi teres eek a lite;*
> *And if thow write a goodly word all softe,*
> *Though it be good, reherce it nought too ofte.'*

The letter is duly written, and conveyed by Pandarus to his niece, whose anxieties and fears instantly revive at the sight of it.

> *Ful dredfully tho gan she stonden stylle,*
> *And took it nought, but al hire humble chere*
> *Gan for to chaunge, and seyde, 'Scrit ne bille*
> *For love of God, that toucheth swich matere,*
> *Ne bring me noon: and also, uncle deere,*
> *To myn estat have more reward, I preye,*
> *Than to his lust! What sholde I more seye?'*

Pandarus hastens to reassure her. How could she think he would do anything to harm her? Disclaiming any knowledge of its contents, he archly enquires if Troilus can write a good letter.

> *How liketh yow the lettre that ye woot?*
> *Kan he thereon? For by my trouthe I noot.'*
>
> *Therewith al rosy hewed tho wex she,*
> *And gan to homme, and seyde, 'So I trowe'.*   [*hum*

97

But the most he can get out of her is a willingness to be a sister to Troilus, and by mutual consent they drop the subject,

> *And fillen forthe in speche of thynges smale,*
> *And seten in the window bothe tweye ...*

The lines are characteristic. Throughout the action the common rhythm of life reasserts itself continually, and in the next section displays a richness and comedy of its own. Pandarus decides that the moment has come for an elaborate plot to confront the pair with one another. He goes to Troilus's brother, Deiphebus, and asks for his support for Criseyde in a threatened lawsuit against her property. The dialogue here is masterly, conveying as it does the mild perplexity of the honest Deiphebus at Pandarus's disingenuously humble approach.

> *Deiphebus hym answerde, 'O, is nat this,*
> *That thow spekest of to me thus straungely,*
> *Criseyda, my friend?' He seyde, 'Yis'.*
> *'Than nedeth' quod Deiphebus, 'hardyly*
> *Namore to speke, for trusteth wel that I*
> *Wol be hire champioun ...'*

Deiphebus decides to give a dinner party so that Criseyde and her supporters can discuss the matter, and suggests that they rope in Helen and Troilus to help as well. An excellent idea, agrees Pandarus. He hurries back to Troilus, tells him what has been arranged, and advises him to sham illness at the dinner so that his brother will offer him a bed for the night. (2. 1520.) Troilus dolefully replies that there will be no need for pretence, and on the appointed evening they go off to the dinner and Troilus duly complains of his fever.

The news is received with concern and he is despatched to bed with appropriate remedies. This provides a talking point and gives a characteristic access of vitality to the conversation.

> *And every wight gan waxen for accesse*
> *A leche anon, and seyde, 'In this manere*   [doctor
> *Men curen folk'—'this charme I wol yow leere'.*
> *But there sat oon, al list hire naught to teche,*
> *That thoughte, 'Best koud I yet been his leche'.*

> *After compleynte, hym gonnen they go preyse,*
> *As folk don yet, whan som wight hath bygonne*
> *To preise a man, and up with pris hym reise*
> *A thousand fold yet heigher than the sonne:*
> *'He is, he kan, that fewe lordes konne' ...*

> *Herde al this thyng Criseyde wel inough ...*

For the first time Criseyde finds herself in a different relation to Troilus than are his relations and friends. She could cure him, she thinks; and surrounded by the cheerful chatter she seems to be alone in a conspiracy with him. The touch shows how his own different awareness of the loved one may be revealed to the lover by a social event and the comments of other people. In fact Criseyde is still not in love, but she is involuntarily undergoing its characteristic experiences: Pandarus is playing deeper than even he is aware. There is the same quality as in the scene in *Anna Karenina* when Vronsky is riding in the steeplechase, and Anna is terribly conscious how different her feelings about him are from those of the party with whom she is sitting and with whom she is outwardly identified.

After dinner they settle down to a serious discussion of Criseyde's supposed predicament which—thanks to Pandarus—is as real to her as it is to the others. Helen suggests that Troilus should be told about it if he is still awake, and adds a graceful little tribute to his 'gentillesse'.

> *For he wol have the more hir grief at herte,*
> *By cause, lo, that she a lady is.*

Pandarus hastens to point out that they had better not all go up—the bedroom is small and they don't want to make him worse. Accordingly Deiphebus and Helen go alone. Chaucer's Helen is an immediately attractive figure, as different from the *femme fatale* of legend as from Shakespeare's enchantress gone to seed whom Paris refers to as 'Nell'. She gives the impression of having an inkling that something is going on, about which she is both discreet and warmly sympathetic; it seems unlikely that she is wholly taken in by the ruse that Troilus adopts to get rid of her and her brother after they have told him of Criseyde's problem.

> *—Quod Troilus, 'Ye two,*
> *Deiphebus and my sister lief and deare,*
> *To yow have I to speke of o matere,*
>
> *To ben avysed by youre reed the bettre—'*
> *And fond, as hap was, at his beddes hed*
> *The copie of a tretys and a lettre,*
> *That Hector had hym sent to axen red,*   [*ask advice*
> *If swych a man was worthi to been ded,*
> *Woot I not who, but in a grisly wise*
> *He preyede hem anon on it avyse.*

Deiphebus gan this lettre for t'onfolde
In ernest greet—so did Eleyne the queene; [manner
And romyng outward, faste it gonne byholde,
Downward a steire, into an herber greene.
This ilke thing they redden hem betwene ...

Just as he continually reminds us of daily living, so Chaucer reminds us of the grim background of the war. His characters are the people at the top, the inner ring who are conducting affairs and debating policy as well as seeing to such unsavoury business as the court-martial of spies and traitors: Helen's position here is that of one of the great feudal ladies of the Middle Ages. The siege is a part of their lives, and war is an instrument of fate as powerful as love, whose violence—in alliance with the Code and their own characters—will eventually kill Troilus and ruin Criseyde. Troilus's convenient letter is an abrupt reminder of this, even though it all seems far away from the garden and the dinner party.

Pandarus meanwhile is reminding his niece that she ought to thank Helen and the rest for the trouble they are taking, and do it soon so as not to keep Troilus from settling down for the night. (2. 1721.) 'Al innocent', she hastens to agree. Their first real meeting is thus an absurdly unromantic one, at least by our standards, though it must be admitted that the Middle Ages appear to have found this particular situation both chivalric and *piquant*. It occurs in *Sir Gawain and The Green Knight*, whose author dwells as lovingly as Chaucer on domestic life in high circles, and who describes how the lady of the castle comes to visit Gawain in bed in the morning: there is a charming picture in the MS of the lady, very smart and self-possessed, standing beside a recumbent Gawain who is decorously rolled up in a sort of tasselled sleeping-bag. In any case, Troilus's pretence of being ill is now a considerable embarrassment to him, and he makes an effort to rise, but she begs him not to, and thanks him for his kindness in undertaking to help with her affairs. Poor Troilus now has to make some sort of declaration of his passion, and his attempt at this is of the feeblest, which endears him to Criseyde all the more. (3. 85–86.) Pandarus, however, feels that he ought to help it out a little.

> And Pandare wep as he to water wolde,
> And poked ever his nece new and newe,
> And seyde, 'Wo bygon been hertes trewe!
> For love of God make of this thyng an ende,
> Or sle us both at ones, er ye wende'.

> 'I! What?' quod she, 'by God and by my trouthe,
> I wot nat what she wilne that I seye!'
> 'I! What?' quod he, 'that ye han on hym routhe,
> For Goddes love, and doth hym nought to deye'.
> 'Now thanne thus', quod she, 'I wolde hym preye
> To telle me the fyn of his entente.   [aim
> Yet wiste I nevere wel what that he mente!'

The badgered girl is driven at last to protest that what she wants to know is just what the pair of them are after. The cards are now on the table, and the moral support of the Code enables Troilus to make a statement that is coherent and even noble. He begs her to grant only that he may be her worshipper and servant: he does not presume to ask anything more. Criseyde is now much more at her ease; the Code gives her too an acceptable and dignified part to play here, and it is with the air of one who at last feels firm ground under her feet that she replies to him, choosing her words carefully.

'Myn honour sauf, I wol wel trewely,
And in swich forme as he gan now devyse,
Receyven hym fully to my servyse ...'

To emphasize her words she switches them from the formal
third person and addresses her suitor directly.

'But natheless, this warne I yow,' quod she,
A kynge's sone although ye be, ywis,
Ye shal namore han sovereignete
Of me in love, than right in that cas is.'

Bolstered by her new role, she expresses herself with the
imperiousness fitting to it; then she takes him in her arms
and kisses him, as she can now do with a clear conscience.
Pandarus falls on his knees and gives thanks to Cupid and
Venus. There is a lyrical decorum in the scene, and it is
slightly ridiculous only in the honourable and delightful
sense in which any sex ceremonial, even a Christian marriage, reveals the incongruity between men and women as
animals and as beings who live by imagination and symbol.

The key in which the scene is pitched is repeated a little later
at what is to us an even more obviously funny moment,
when the positions of the lovers are reversed, and Pandarus
runs to get Troilus a cushion to kneel at his lady's bedside.
Chaucer comments here that Pandarus 'so wel koude feele
in everything.' *Feel* may seem to us a surprising word, for
apart from the buffoonery of the business, Pandarus might
seem to show himself here only as what the Elizabethans
would have called 'a wondrous necessary man', a man who
to-day would be in great demand to bid at auctions and
organize club dinners, and we associate his kind of assurance
with insensitivity rather than with feeling. Romanticism

dies hard, and we still tend to assume that it is as improper to groom the feelings and improve them with use as it was for Wordsworth to cultivate a 'taste' for poetry. In some ways the Code has more in common with the 18th century cult of sensibility than with present-day manners.

Troilus's troubles are by no means over yet. Criseyde has made it clear that she has no intention of becoming his mistress, and according to the Code he may have to be her servant for a life-time without getting any further. So the laborious siege must continue, and the hopes of the besiegers are kept up only by the knowledge that *Pité*—as in the *Roman de La Rose*—is the weak spot in the lady's defence. Boccaccio by this time has brought his lovers to bed. Even as she was persuaded to write Troilo the letter, Griseida had confided to her cousin Pandaro: 'Would I were in his arms, clasped face to face!' She is not, like Shakespeare's Cressida, 'a daughter of the game', but she has a bold and simple Renaissance appetite which she doesn't trouble to conceal from the go-between, and which is complemented by Troilo, who cries when he first sees her—'Would I were with her for one winter's night, and then to spend a hundred and fifty in hell!' These are the exclamations of a franker feeling than the Code allowed for, though they found as vivid expression in the Middle Ages as at any other time, as we can see from *Aucassin and Nicolette*, from the lyrics of the Harley MS and 'O Western Wind'!, and from the cry of that anonymous German student who saw Eleanor of Aquitaine at Cologne—'If the world were all mine from the sea to the Rhine I would give it all away to have the Queen of England in my arms!'

The point is that Boccaccio keeps his lovers in the world of love *poetry*, with its traditional yearnings and hyperboles, while Chaucer releases them into the world

of the everyday consciousness, where everything is shapeless and undemonstrable and unique. 'The more I think
the less I am,' mourned Kierkegaard, and indeed Troilo and
Griseida simply *are* when they utter these cries, as other
lovers in life and poetry had been before them. But like ourselves, or like the characters in a great novel, Chaucer's
lovers have no such absolute identity. What makes their
story so much more absorbing is that their consciousness cannot be grasped; it hovers and broods like the spirit on the
water—again, as our own consciousness does to ourselves—
and will not enter finally into words and be fixed externally
by them.

As I have already suggested in the last chapter, the
wholly successful fictional character—that rarest achievement
—is seen from outside as well as from inside, and Criseyde is
also presented to us externally in a number of subtly un-
assuming touches, very different from the stock poetic
exclamations which place Boccaccio's lovers from the outside. We see the strangely and terribly feelingless Criseyde
at the end of the story, 'mild and mansuete' by her father's
tent; the Criseyde who asked her niece about love; and who
greeted her fussy and business-like uncle with the artless
quip—'your maistresse is nat here'. It is the Code which
helps Chaucer to produce the inside and outside creation,
just as it is the Code which enables him to make his inherited
story more consistent and inevitable in itself. For I am naturally not suggesting that Chaucer saw the question of character in these theoretical terms, but by a *curiosa felicitas* the
Code enabled him to work as if he did, and it is clear that the
distinction between a lover whose sensibility was in line with
the Code, and the lover who simply responded to his
instincts, was very much in his mind. *The Knight's Tale*
makes this plain: Palamon, an elementary sort of Troilus, is

contrasted with Arcite, a Troilo figure who exclaims deris-
ively to his friend,

> *Thyn is affeccioun of hooliness,*
> *And myn is love, as to a creature.*

Here Chaucer makes the difference ironic, but in the bigger
poem there is no need for irony.

It is extraordinarily convincing, by any standards, that the
physical desire which beckons Griseida on is quite absent
from the many pros and cons that fill Criseyde's mind when
she is confronted with the prospect of love. What fits the
Code is also most psychologically realistic. The problems of
falling in love are too complex for her to be able to spare a
thought for the actual pleasures of love-making. And her
chastity is a sort of accident of this complexity—it does not
mean that she is either frigid or hypocritical: merely that in
the situation she finds herself it makes life simpler and pleas-
anter. 'Vacant heart and hand and eye, easy live and quiet
die.' Chaucer makes it clear that this has nothing to do with
religion or morality: Criseyde has not got much more sense
of the first than a modern heroine, and the Code gave no
encouragement to chastity as such. The good sense that
inspires her attitude is for us an accurate and ironic indicator
of the passions and aims of love, but for her its weakness is
that it cannot be an end in itself. The news of Troilus's
passion makes her ask herself 'To what fyn live I thus?'—
what is the purpose of her present existence? It is a fatal question. She is upset at the idea of love, but she is also upset by
the fact that it levels a criticism at her present mode of life.
 Although one hesitates to disagree with so great an
authority, C. S. Lewis is surely taking too short a cut when
he announces that timidity is Criseyde's ruling passion. The

very idea of passion is out of place in Chaucer's unfolding of
a consciousness at once so complex and so simple—simple in
itself but complex in its response to the demands of circumstance and Code. Her trouble is rather the absence of a
passion. I have commented on the subtlety with which
Chaucer shows us the incidents that elbow her in the direction of romance—her niece's song in the garden, the nightingale, her dream. It is her sudden awareness of these things
in the light of Troilus's infatuation which makes her reflect,
'To what fyn live I thus?' She has great good sense, but it is
her misfortune (as it was emphatically not that of Jane
Austen's heroines), that her good sense can be thrown off its
balance by the reflection: what is there to be sensible about?
The sense of Elinor Dashwood strikes us as being a little
priggish because it is so firmly rooted in religious and social
convictions that are hardly ever discussed and hardly felt
even, but which are none the less deeply there. We could
not shake Elinor a hairsbreadth by saying to her, '*why* do
you need to be sensible about this?—but we could throw
Criseyde into a terrible dither at once. In this she strikes us
as a more modern, or perhaps a more timeless, character;
certainly a more comprehensive one. A loss by the imagination of its confidence and initiative is a common fate in any
age, and one that cannot be countered by any amount of
good sense. In the 18th century Criseyde might have enjoyed
a serene existence, for her good sense would then have had
a whole society to support it, but in any other time she
would have to tag round forlornly after the prevailing
mores, continually suffering shocks to her natural prudence
and her nervous system which would demoralize her and
make her ask, 'To what fyn live I thus?' Life, the imaginative
possibilities of the time, would give her no peace until she
let them do with her what they wanted.

Ironically enough it is her good sense which helps on the final capitulation. The indefatigable Pandarus has asked her to supper and she inquires if Troilus will be there. Pandarus assures her that he is out of town,

Nought list myn auctor fully to declare
What that she thoughte when he seyde so ...

In fact Boccaccio says nothing about it, but Chaucer always enjoys these 'appeals to incalculability' which the convention of following a source allows him. Did Criseyde have some suspicion of what might have been arranged? Certainly she now feels very tender towards Troilus. The respect and fidelity which he has shown during his period of 'service', and the feeling of protective adoration with which he has surrounded her, have made her much less haunted by the idea of being used and let down: she is beginning to let herself be led by her natural sweetness and affection to the point where she may be willing to humour her uncle's attempts on her virtue. But in all sophisticated works there is, as James put it, 'a charm in any ambiguity of appearance that is not by the same stroke an ambiguity of sense'. If we are left in doubt here about her exact state of mind we are not therefore to suppose that she divined her uncle's intentions all along and has been leading her pursuers at her own leisure to the place she wanted to go. She has very little sense of the past and none at all of the future, but by now she is familiar with her uncle's tactics and they seem much less invidious than they once did.

Chaucer does not tell us whether Pandarus was an amateur astrologer and was thus able to forecast the cloudburst which would take place that evening, caused by the coincidence of the crescent moon in Cancer with Jupiter and Saturn. From all we know of his inquiring temper it seems quite likely, but if he was not it would be proof that his scheming needed liberal assistance from Fortune, 'executrice of wierdes', before it would bear fruit. As it is, when she sees the downpour and Pandarus urges her to stay the night, Criseyde sensibly decides to make the best of it.

> And syn it ron, and al was on a flod,　　　　　[rained
> She thoughte, 'As good chep may I dwellen here,
> And graunte it gladly with a frendes chere,
> And have a thonk, as grucche and thanne abide;
> For hom to gon, it may naught wel bitide.'

When the after-dinner talk and stories are over, and a nightcap drunk, they set about preparing for bed. The excitement in the air which the reader feels so strongly, and which Keats was to remember and reproduce so well in *The Eve of St Agnes*, is suggested by the contrast between this warm domestic ritual within and the wild weather outside.

> ... swych a reyn from heven gan avale,
> That every maner womman that was there
> Hadde of that smoky reyn a verray feere.

But, as Pandarus points out, 'this were a weder for to slepen inne'. He bustles about, allotting Criseyde his own closet and arranging mattresses on the floor outside it for her maids, as if they were so many dormice about to hibernate. He finds a moment to visit Troilus in the cupboard where he has been immured all day, and tells him that the great moment is at hand. With that sense of the mythological general always hovering behind the human particular which was shared by both the Middle Ages and the Renaissance—though the former may have given it more earnest and less adroit expression—Troilus calls on all the Olympic lovers for support, and implores Apollo to assist him by the memory of that sad moment when Daphne hid herself

> *Under the bark, and laurer wax for drede ...*

His prayers are abruptly cut short by Pandarus.

> *Thow wrecched mouses herte,*
> *Artow agaste so that she wol thee bite?*
> *Why, don this furred cloke upon thy sherte,*
> *And folwe me—*

In spite of Pandarus it is a heroic moment and it is fittingly accompanied by the storm.

> *The sterne wynd so loude gan to route*
> *That no wight oother noise myghte heere ...*

Shakespeare in *Othello* also provides a storm which is not in his source to herald the brief union of the lovers, and perhaps it is not too fanciful to remember the deluge in *The Golden Bowl* beneath which Charlotte stands macintoshed outside the windows of Portland Place. The weather seems to find its way into the dramatic imagination of love.

In spite of my admiration for the brilliance and complexity with which Chaucer expands his theme, I am sometimes inclined to feel that he lingers a little too long over the ensuing scene, and that something like simple burlesque does rear its head at the famous moment when Troilus swoons away under the mild rebuke given him by Criseyde for being jealous. It is in any case a fictitious jealousy, invented by Pandarus to explain Troilus's presence in the house, but characteristically Criseyde is taken in by it at once. (3. 806–808.) She will tell him in the morning how absurd he is being. The whole idea of jealousy quite upsets her and she speaks her mind about it. Thwarted by the theoretical turn the conversation has taken, Pandarus accuses her of not really being fond of Troilus. She replies warmly and they almost come to 'words' over it. Will she see him then at once, as he is very upset? Poor Criseyde is in a strange house and she has been abruptly woken out of a sound sleep; though it is clear that she has accepted the idea of going to bed with Troilus in the near future, for she loves him dearly, she does not want—exquisitely human as always—to have to see him now and prove it on the spot. Yet in the struggle between her desire to go back to sleep and her pity for Troilus, pity wins. He is fetched in, and she repeats her views on jealousy in no uncertain terms.

> 'Ek al my wo is this, that folk now usen
> To seyn right thus, "Ye jalousie is love",
> And wolde a busshel venym al excusen
> For that a greyn of love is on it shove.'

Troilus is so abashed that he faints away and has to be restored in Criseyde's bed by the united efforts of niece and uncle. The humour of the episode certainly stands out with the simplicity of a reef-knot in a tale whose texture is so finely and elusively interwoven, and it leaves an unfortunate impression on the casual reader that the whole of a poem must be farcical with so clear a joke in the middle of it. But the climax of love is also a sexual climax, and though Chaucer takes love very seriously indeed his sense of proportion cannot see the actual business of copulation as anything but delightfully ridiculous. Nor has the earnest care with which latter-day fiction describes the sexual act disproved Chaucer's implication that this is no subject to which art can devote itself 'with full devout corage'. In any case, once we are properly absorbed in the social world of the Code—and Troy is not really so different from Proust's Paris or Henry James's London—the moment sinks back into the narrative and becomes no more than a richly-prepared comic incident, like the extraordinary behaviour of Charlus when the narrator first visits him in Paris.

The rest of the scene calls for no other gloss than Chaucer's own words,

> *Though that I tarie a yer, sometyme I moot*
> *After myn auctor, tellen hire gladnesse,*
> *As well as I have told hire hevynesse.*

But he does not linger over the settled pleasures of the next three years. They were too happy to have any history. He merely observes, in accordance with the Code, how immensely the state of love improved their natures. Troilus's natural largeness of spirit is still further increased, and when he went hunting it was only after the boar, bear, or lion— he spared the 'smale bestes'.

> *But al to litel, weylaway the whyle,*
> *Lasteth swich joie, ythonked be Fortune ...*

Antenor is taken prisoner, and in order to ransom him it is proposed to send Criseyde back to her father in the Greek camp. There is nothing Troilus can do about it, and he is forced to sit silent while the agreement is ratified in 'parlement', racking his brains for a solution that will solve both problems,

First, how to save hire honour, and what weye
He mighte best th'eschaunge of hire withstonde.

Pandarus cannot help him, except with the forlorn advice to
think that it was fun while it lasted, advice that is ironically
in contrast with the caution from Boethius that he impressed
three years before on a Troilus incoherent with gratitude.

> 'For of fortunes sharp adversitee
> The worste kynde of infortune is this,
> A man to han been in prosperitee,
> And it remembren, when it passéd is ...'

Like his comment on the just suspicions of women, this
advice shows the real gravity there is in Pandarus; and we
remember that he has a 'story' of his own, a story which
exasperation and despair make Troilus bring up now against
his old friend.

> 'But telle me now, syn that thow thynketh so light
> To changen so in love ay to and fro,
> Whi hastow not don bisily thi might
> To chaungen hire that doth thee al thi wo?
> Whi nyltow lete hire fro thi herte go?'

Pandarus is convincing neither as an advocate of promiscuity
nor when he makes an effort to be tough, exhorting Troilus
'to manly sette the world on six and sevene' in order to keep
his lady.

Criseyde's reception of the news is very different from the
frenzy of Troilus but no less moving. She is surrounded by
chattering women.

Quod first that oon, 'I am glad trewely,
Bycause of yow, that shal youre fader see'.
Another seyde, 'Ywis so am nat I,
For al to litel hath she with us be'.
Quoth tho the thridde, 'I hope, ywis, that she
Shal bringen us the pees on every syde,
That when she goth almyghty God hire gide'.

Tho wordes and tho wommanysshe she thynges,
She herde hem right as tho she thennes were;
For, God it woot, hire herte on othir thyng is ...
So that she felte almost hire herte dye
For wo and wery of that compaignye.

When she is alone and gives way to her tears her uncle
rushes in to distract her again. Fatally, he has decided to take
a brisk, no nonsense line. He urges her not to cry when
Troilus comes but to keep calm and think up some way of
rejoining him from the Greek camp

soon after ye be wente.
Women ben wyse in short avysement,
And lat seen how your wit shal now availle.

We can almost see the frozen despair of poor Criseyde when
her uncle, who has always urged her to leave everything to
him, says it is all up to her now. She strives to collect herself.

I shal don al my myght me to restreyne
From wepyng in his sighte ...

but the damage has been done, and isolation seems to gather
round her. The sight of Troilus's grief makes her so miserable that she sinks down in a faint, but when he pulls out his

sword to kill himself she recovers at once. The theatre is
entirely suited to him and to the moment, but Criseyde cannot rise to it, it makes her feel all the more wretched and shut
out: she cannot soar to the idea of a *liebestod* with Troilus,
though she makes a forlorn attempt (1240) to say the right
thing. But his despair merely terrifies her and makes her the
more anxious to soothe and comfort him somehow. The
poem shows how their different ways of expressing grief
drive a wedge between them at this moment, and how the
hysterical violence of Troilus makes Criseyde shrink into
herself. Their *rapport* in love was complete, but the crisis
reveals the great weakness of a Courtly Love affair (or perhaps
any affair): they do not know each other well enough to
maintain their intimacy at a moment like this. Poor Criseyde
tries to re-establish it by an appeal to their old habit of joyful
mutuality.

> *we han right ynough of this,*
> *And lat us ryse and streight to bedde go,*
> *And there lat us speken of our wo.*

After the drama of the suicide threat this prompt appeal to
bed has all the inconsequence of life, but so miserable is the
moment that we can hardly raise a smile.

> *Whan they were in hire bed, in armes folde,*
> *Naught was it lyk tho nightes here-byforn,*
> *For piteously ech other gan byholde ...*

Remembering her uncle's words, Criseyde does her best to
take the initiative and restore their disaster to a manageable
size.

> *'I am a womman, as ful wel ye woot,*
> *And as I am avysed sodeynly ...*

Me thynketh thus, that nouther ye nor I
Ought half this wo to maken, skilfully ...
... men ful ofte, ywis,
Mote spenden part the remenant for to save.'

She will tell her father that the family property in Troy must
be kept an eye on, and that will give her an excuse to get
back. Though he does his best, as a good 'servant', to bear
up and accept the situation, her efforts at calm and reason are
infinitely lowering to poor Troilus. Feverishly he points out
what is probably quite true: her father has been at such pains
to get her back that he won't let her go again easily—he no
doubt has some plan for her, like a rich marriage. Besides,
the Greeks are delightful and cultivated people; seeing her
beauty they will lay themselves out to distract and entertain
her. He implores her not to go, but to put her trust in him
and let them 'stele away' together. For as well as hysteria,
grief has bred in Troilus a capacity for urgent practical
decision. He is prepared to sacrifice everything, his rank, his
friends, his position in the army, if they can only get away
and live quietly somewhere. He has even given thought to
the important question of money.

> *'And vulgarly to speken of substaunce*
> *Of tresour, may we bothe with us lede*
> *Inough to lyve in honour and pleasaunce*
> *Til into tyme that we shal ben dede;*
> *And thus we may eschuen al this drede.*

It is at this moment that Pandarus has much to answer for.
He has convinced his niece that her 'wal of stiel and shield
from every displeasaunce' can do nothing for her in this
crisis: she will have to surmount it herself. And quite apart

116

from her uncle's instructions, her own imagination simply will not respond to Troilus's vision of the future. It is only the reader's imagination that grasps his desperate urgency and sincerity. But the love he gives her is too much a part of the present discreet régime for her to imagine it in any other setting, though while that régime lasted it would never occur to her to be anything but devoted to him in return. She cannot imagine a future in which he has given up his princely splendour and his military responsibilities—all the absorptions which do not concern her directly and which she has been happy to watch from outside. How can she supply anything in place of them?

> Criseyde, with a sik, right in this wyse,   [*sigh*
> Answerde, 'Ywys, my deere herte trewe,
> We wel may stele awey, as ye devyse,
> And fynden swich unthrifty weyes newe;
> But afterward ful soore it wol us rewe.
> And helpe me God so at my mooste nede,
> As causeless ye suffren al this drede.'

It is a damning refusal to meet him squarely, and 'unthrifty' is a hard word, when Troilus has already gone into the practical details of the scheme. Psychologically it is—as I have already suggested—the climax of the tale. That sigh is the end of Criseyde. She goes on to ask what would people think?—they would say he was a coward, and what about her reputation?—but the decision is already made, and Troilus knows it.

> For when he saugh that she ne mighte dwelle,
> Which that his soule out of his herte rente,
> Withouten more, out of the chaumbre he wente.

Though it is deeply true to the nature of the love affair he is writing about, Chaucer's timing to some extent removes suspense from the sequel. In Boccaccio we watch Griseida, when she is introduced to Diomede, with the intrigued unsympathy with which we might watch a tête-à-tête at a cocktail party. Will she, or will she not? We know the answer when she says to him, 'I wonder that you set your heart on a *feminella* like me'; and after she has reached her father we hardly need Boccaccio's gloating comment: 'her heart was still faithful, but not for long'. But in Chaucer's melancholy coda everything is flat; we feel the weight of every moment and the mechanical acceptance of life and its duties. Numbed but compliant, Criseyde greets her father.

> *She seyde ek, she was fayn with hym to mete,*
> *And stood forth muwet, milde, and mansuete.*

Troilus meanwhile is frantic, cursing all the gods and goddesses, nature, fate, and his birth,

> *And, save his lady, every creature.*

He reads her letters a hundred times a day, 'refiguryng hire shap, hire wommanhede'. He feels so wretched that he cannot help wondering if anyone has been struck by his sad state.

> *Another tyme ymaginen he wolde*
> *That every wight that wente by the weye*
> *Hadde of hym routhe, and that they seyen sholde,*
> *'I am right sory Troilus wol deye'.*

In fact we are shown her mere *existence* in deprivation, and his male capacity, and also freedom, to act the part.

For Chaucer, hitting off the type of Diomede—Troilus's

supplanter—is almost too easy. He exists unchanged in any age, and though he of course goes to work by the Code his smooth approach topples the poem's whole precarious structure of civility in love. With his usual straightforwardness Boccaccio records that he 'took a fancy to her' as soon as he saw Griseida, but Chaucer's Diomede reflects only that he may as well keep his hand in—it will 'shorte the weye'. Besides, he has noticed that Troilus seems to be in love with Criseyde and this stirs him to an automatic emulation. His technique is in revolting contrast to Troilus's lack of it. He shrewdly sizes her up even as they are riding to the camp, and asks her to think of him as a brother. We remember how she first told Troilus she would be a sister to him. The next day he suddenly declares himself her servant, and makes a special parade of saying that he never spoke like this to a lady before, and was never in love with one either. Criseyde accepts this flagrant remark in a bemused way; she summons up her politeness and thanks him, but she has hardly heard what he has been saying. In the next few days she has her share of 'the worste kynde of infortune'; she bitterly regrets that she did not accept Troilus's offer, and she tries to find some way of getting back. But then Diomede calls again and she is confronted with a new and appalling situation. He asks her casually what she thinks about the war,

> And of th'assege he gan hire ek biseche   [siege
> To telle hym what was hire opinyoun.

It is typical of Diomede that he should pretend to ask her first before telling her what he wants her to feel.

> 'The folk of Troie, as who seyth, alle and some
> In prisoun ben, as ye youreselven se;

Nor thennes shal nat oon on-lyve come
For al the gold atwixen sonne and se.
Trusteth wel and understondeth me!'

He proceeds to curdle her blood with accounts of what will
happen to the inhabitants when the Greeks take the place,
and ends by remarking that she should get a lover among her
new friends and—'I wol ben he to serven yow myselve'. His
parody of a gentle lover is so gross that it is almost comic
relief.

And with that word he gan to waxen red,
And in his speche a litel wight he quok,   [*stumbled*
And caste aside a litel wight his hed,
And stynte a while: and afterward he wok,
And sobreliche on hire he threw his lok,
And seyde, 'I am, al be it yow no joie,
As gentil man as any wight in Troie.'

But Criseyde is indifferent to his manners; her whole attention is fixed on the dreadful information he has casually
given her. In Troy the war was like a volcano under which
she had grown used to living, and Troilus's love had been a
tacit assurance that nothing terrible would happen. As cunning as Iago, Diomede demands why it was her father was so
keen to get her back, notwithstanding the loss of their
property in the town,

If he ne wiste that the cite sholde
Destroied ben?

As it happens Diomede's prediction is wholly accurate, but
this has no bearing on her aghast and immediate acceptance
of it. She would believe his assertions, however implausible,

because his concealed motives give them such a confident ring.

What follows is as rapid, as mutual, and as gruesomely perfunctory as a seduction in an early Anthony Powell novel. Chaucer now presents the Criseyde whom we have come to know so well as a figure seen wholly from the outside. It is significant that he postpones to this point a physical description of her.

> *Criseyde mene was of hire stature ...*

and he notes that her only defect of beauty was that her eyebrows met in the middle. He adds similar descriptions of Troilus and Diomede, for we are quite separated now from the consciousness of love that ignores external appearances. 'This is, and is not, Cressid'—Shakespeare makes a great scene of it, illuminating and almost uniting the lovers again in Troilus's metaphysical astonishment, but in Chaucer their isolation continues unbroken to the end. We catch a last glimpse of the old Criseyde when she suddenly bursts out crying at the thought of Troilus's 'gentillesse' and then reflects, 'to Diomede algate I wol be trewe'. This is the Criseyde who pretended to misunderstand the solicitude of her bustling uncle—

> *'Uncle,' quod she, 'Youre maistresse is nat here.'*
> *With that they gonnen laughe ...*

—and who assured a triumphant Troilus when they were at last in bed together that she would not be there if she had not already yielded to him in her heart. But that is the end of her. The letter she writes in reply to Troilus's frantic pleas to return is a sort of anti-love-letter, a masterpiece of querulous evasion. She will try to come some time, she says, but she is in difficulties because of bad gossip about herself and him, which is obviously his fault—she cannot say more about it for the present. From this letter Troilus

> *wel understood that she*
> *Nas nought so kynde as that hire oughte be.*

It is the moment for such understatement. She disappears from view. Troilus meets his death in battle. But the meaning of love has disappeared before death comes, and it is this chill of total indifference and meaninglessness, spreading like fog over the end of his poem, that Chaucer dispels in his palinode. The love of God is unchanging and incorruptible, and it is towards Him that we must turn,

> *For he nyl falsen no wight, dar I seye.*

The completeness of the human failure to make love endure, so movingly implied by Chaucer, is made quite explicit in *The Testament of Cresseid*, a poem written by the Scottish schoolmaster Henryson more than fifty years after Chaucer's death. He emphasizes that Diomede soon tired of his conquest and discarded her, and goes on remorselessly to describe how she then became a leper, living in the extremity of wretchedness. Begging between the lines one day she sees Troilus ride past with his train of followers.

> *Then upon him scho kest up baith hir ene,*   [*eyes*
> *And with ane blenk it come into his thocht,*   [*a flash*
> *That he sumtime hir face befoir had sene,*
> *But scho was in sic plye he knew hir nocht;* [*such a state*
> *Yit than hir luik into his mynd it brocht*
> *The sweit visage and amorous blenking*
> *Of fair Cresseid, sumtyme his awin darling.*

Neither recognizes the other. Criseyde asks her companions who the knight was: Troilus thinks, where have I seen that poor creature before? It is an effective and justly famous moment, but like similar moments in celebrated films it is rather too insistently graphic. At the back of it is a hint of something exultant, as there is in Boccaccio's finale, and the satisfaction of the author is a certain sign that truth is being led off in a particular direction. Before the last great notes of the palinode, Chaucer's poem sinks into an emptiness and silence that contain the idea that human memory is as uncertain as human love, but do not pronounce it for a fact. As my comparison with the films implies, Henryson's effect seems modern to us and perhaps takes our fancy for that reason; we have a relish for the kind of definitive insight involved, and it is just this kind of insight that Chaucer does not give us. Even 'the worste kynde of infortune' has nothing infallible and universal about it. What destroys poor Troilus, that most vulnerable and Boethian of heroes, is a source of deep satisfaction to the Wife of Bath.

> It tikleth me about myn herte roote.
> Unto this day it doth my herte boote
> That I have had the world as in my tyme.

Like Shakespeare, Chaucer shows us the resources of human freedom so naturally that we take them for granted. Both give us the impervious as well as the tragic man, the Wife of Bath and Parolles as well as Troilus and Othello, resilience and unmeaning as well as shape and destiny. And their awareness of separate people goes deeper than any insight into abstractions like love and grief and the 'truth' about men and women.

CHAPTER THREE

LOVE AND IDENTITY:

Othello

CHAPTER THREE

Love and Identity:

OTHELLO

IT MAY seem odd that *Othello* should follow Chaucer's poem. If Shakespeare, why not *Troilus and Cressida* itself, or *Antony and Cleopatra* even more? Is not *Othello* the most deliberately restricted of all Shakespeare's mature plays, a dramatic study in jealousy, the most dull and infertile concomitant of love? It seems to me on the contrary that the treatment of love in *Othello* is of a singular fullness and depth, and that this can best be shown by contrast and comparison with works of a similar comprehensiveness. For by an odd paradox the seemingly pure, almost classical, theatre of *Othello*, its economy of exposition and crisis unique in Shakespeare's work, have blinded us to the fact that Shakespeare is writing about the private life—personal relations and problems of domesticity and daily living—in a way that he does nowhere else. The subject matter of *Othello* is the subject matter of the domestic novel, the subject matter of Jane Austen, Proust, and Henry James. It is of course also the subject matter of French farce. But the characters of the novel share with those of *Othello* the same mode of individuality, the ungraspable element in the live and familiar person, the quality of uniqueness which means that though they are subject to the partial viewpoints of other individuals they cannot in the nature of things be seen all round and summed up. And such characters are very different from those employed in the kind of demonstration which ends with a pronouncement like, *il y a toujours celui qui aime et celui qui se laisse aimer*, a pronouncement made by the author as if he were a god.

All great writers seem agreed that the private life and its problems requires the relative view, and we should certainly expect to find it in Shakespeare. We are inured to the freedom of *Hamlet*, whose drama is the sphere of action and public life, but the theatrical simplicity of *Othello* has led us to assume that this most private of the plays is also the least complex and the least full of possibility. And yet the argument over the characters at once suggests that this is not the case, for it is recognizably the same conflict that is perennially taking place, at all levels of sophistication, about the great figures of domestic fiction. What are they really like? Should they have behaved as they did? The queries continue about Othello and Iago as they do about Anna and Vronsky and about the characters in *The Golden Bowl*. And they take the form of a personal response to the characters: the reaction, whether of admiration or animosity, is like that of one personality upon another. The critics approach the play as if the characters were members of their clubs or colleges. Rymer is disgusted; Swinburne adores; Bradley is covertly fascinated; T. S. Eliot and F. R. Leavis disapprove. But there is a distinction to be made between them, for the last two also claim what they imply none of their predecessors showed—a balanced, analytic, and judicious viewpoint. They imply that while the earlier practice was to be carried away by the distaste or enthusiasm inspired by a *coup de théâtre*, their own approach is a well-weighed post-mortem on what is really in the play. Latter-day critics, in fact, are not emotionally 'taken in'.

Critics who are not taken in by the personality of *Othello* do not go so far as to suggest that the author was. They assume that Shakespeare's conception of the hero must be the same as their own: that he also sees Othello as a bogus great man, whose masterfulness and nobility are really a thin covering for 'the obtuse and brutal egotism' which readily leads to an 'insane and self-deceiving passion'. The phrases are those of Dr Leavis, Othello's harshest critic, and he continues: 'the habitual nobility is seen to make self-deception invincible, the egotism it expresses being the drive to catastrophe'.[1] This then is the effect that Shakespeare had in mind, though it is not apparent to the readers and audiences who are taken in by what Leavis calls 'the sentimentalists' Othello'. We might notice at this point the odd irony that those who decline to be taken in by Othello find themselves in the company of Iago. Iago too is in no doubt about Othello's real nature, and he is not a tolerant man: his opinions about life, morals, and society are very definite indeed. Moreover his tone suggests now and then that though he has 'placed' Othello he remains exasperated with him, indeed envious of him, for although Othello's masterfulness and nobility are a fraudulent pretence they are imposed with such maddening conviction and success upon the world at large. To one who prides himself upon being a master dissembler —'I am not what I am'—what could be more insufferable than the spectacle of someone dissembling far more magnificently and effectively than himself, and—crowning insult—without even being aware that he was doing it?

I imagine that no critic who feels that Othello is fatally 'placed' in the play would disagree that Iago is placed as well,

[1] This and subsequent quotations are from 'The Sentimentalists' Othello' in the essay collection *The Common Pursuit*.

But then so is Iago's conception of Othello. And here the confident summer-up of Othello might become a little uneasy, finding that his own verdict on Othello is already placed, and damningly so, in the presentation of Iago's view. The author with whose intentions he imagined himself to be in a minority of understanding appears to have situated this kind of understanding in the Iago consciousness. So far from being in with Shakespeare on the truth about Othello, he finds himself left in the dubious company of those who can see through and all round the hero, while the author retires in his elusive way to a more remote and more enigmatic viewpoint. The insight of Iago is clearly a double-edged asset, and in whatever light we are intended to view Othello there can be no doubt of the repellent nature of his betrayer. Apart from the horror of what he does, Iago's outlook is simple, brutal, and dull; his insight is of the sort which reduces all impulse and motive to baseness; he claims to know exactly what human beings want and why. He is too self-assured to find anything mysterious, and he is himself a totally unmysterious character, in fact he is deadeningly trivial. For him, people are either wholly discerning or complete fools: the discerning ones, like himself, are trying something on, and the most contemptible, like Othello and Roderigo, are in the grip of a force which they cannot control, a force which they laughably think of as 'love', but which Iago knows to be 'a mere lust of the blood and permission of the will'—something, like the rest of life, to be made use of and despised. 'Our bodies are our gardens to which our wills are gardeners ...' his speeches to Roderigo set out his absolute morality very clearly. Sure that he knows himself, he is equally convinced that he knows others. 'And knowing what I am,' he says to Othello when pointing out the elementary facts of infidelity, 'I know what she shall be.'

His pride in his powers of analysis and worldly common-sense uncannily anticipate some of the features of the Augustan spirit, and as if to clothe this spirit in its appropriate diction Shakespeare provides him with a speech which might come straight out of an 18th century poem.

> *She that was ever fair, and never proud;*
> *Had tongue at will, and yet was never loud;*
> *Never lackt gold, and yet went never gay;*
> *Fled from her wish, and yet said 'Now I may';*
> *She that, being angered, her revenge being nigh,*
> *Bade her wrong stay and her displeasure fly;*
> *She that in wisdom never was so frail*
> *To change the cod's head for the salmon's tail;*
> *She that could think, and ne'er disclose her mind;*
> *See suitors following and not look behind;*
> *She was a wight, if ever such wight were,*
> *To suckle fools and chronicle small beer.*

It is a striking forecast of a commonplace Augustan idiom, with the stock cynicism and the tough louche discernment that will be echoed in a hundred satires, in the *trivia* of Swift and Mandeville, and the wit of the restoration stage. Indeed Iago, whose honesty impresses the other characters so much, is in many ways a terrible parody of the Augustan *honnête homme*, without a vestige of romanticism in his outlook.

All this indicates that whatever we think of Othello, he is at least very unlike Iago. There is an immense gulf between them. Such a gap between the mode of being of two characters is itself unique in Shakespearean tragedy, for in some way Cordelia and her sisters, Antony and Octavius, even Hamlet and his mother, are kept in close *rapport* by the mode of their tragic relation: they are never incomprehensible to each other; the experiences they undergo give them a kind of mutality and cohesion, the kind of cohesion that Mr Wilson Knight no doubt has in mind when he remarks on its absence in *Othello*, 'where the dominant quality is separation'. Certainly, but Mr Wilson Knight goes on to say that 'the thought of *Othello* does not mesh with the reader's: rather it is always outside us, aloof'. Surely it is the 'thoughts' of the characters that do not 'mesh', and it is they who remain always outside one another, not we outside them? The gulf between Iago and Othello is like that between Hinton and Heathcliff in *Wuthering Heights* or that between Anna Karenina and her husband.

These novels are not 'aloof' from us, but it is significant that they are novels. In Shakespeare's source a *novella* of the private passions, *Othello* retains as a play characters who remind us of its origin by reminding us of the characters we meet in great fiction. The gap between Othello and Iago is duplicated by the gap between the world of a novel and the world of a play; by the gap between the swift dramatic time of the plot and the lingering fictional time of the domestic psychology which it depicts; by that between the heroic and romantic poetry of Othello and the Augustan couplets and incisive prose of Iago; and most of all by the gap between the impact of the *coup de théâtre* on our emotions, and the effect of the analysis of love and jealousy upon our minds. *Othello* is constructed on a whole series of such tensions and contrasts, which must be understood if we are to appreciate its riches fully, and which must be traced to their source in the initial contrast between story and theatre.

It is all the more important to understand this because *Othello* is on the face of it so very much of a play. Mr Wilson Knight's remarks imply indeed that it is *too* much of one, that it does not resemble enough the spacious and crowded dramatic universe of the other tragedies. But in turning towards them in search of a contrasting congeniality and bounty he is turning in the wrong direction: it is the fictional universe, not the dramatic, which will give us the key to the bounty of *Othello*, in its own way as copious and imponderable as that of the other great plays. It has had to become so very much a play because it is in its source so uncompromisingly a seamy cautionary tale, a tale that presented Shakespeare with a uniquely difficult problem of adaptation. Cinthio's *novella*, as he found it, takes place wholly in an Iago-world. Othello, Iago, and Cassio are much the same sort of person; their desires and motives are similar, and they are equal in their assumptions and in the brutish 'pluming up of the will'. Desdemona alone, a figure of rather Dickensian saintliness, is outside and above this prevailing atmosphere. Iago and Othello murder her together, and then pull down the ceiling of the chamber to make their crime look like an accident. And they are accomplices in motive as well as in deed: both do it 'for love'—Othello in jealousy, and Iago in envy and hatred because his love overtures to Desdemona were rejected. It is this unprepossessing tale which Shakespeare set himself to jack up to the level of the highest tragic art. The technical problems involved are enormous. How did he set about solving them?

A preliminary point to notice is that if the audience often tends to travel, in some sense, from the Othello to the Iago viewpoint, Shakespeare himself travelled in the opposite direction. He started with a world in which Iago's values and outlook are supreme, and he ends with one in which Othello—by his very existence—affirms the existence of a totally different outlook and a different world. For the flat and mean uniformity of the story he substituted the twin poles of significance on which the play rests. He piles up on

one side in a glowing mass the warmth, colour, and magnificence of life; all its intermittent splendour and its 'bright
things that come to confusion'; all—one has no objection to
adding, in deference to Mr Eliot and Dr Leavis—its open
vanity and absurdity, its generous illusion and self-bolstering
dramatics. Opposite this Shakespeare concentrates Iago's
world, which my comments on his nature have already
sufficiently pictured. Of course there is nothing symbolic in
this opposition. The idea of a bright brave world of acceptances and aspirations confronting a drab world of brutal
fact might appeal to an Anouilh or a Fry, just as the idea of
a monstrously self-deceiving egotist might have appealed to
Ibsen: there is no reason to suppose that either pattern suggested itself to Shakespeare—indeed, this kind of exclusive
consciousness seems quite foreign to all we can guess of his
creative powers.

But he must have been aware of the contrasts he
was creating between the story he had borrowed and
the play that would burst upon his audience. The time
problem he overrides by putting a paralysing speed and
force into the impact of the plot and its *dénouement*—(the
novella, naturally enough, lingers into weeks and months)—
while leaving a *sense* of time to work quite openly in the
minds and reactions of the characters. As Bradley observed,
this doubleness of time is evident to any spectator who
reflects on the action of the play. Physically there is neither
time nor occasion for adultery; but this does not stop
Othello being convinced that Desdemona 'has the act of
shame a thousand times committed', nor Iago asserting that
Cassio has talked in his sleep about it. These are apprehensions that only the novel, with its unremittingly quotid-
ian effect, could produce, and Shakespeare has retained them,
hinting only one slight link with the swiftness of drama in

the suggestion that these things *might* all have happened in
Venice before the marriage. An even more significant
change is made in the Iago of the *novella*, whose love for
Desdemona changed to hatred because she rejected him.
Dramatically, Shakespeare's Iago must have nothing in
common with Othello; love must not be a link between
them, and Iago must not be subject to the common human
passion. All that remains of it in the text is made subtle
use of to suggest that what Iago calls love is not what the
word usually means. 'Now I do love her too', he says of
Desdemona—

> *Not out of absolute lust—though peradventure*
> *I stand accountant for as great a sin—*
> *But partly led to diet my revenge,*
> *For that I do suspect the lusty Moor*
> *Hath leapt into my seat.*

It is an astonishing reflection. We would assume that Iago
would feel an automatic lust for Desdemona—all rational
men, in his view, feel thus about attractive women—but he
adds that he 'loves' her out of revenge, because he thinks
Othello has cuckolded him. His conception of love assumes a
kind of nightmarish absurdity; apart from normal lust he
proposes to himself to 'love' Desdemona in order to get his
own back on her husband! It is an effect that we shall be
noticing continually in the play—the isolation of the characters in their separate conventions of understanding, and
the shock that is produced by the collision of words used
with different meanings. As we shall see, one of Iago's chief
weapons is the suggestion that Othello and Desdemona
speak a different moral language, and that what is dreadful

to him seems normal enough to her (and by implication to Iago himself): she goes to bed with Cassio innocently, 'not meaning any harm' (Act IV, Scene 1. 5).

Coleridge's famous phrase for Iago's reasoning—'the motive-hunting of motiveless malignity'—does indicate very aptly the psychological impression left by Shakespeare's technical need to deprive Iago of his love motive. But it should not be allowed to start a chain of psychological criticism based on the idea that such a motiveless evil must be fascinating and absorbing in itself. The reasons he gives for what he does are admirably consistent with the deadly triviality of his outlook, and that outlook—and indeed the framework of the play—is based on his non-comprehension of love. It is this that is the real point of Iago. It goes with his mode of utterance as contrasted with Othello's, and with the whole antithetical movement of the play: even the movement of single scenes is founded on these antitheses, as in Act II, Scene 1, where the triumphant chorus for Othello's arrival is succeeded by the Iago idiom, which returns again at the end of the scene after the duet of the lovers' meeting. As I have suggested, the antithesis is even carried into the mind of the spectator: the effect on him of the *coup de théâtre* is quite separate from his subsequent rational analysis of behaviour and plot; and it is this curious split in appraisal which has contributed more than any other factor to the critical marking down of *Othello*, to the variously oblique depreciations of Bradley, Eliot, and Wilson Knight, and the franker verdict of Leavis—'with all its brilliance and poignancy it comes below Shakespeare's supreme, his very greatest work'.

It is a verdict that is based on the same premise as Wilson Knight's insistence that the greatest Shakespearean tragedy is 'cohesive', and T. S. Eliot's suggestion that Othello's tragic stature is jeopardised by his *Bovarysme* and his wish 'to cheer himself up'. This premise is that the great play should be impersonal, that the quirks and undercurrents of individual psychology should be swallowed up in a grand tragic generality. It is significant that admirers of this impersonality in Shakespeare find it at its height in *Antony and Cleopatra*, which is of all his plays the closest to its source. The admired qualities are already implicit in Plutarch and in historical tradition; already the theme is noble, archetypal, while that of *Othello* might well have been turned into comedy, as Shakespeare converted similar tales in *Much Ado* and *All's Well*. The nature of this gap between story and play, and the steps taken to span it, are ignored by the purists of tragic completeness.

Moreover every critical formula for supreme tragedy contains the possibility of abuse. Thanks to modern Shakespearean interpretation we are well indoctrinated to-day with the notion that each tragedy is a 'spatial' and self-ordered universe, out of time, unimpeded by the trailing umbilicals of consistency and characterization, and having a peculiar power which can profoundly illuminate our unpeculiar world. This way of looking at the tragedies can be very valuable, but like all such conceptualizations it falsifies not only by substituting critical symbol for actuality, but also by tacitly excluding the possibility in Shakespeare of other and equally valid tragic modes. Wilson Knight's approval of *Lear* or *Timon* is well expressed in his phrase 'a visionary statement', and he tells us that *Othello* is 'a story of intrigue rather than a visionary statement'. This description would certainly fit Cinthio's *novella*: applied to the play it seems to ignore everything that has been achieved between the two. Dr Leavis feels that 'even *Othello* is poetic drama and not a psychological novel written in dramatic form and

draped in poetry, but relevant discussion of its tragic significance will nevertheless be mainly a matter of character-
analysis.' He adds that the play is well fitted to Bradley's
critical approach 'if he had made it with moderate intelligence'. This depreciates *Othello* as much as Bradley: we
infer that any play which is suited to his methods cannot be
of the highest quality.

In applying their strictures of 'intrigue' and 'character',
both critics confirm *Othello's* status as a second-class play.
Dr Leavis's verdict follows logically enough from his conviction that Shakespeare's aim in this 'brilliant piece of
workmanship' was the portrait of a particular kind of egotist, and that this is not the highest kind of tragic preoccupation, however successfully worked out. Its nature as a psychological study automatically diminishes it. Realistic,
analysable characters are apparently the sign of an inferior
play. Coleridge and Bradley are fascinated by the personality
of Iago, and Eliot and Leavis repelled by the personality of
Othello. But whatever our views on the place of character
in tragedy, it is impossible to avoid the intimacy of the
personal contact in any work which, like *Othello*, carries us
into the heart of private life. We cannot feel about Hamlet
or Macbeth the same animus which we bring to Othello,
because the duties and ambitions of kings and princes are
not, like jealousy and adultery, matters of which we daily
take note and on which we daily sit in judgement. *Othello* is
as close to us as the Sunday newspaper; and its story, like
that of newspaper or novel, could be our own story. Yet it is
a poetic drama, and it is precisely its success as such that
prevents, or should prevent, our response becoming trivial-
ized into too narrow a reaction to personality. Dr Leavis's
concession that 'even *Othello*' is a poetic drama does not in
practice alter his appraisal of it and his conviction that 'for

those who take what Shakespeare has to offer' it is essentially a study in personality. For him, as for Bradley, who made the point by commenting on *Othello's* lack of 'symbolic' quality, it offers what the novel offers.

Now I have already suggested that a comparison of *Othello* with the novel can be extremely illuminating, provided that we are scrupulous about which points of comparison are relevant and which are not. The common ground is the subject matter—human relations in the domestic sphere —and thus it is as relevant to ask ourselves what was the nature of Othello's and Desdemona's love, and what were their chances of happiness, as it is to wonder whether Isobel, in *The Portrait of a Lady*, would ever have left her husband, or how Elizabeth and D'Arcy would have got on after marriage. These queries are relevant because the resonance of such situations can never be stilled; as Henry James well knew, 'such relations, properly considered, end nowhere', and the author who invokes them is automatically invoking our speculation as a further enrichment of his effect. In these relationships, moreover, a speaker may reveal one thing while saying another, or may be quite ignorant of the nature of a person he thinks he knows, or—(a favourite device of Proust's)—may have to alter a fixed opinion about someone in the light of fresh and unexpected evidence. All these considerations are as relevant to *Othello* as they are to the novel, and their freedom of range within their proper field can be shown by contrast with their irrelevance in a different setting. We all know that it does not much matter how many children Lady Macbeth had, and there is no point in our asking if she would have been a good mother to them, or if she would have left Macbeth for a more ruthless husband if he had refused to kill Duncan. But the fictional analogy can be more subtly irrelevant than this, and a great deal more falsifying. Both Bradley and Leavis treat *Othello* as a psychological *roman à clef*. Convinced of its simplicity and lack of complex effects, they look for the crucial aspect of the play, the factor which shall determine the nature of their appraisal. Both find it in a single personality. Bradley devotes most of his study of the play to Iago, and to asking questions like: what did he hope to gain from his crime? Such a question shows the wrong sort of fictional analogy, for it makes a demand on plot which the novel by convention upholds but which the poetic drama need not. Bradley also asks the proper question: Without Iago, would the lovers have achieved happiness?—proper, because it sets us to consider the nature of that love and how Shakespeare portrays it, and these considerations are deeply relevant to the world of the play. But it is Iago who principally attracts him and draws his real emotional response. The humane and bookish Victorian is both fluttered and spellbound by what he feels to be the problem of Evil; and his emotion, which echoes from its own individual but no less immediate quarter the fury of Rymer and the adoration of Swinburne's '*we love Othello*', is itself echoed by the distaste with which Leavis, whose conception of a lover's conduct is framed in the exacting school of D. H. Lawrence, animadverts on the nature and behaviour of the hero.

Leavis perceives clearly the nature of the vicious circle in which Bradley and his supporters have trapped themselves, pointing out that their interest in Iago proceeds from their assumption of a noble-hearted unjealous Othello who must require for his undoing an Iago of dazzling intellect and fiendish skill. Or (to go round the circle in the opposite direction) *because* Iago is a diabolic superman, Othello can still retain his great and wronged nobility and virtue. Leavis breaks out of the circle at one blow by taking it that Othello is the kind of man whom we should in any case expect to find brutally assaulting his wife in a fit of jealousy and in a mood of outraged justice, so that Iago's task is therefore a trivial one and he himself a repellent but by no means a diabolically clever person. His blow (if we accept that it has force behind it) also loosens the great edifice of the tragedy and sends it sliding back towards the original mire of Cinthio. The Shakespearean differentiation is lost; Othello the egotistic brute, and Iago his rancorous subordinate, are reunited on the same plane of being. Although Leavis calls the play 'a marvellously adroit piece of workmanship', he shows no sign of interest in the technical problems of its genesis, and the mere study of egotism which he concludes it to be quite justifies his verdict of second-rate.

While Leavis shrinks Othello, Bradley expands him, and of the two attitudes it seems likely that the second is more likely to do Shakespeare justice. All his characters, even the minor ones, have the air of being larger and more realized than their rôle in the play requires. Leavis accuses Bradley of 'denaturing' the play, but it is hard to see how a misinterpretation which admits the size of the play, and its capacity to grow in the mind of the critic and his readers, can 'denature' it as effectively as a treatment which reduces it to the dimensions of Ibsen. Leavis's perception, like that of Eliot, is essentially negative: their distaste makes them wish to contain the subject within the most finite limits.

The clue to this rejection is to be found in the concept of impersonal tragedy which I have already mentioned. Eliot's *Shakespeare and The Stoicism of Seneca*, and his dialogue on tragedy, make the same point as Leavis's essays on *Othello* and on *Tragedy and the Medium*. All emphasize that in great tragedy there occurs a breaking down of character, a merging of individuals into a transcended human whole; there must be an 'emancipation from the ready-defined self', and no 'exaltation of the established ego', no 'cheering oneself up'. Leavis quotes a letter of D. H. Lawrence to the effect that he is 'sick of people' because 'they preserve an evil bad separating spirit', and all 'want the same thing ... to be a free agent' in a state where 'each separate little ego is an independent principality by itself'. Leavis says Lawrence is implying that such desires are 'incompatible with tragic experience' which must be 'an escape from all attitudes of self-assertion'. There are occasions when this doctrine can be helpful and revealing, but—like all attempts to isolate the essence of tragedy—it makes me feel that no tragic experience can survive a verdict on whether it is or is not doctrinally sound without becoming artificialized. The merits of tragic presentations can obviously be measured, but not in accordance with a single criterion. Why should a tragedy of personality automatically be slighter than an impersonal one? If we feel that the Duchess of Malfi is a less tragic figure than Phèdre, or Hotspur than Oedipus, it is not because Hotspur and the Duchess strike us as more commonplace, more selfish, more endearing—more generally 'human' in fact—but because the whole complex of their drama is on a lesser scale or involves less deeply perturbing issues. Antigone is not less human than Lady Macbeth, nor Achilles—whose tragic wrath arose from his disappointment over a slave-girl—more impersonal than Hamlet.

Like Matthew Arnold's doctrine of high seriousness, the doctrine of tragic—or more widely of poetic—impersonality, is apt to become an imposition of near-religious uniformity for a particular end. It is also highly ambiguous, as its advocates involuntarily reveal. Thus I. A. Richards, whose views are cited by Leavis as being 'in harmony' with his own, writes that in the full tragic experience 'the mind does not shy away from anything, it does not protect itself with any illusion, it stands uncomforted, unintimidated, alone and self-reliant'. An un-prejudiced reader might be excused for getting confused here between the mind that is enjoying 'the full tragic experience', and the established ego striking its deplorable 'attitude of self-assertion'. Much will presumably depend on self-consciousness, upon whether the mind knows itself to be standing uncomforted, unintimidated etc.: for to *feel* un-comforted, alone, and self-reliant, is itself a means of obtain-ing comfort. The more we look into it the more we find that there is only a phantom antithesis between a calm com-munal unillusioned state of mind and an exalted, separated, and ready-defined one. Both show a conscious attitude towards tragic experience, and which we prefer will depend on our total view of how human beings should behave. Both Eliot and Leavis have very definite views here, and their attitudes to tragedy reflect them. We might notice as possibly significant, too, the approval of a quotation in which Lawrence announces himself as 'sick of people'—not a very auspicious frame of mind in which to appraise the populous world of Shakespeare.

But where *Othello* is concerned there is a still more cogent reason for not applying the criterion of tragic impersonality. *Othello* is not an impersonal tragedy because sexual love is not an impersonal emotion. Leavis's criticism of Othello's temperament is a highly realistic one, and since the nature of sexual love is explored so realistically in the play this seems an excellent thing. Indeed it is remarkable how much criti-cism of the play has ignored its main theme. But as well as being realistic the treatment of love is many-sided; Shake-speare enters into and celebrates its most soaring emotions as well as showing us its weaknesses, its cruelty and incom-prehension. No point is made and no challenge extended;

no obvious judgement is involved, and there is certainly no moral standard proffered by which we are to assess the behaviour of people in love. Leavis, however, thinks that 'for those who take what Shakespeare had to offer' the issue is quite simple and clear-cut; he propounds a moral standard and he deplores the fact that Othello comes nowhere near it. He sees the play with the eye of a man who has made up his mind how people in love should behave: we have noticed that Iago is equally absolute in such matters.

> It is plain that Othello's love is composed very largely of ignorance of self as well as ignorance of Desdemona: how-ever nobly he may feel about it, it isn't altogether what he, and Bradley with him, thinks it is. It may be love, but it can only be in an oddly qualified sense love of her: it must be much more a matter of self-centred and self-regarding satisfactions—pride, sensual possessiveness, appetite, love of loving—than he suspects.

This is very acute, but Leavis seems to feel that Shakespeare, like George Eliot, owed a perpetual obligation to his per-ceptions and opinions—opinions necessarily of the most enlightened and inflexible kind. As a comment on the play, preliminary to 'placing' it, the acuteness loses its edge, for isn't the whole tragedy and the whole poignancy of sexual love precisely that it is so often like this—like this among many other things? Othello shares his tragedy with all of us, but Leavis seems to feel that in indicating this aspect of love he is passing a final judgement on Othello personally, while audience and critic stand censoriously by with their withers unwrung. This is all the odder because of his com-ment elsewhere that we are drawn to identify ourselves with Othello, with the Othello of his own—and Bradley's—imagination that is: but the correct response to *Shakespeare's*

Othello is evidently a distant appraisal of his shortcomings, and a lack of tragic communion which indicates the comparatively minor status of the work. We are to feel nothing but alienation, a Brechtian *Verfremdungseffekt*. And Leavis will not allow that a love containing the elements he analyses might also contain the qualities of greatness, nobility, and self-sacrifice. He concedes that Othello possesses nobility of a sort:—'with external stress the noble Othello is well qualified to deal. If he went down (in the storm), and we know he won't—he would go down magnificently.' He might have added that if there had been the need to sacrifice his life for Desdemona's—and we know there can't be—he would have done it without hesitating. The constantly imputed grandeur in positive action (and therefore in love), which is a vital part of the play's tragic richness, is ignored by Leavis, who merely remarks that it has dazzled the inactive and secluded critics, and hints darkly that the admiration of the academic for the life of action is connected with 'the cult of T. E. Lawrence'.

To sum up, the initial fallacy of much *Othello* criticism is the assumption that it is a simple clear-cut affair, and that the task of the critic is to determine what kind of simplicity, so to speak, is involved. For Wilson Knight it is the simplicity of intrigue; for Leavis, that of a special kind of character study; for Bradley (whose approach is less narrowly perspicacious and therefore less inadequate), the more exciting simplicity of a fathomless evil corrupting, though not eclipsing, good. The strong feelings aroused are all directed to one of these particular ends. But if we rather assume, from the nature of the subject and of the response we give to it, that the play is likely to be a highly complex affair, with a Shakespearean variety of perceptions and significances, then we shall cease to be merely pro- or anti-Othello, or under the spell of a *coup de théâtre*, and instead be more receptive to its totality of effect. It is this effect that we must now look at in greater detail.

In claiming for the play a far greater degree of complexity than is generally assumed, I am not saying that it closely resembles Shakespeare's other great plays, or that it works in the same way as they do. *Othello* is a tragedy of incomprehension, not at the level of intrigue but at the very deepest level of human dealings. And one would expect that the effect of such a tragedy would be significantly different from those in which a kind of understanding links the actors ever more closely as they suffer or inflict suffering; that it would be, in fact, more like that of a great novel. No one in *Othello* comes to understand himself or anyone else. None of them realize their situation. At the centre, between the poles of the play, Desdemona, Cassio, and Emilia show common sense and humanity, but it is more a matter of good instinct than illumination. Iago maintains to the end the dreadful integrity of his own ignorance, and in spite of—or perhaps because of—the revelation of Desdemona's innocence, Othello retains to the end his agonized incomprehension —the incomprehension which is so moving an aspect of tragedy in sexual love. His love for Desdemona was to him a marvellous revelation of himself rather than a real knowledge of her. And the proof of her innocence is no substitute for such an awareness. This is the final tragic separation, intensified by the conviction that she is going to heaven and he is going to hell. But although the characters never achieve understanding, and although our response to them—as theirs to each other—shifts with the successive and conflicting pulls of emotion and analysis, so that we see Othello through his own eyes and Iago's as well as with our own, yet if we wait for the fullness of what the play has to offer we do reach a state of tragic comprehension; we are left with a greater insight into the passions and the will, and how they operate to cut us off from each other and from ourselves.

The way this happens is however, as I have suggested, unique in Shakespeare. The tragic atmosphere offers none of that harmonious and formal communion in sorrow which plays at the end of *King Lear*,[1] or the participation in *Macbeth* at the re-establishment of spiritual order. Othello's tragedy is personal, ending in a total loneliness of spirit, and our recognition of it can only be correspondingly solitary. A parallel with the essentially private revelation of the novel form is always making itself felt. The critical approaches we have been considering imply that the other tragedies are more characteristically and greatly Shakespearean because they are more susceptible to the kind of exegesis which the criticism prefers. Because of his enthusiasm for what he regards as its symbolic presentation of Renaissance Man, Wilson Knight leaves us with the impression that *Timon of Athens* is the most remarkable of Shakespeare's tragedies. His interpretative method finds so much to elicit that the sense of proportion overreaches itself. It is this feeling for the material available to criticism which has produced the concept—now almost a cliché in Shakespearean criticism—of 'different imaginative levels' within the working of the greatest kind of tragedy. Thus Hamlet, for instance, is at the surface a gripping masterpiece of suspense and murder; rather deeper down it reveals the psychological relationship of father, mother, and son; deeper still, perhaps, the quasi-religious dilemma of a man who suddenly finds himself at

[1] KENT: Is this the promised end?
EDGAR: Or image of that horror?
ALBANY: Fall, and cease.

odds with the seeming reality of the world. Except at the surface the exact nature of these 'levels' will of course be perpetually disputed and seen in different lights, but the idea of them does suggest the inexhaustibility of our experience of Shakespeare. Their chief drawback, like the critique of 'impersonality', is the tendency to be invoked as a tragic standard which Othello, simple and undifferentiated as befits a story of intrigue, is again found to fall short of.

Modern criticism here is ignoring the unfamiliar effect because it does not see the familiar one it is looking for. The 'levels' of Othello are temporal (to use Wilson Knight's terminology), not spatial; and they are not those of mutually inclusive 'meanings' but of successive and at first mutually exclusive points of view. Hamlet is at one and the same moment a revenge hero, an Œdipal hero, and a religious hero: the rôles can all be played together and all are in some sense true; and though an audience could hardly in practice take them all in simultaneously, the possibility of this is a valid aim and convention. Moreover, while for Leavis, as for Bradley, Othello is either a jealous brute or he is not, the most opinionated critic would concede that most attitudes towards Hamlet and most qualities imputed to him are reconcilable in the total tragic effect. But the whole tendency of *Othello* is to make us partisan, to underline the incommensurability of opposed emotional stances. Just as Desdemona can never see Othello as Iago does, or Iago as does Desdemona, so our own succession of responses follows and reflects the partial and solipsistic attitudes of the protagonists. We are in the bafflingly relative world of social observation, where our own passions and prejudices distort reality as much as those of the people we are watching; and where our discernment of an unconscious motive or a comical lack of awareness—'A's good nature is really selfishness', or, 'Does B ever realize how he bores?'—also reveals our own nature and desires to others who may themselves be noting our unawareness of the fact. In *Othello* love is the agent which precipitates and co-ordinates these responses, keeps them moving, and forces us to reflect in the privacy of our own feelings the stages of an isolated and mysterious struggle.

For love is of all forces in society the most confusing and the most revealing; it stands both for the frightful difficulty of knowing other people and for the possibility of that knowledge; its existence implies the ideal existence of under-standing and its absence the total removal of it. The stages of our response to *Othello* compel us to see both with the eye of love and without it, and it is our awareness of what this means that leads us at last to a settled appraisal. The fatal thing is to get stuck at some point, to come to a halt on some premature conviction about the nature of the play, an easy course for the critic whose instinct it is to make up his mind about the nature of the experience he is having. Like all great works of art, *Othello* deprives us of the confident sense of ourselves *vis-à-vis* the rest of the world.

'Mutually exclusive points of view' is a phrase which might seem to imply an almost Shavian dramatic mode—lively argument about the nature of sexual love. But an audience gives an 'interested' and 'stimulated' response to *Candida*, while—as the critics have shown us—Othello arouses passionate and complex emotions. The 'points of view' in *Othello* have the whole man behind them and not just an argument; an obvious distinction, but worth making in view of the contrasts in the play between poetry and prose—the most important of our pairs of 'opposing poles' already mentioned. Poetry has a great deal more to do here than in the more organically conceived tragedies, the more so because it is not so native to the world of Othello as to the court of Lear and the castle of Macbeth. *Othello* begins at the moment when the fairy-story ends, and the great 'love-duet' at the beginning of Act II announces what should be the post-marriage *détente*: it is the prelude to domesticity, 'suckling fools and chronicling small beer'. The verse must celebrate in heroic terms a domestic situation too realistic even for comedy. But it does not only celebrate it and lift it to a heroic plane, it also analyses it. Although poetry and prose are so sharply differentiated both have the power to dissect and reveal. The antithesis is not, as might be supposed, between simple colourful heroic poetry, and mordant prose, but between the natures of the prose speaker and the poetry speaker. The poetry can be complex and pointed, but it also exalts—as the prose cannot—the bountiful glory and excitement of love. That this excitement has its dangers, even its ugliness and absurdity, both poetry and prose can convey in their separate ways. In using the term 'love-duet' I am suggesting that the unique indicative function of the poetry is indeed comparable with the *aria*: Verdi's *Otello* is the most successful of all operas based on poetic drama, and the greatest performance of Othello was given by Salvini, an actor whose voice and bearing were trained in opera. The magnificence of the poetry embodies the vital splendours of love— Desdemona's as well as Othello's—and is used by those who, like Cassio and the Gentlemen at the beginning of Act II, admire and extol such love. It is not used, except as a conscious and horrible parody, by Iago, who as we have seen produces his own style of verse in deliberate opposition to the love-idiom, a style uncannily prescient of the 18th century. Emilia has her own idiom, essentially prose though formally in blank verse, for her important and trenchant speech (Act IV, Scene 3) on the need for give and take between men and women.

Act II, Scene 1 illustrates these points in detail. First Montano and the Gentlemen celebrate in the language of love the storm at sea, that 'storm of fortunes' which the lovers expected and surmounted with such triumphant confidence.

> For do but stand upon the foaming shore,
> The chiding billow seems to pelt the clouds;
> The wind-shaked surge, with high and monstrous mane,
> Seems to cast water on the burning bear,
> And quench the guards of the ever-fixed pole:
> I never did like molestation view
> On the enchaféd flood.

In Cinthio's story the couple arrive 'on a perfectly tranquil sea', a detail only too much in keeping with the humdrum setting and the harmony of their previous conjugal life. Shakespeare's contrasting storm brings in the powers of love and danger—the latter in both its new and old senses. Cassio now arrives and thanks the previous speakers.

> Thanks, you the valiant of this warlike isle,
> That so approve the Moor! O, let the heavens
> Give him defence against the elements,
> For I have lost him on a dangerous sea.

Valiancy and love are connected, their language the same: and with the entry of Cassio the chorus swells to include Desdemona in a paean of praise.

> ... he hath achieved a maid
> That paragons description and wild fame;

> *One that excels the quirks of blazoning pens,*
> *And in the essential vesture of creation*
> *Does tire the ingener.*

The storm is emphasized once more:

> *Tempests themselves, high seas and howling winds,*
> *The gutter'd rocks and congregated sands—*
> *Traitors ensteept to enclog the guiltless keel—*
> *As having sense of beauty, do omit*
> *Their mortal natures, letting go safely by*
> *The divine Desdemona.*

And the power of love is invoked for all its votaries:

> *Great Jove, Othello guard,*
> *And swell his sail with thine own powerful breath,*
> *That he may bless this bay with his tall ship,*
> *Make love's quick pants in Desdemona's arms,*
> *Give renew'd fire to our extincted spirits*
> *And bring all Cyprus comfort!*

The paean reaches its climax with the appearance of Desdemona herself,

> *O, behold,*
> *The riches of this ship is come on shore!*
> *Ye men of Cyprus, let her have your knees.*
> *Hail to thee, lady, and the grace of heaven*
> *Before, behind thee, and on every hand,*
> *Enwheel thee round!*

It is then abruptly checked and reversed by the presence of Iago. The whole atmosphere of the scene changes at once.

Cassio, the noble and enthusiastic leader of the chorus, now appears almost absurd as he administers a gallant peck to the cheek of Emilia, observing

> *'tis my breeding*
> *That gives me this bold show of courtesy.*

The little fatuity is endearing enough in its way, but with Iago there Cassio appears in a different light: we see him to some extent through Iago's eyes. We also realize that Cassio has an idea of himself as a well-bred person which can appear fitting and noble or as something a bit vulgar and even—in a comical way—calculating. Conscious as we are of ideas about personal identity, the *persona* and so forth, we should recognize the swiftness and accuracy with which Shakespeare makes his point about them here and connects it, *via* the realistic and operatic contrasts of the scene, with the enthusiasm and the poetry of love. Love, we might say, brings to a head this problem of identity, and also makes it seem to those in the grip of love a problem to which the answer must instantly be found. Our awareness of Cassio in this scene foreshadows the sense of him that Othello will soon come to have, and furthermore our mixed impression of Cassio as the celebrant of love foreshadows our impressions of Othello himself.

For the next hundred lines or so Iago dominates the gathering. The theme of the passage is 'placing' people in terms of parlour witticisms.

> DESDEMONA: *What wouldst thou write of me if thou*
> *shouldst praise me?*
> IAGO: *O gentle lady do not put me to't,*
> *For I am nothing if not critical.*

Desdemona enters the game in order to conceal her anxiety for Othello.

> DESDEMONA: *Come on, assay.—There's one gone to*
> *the harbour?*
> IAGO: *Ay Madam.*
> DESDEMONA: *I am not merry, but I do beguile*
> *The thing I am by seeming otherwise.*
> *—Come, how wouldst thou praise me?*

In concealing her fears from the two men Desdemona shows her instinctive consideration. She will not embarrass them by making them feel they should try to reassure her, and what she feels for Othello is no affair of theirs. The coarse common sense and home-speaking of Iago is at the furthest possible remove from her love and anxiety: it is soothing at a crisis as neutral and indifferent things are. It is conveniently to hand and she embraces it with something like zest. Again the realism of the touch makes just the right point. Unlike Cassio, whose case is more ambiguous, Desdemona 'by seeming otherwise' only reveals more clearly and poignantly to the audience 'the thing she is'. But her behaviour *could* be seen in another light: through Iago's eyes we see her responses merely reflecting his own *idées fixes* about women, and behind Iago the anguish of Othello again begins to take shape.

At the end of the Iago passage Cassio again becomes the noble chorus introducing the entrance of Othello. *Lo, where he comes!* The phrase is often met in the tragedies and establishes an entrance with wonderful economy: our obligatory use of the continuous present has deprived us of such naturally ceremonial effects. Iago will use the same phrase when he sees Othello upon the rack.

Look, where he comes! Not poppy nor mandragora
Nor all the drowsy syrups of the world
Shall ever medicine thee to that sweet sleep
Which thou owedst yesterday.

Iago is deliberately parodying the ceremonial love-idiom of
Othello, Cassio, and the others, and the lines reminiscent of
Othello's own sonorous style are spoken with mocking glee.
The note of parody is emphasized further on in the scene,
where Iago produces a horrible simulacrum of Othello's
oath of vengeance:

OTHELLO: *... Like to the Pontic sea*
              Whose icy currents and compulsive course
              Ne'er feels retiring ebb, but keeps due on
              To the Propontic and the Hellespont;
              Even so my bloody thoughts, with violent pace,
              Shall ne'er look back, ne'er ebb to humble love
              Till that a capable and wide revenge
              Swallow them up. Now, by yond marble heaven,
              In the due reverence of a sacred vow
              I here engage my words.
IAGO: *Do not rise yet.*
              Witness, you ever-burning lights above,
              You elements that clip us round about,
              Witness that here Iago doth give up
              The execution of his wit, hands, heart,
              To wronged Othello's service. Let him command,
              And to obey shall be in me remorse,
              What bloody business ever.

The difference between the monumental fervour of
Othello's love-hate, and Iago's melodramatic imitation of it,
would hardly need commenting on if Eliot and Leavis had

not suggested that this liability to parody is the weakness of Othello's poetic idiom, a weakness that reveals the hollowness of the man. Leavis takes Bradley to task for saying that Othello is 'the greatest poet' of all Shakespeare's heroes, and observes very justly that not only do other people in the play speak in the characteristic Othello style, but that 'if characters in poetic drama speak poetry we ought to be able to notice the fact without concluding that they are poets'. Certainly we ought, but where *Othello* is concerned we might also reflect that if certain characters speak poetry it is because it is the idiom of the love theme in the play. This is so obvious that the evasion of it by Eliot and Leavis seems inexplicable, until we remember their essentially negative approach to the play's presentation of love. The poetry of *Othello* is firmly and positively poetic, and so convinced is Leavis of the negative psychological purpose of the play that he is compelled to distinguish between Othello's poetical utterance when it shows 'an attitude *towards* the emotion expressed—an attitude of a kind we are familiar with in the analysis of sentimentality', and the poetry—spoken either by him or by others—which is impersonally 'in the heroic mode', and therefore genuine, its 'firm outline' not concealing an underlying softness. This distinction has no real existence. The 'heroic mode' *is* the love mode, as Dr Leavis must surely have seen if he were not so determined that love in the play is a negative and hollow thing, existing only to be shown up. The power of which the poetry is the expression and symbol is all of a piece, and conveys love in all its aspects—terrible, tender, romantic, domestic, etc. Leavis's contention that 'the heroic mode'—as distinct from the hollow and self-revealing rhetoric of Othello—has only a comparatively simple magnificence, is not borne out by a speech like Desdemona's before the senate.

> *That I did love the Moor to live with him*
> *My downright violence and storm of fortunes*
> *May trumpet to the world: my heart's subdued*
> *Even to the very quality of my lord:*
> *I saw Othello's visage in his mind*
> *And to his honours and his valiant parts*
> *Did I my soul and fortunes consecrate ...*

The tone is certainly joyous and magnificent, but it is also as 'revealing' as Leavis claims Othello's rhetoric to be. It reveals Desdemona's mode of being in love, just as Othello's speeches reveal his. As well as being lyrical and romantic, the love-idiom is an expository medium so sensitive that the characters who use it cannot open their mouths without revealing their emotional bias, and their conscious or unconscious conceptions of love. The criticism that emphasizes its romantic simplicity—(Wilson Knight's phrase, *The Othello Music*, suggests the Paterian idea of poetry aspiring towards the musical condition)—fails to see its dramatic point.

The reason for this failure lies in Iago's parodying, for I. A. Richards made what has proved to be an influential critical pronouncement when he declared that poems which can be parodied by a 'confrontation with their opposite' are necessarily on a lower poetic level than poems which have, so to speak, a built-in irony that anticipates other responses and contains many shades of feeling. Thus Landor's *Rose Aylmer* is intrinsically inferior to Scott's *Proud Maisie*, because its author sticks his neck out in a simple attitude that invites mimicry. But whatever we may feel about this criterion, it clearly cannot have any relevance to Shakespeare's dramatic poetry, whose simplicity (if it is simple) is not that of the author. Moreover we must remind ourselves again of the peculiar operation of the play, its mode of involving us in successive emotions and attitudes comparable to those of the characters themselves, and its sequential rather than simultaneous mode of illumination—a mode entailed on Shakespeare, as we have seen, by the intrigue at its roots. The magnificence of the love-choruses may indeed hypnotize us at the outset, and postpone our reception of the vital information they contain, but we shall understand them later as part of the full complexity of the *Othello* world, the world of human love and lovelessness, of the inability of one kind of love to understand another, and of the persistence with which human beings cling to the conception of their love as a part of themselves.

As her speech before the senate shows, Desdemona's way of being in love is as clearly revealed as that of Othello. The love-duet in Act II, Scene 1 adds further touches of significance.

OTHELLO: *O my fair warrior!*

DESDEMONA: *My dear Othello!*

OTHELLO: *It gives me wonder great as my content*
To see you here before me. O my soul's joy,
If after every tempest come such calms
May the winds blow till they have wakened death!
And let the labouring bark climb hills of seas
Olympus-high, and duck again as low
As hell's from heaven! If it were now to die
'Twere now to be most happy, for I fear
My soul hath her content so absolute
That not another comfort like to this
Succeeds in unknown fate.

DESDEMONA: *The heavens forbid*
But that our loves and comforts should increase
Even as our days do grow!

OTHELLO: *Amen to that, sweet powers!*
I cannot speak enough of this content,
It stops me here, it is too much of joy:
And this, and this, the greatest discords be (kis-
sing her).
That e'er our hearts shall make!

Two different kinds of love are movingly displayed here.
Othello's is the masculine and romantic: his opening hyperbole invokes the romantic commonplace—'Love calls to
war'—and also receives Desdemona into his wholly martial
personality, just as she had wished in refusing to remain 'a
moth of peace'. The glory of the achievement is carried
buoyantly on in the image of the ship riding the waves.
What battles and dangers wouldn't they undergo for this?
But then with the imagined calm a note of brooding appears;
the tone changes and deepens; 'If it were now to die ...'
Othello has withdrawn his delighted gaze from Desdemona
and is addressing himself and his own vision of love. And in
the romantic context that vision has an alarming familiarity.
Having achieved his desire, Othello turns naturally to the
idea of the *liebestod*, death as the only fit and comparable
peer of love. How can the tension otherwise be kept up and
the lover remain at the summit of his happiness? Unknow-
ingly Othello is applying this fatal romantic logic, which
will not compromise possession with the trivialities of
domesticity. And it is of course as a possession, a marvellous
and unexpected conquest, that he sees Desdemona. He has
won her like a fortune or a battle.

If heaven had made me such another jewel,
One whole entire and perfect chrysolite,
I'd not have changed her for it.

This attitude earns him the disapproval of Eliot and Leavis; but so far from singling out Othello as a type of the ignorant and ungentle lover, Shakespeare portrays him as epitomizing the positive glory of love, which like the glory of war includes and assumes the fact of suffering and injustice. Both love and war are summed up in the image of storm, a manifestation both glorious and terrifying. Yet, as we are finding, there is more in the love-duet than the poetic symbol of the storm and the poetic prolepsis of the lovers' death: there is also the sharp illumination of what men and women in love are like. Othello's sentiments are magnificently commonplace; for he shares with most men the delight of achievement and possession and he feels too the loss of freedom, of the 'unhoused condition', a loss which he has already faced in his large way and put aside. The romantic dangers are there, as with most men, but they do not diagnose his amatory weakness or label him finally. He is not a Tristan or a Lancelot, wholly committed to an intensity in love which is unaware of any freedom outside itself.

Indeed the possibility of development, and the sense of freedom that goes with it, is precisely what the duet most poignantly holds out. Desdemona's love for Othello is also of course wildly romantic—he personifies for her all the romance she has discovered to exist in life—but committing herself to this vision is for her a more matter-of-fact business than it could be for him. Her greeting is as whole-hearted as his, and as characteristic. 'My dear Othello!'—the simple warmth reveals a whole world of feminine actuality behind the male need for hyperbole and symbol. She takes his speech lightly, as the sort of wonderfully gratifying and romantic thing he *would* say—its deeper note doesn't mean much to her except as a stimulus to 'touch wood' and to give her own settled and happy conception of the future. She takes up the word 'comfort' from his speech, the sort of word which in her vision of things presents a concrete and lasting reassurance and satisfaction. The situation has a joyful sense of mutual possibility, the spaciousness which throughout the play is the atmosphere and element of love. Othello's unconsciously romantic sense of an end rather than a beginning is not final: Desdemona's placid confidence touches and lights his own, and he shows the beginnings of a readiness to draw certainty and stability from her, just as she had drawn fire and enthusiasm from him. But this interdependence is not the same as understanding: the singers in the duet are too preoccupied with the vision of their own love really to perceive the nature of their partner's. Desdemona is as much imprisoned in her assumption of love as is Othello in his, and for the same reasons: their kinds of love have produced the relationship in which they find themselves. The helplessness of Desdemona as the tragic climate darkens round her is as much emphasized as is that of Othello in the grip of his jealousy, and it proceeds from the same cause. She cannot break out of her kind of love to tell him what a monster he is being any more than he can break out of his to reflect that after all she is a free agent, and that perhaps a quiet talk would clear the matter up.

I may seem here to be seeing Shakespeare through the spectacles of Proust, for whom A can never love B but only his idea of B, and *vice versa*, with confusing and depressing results. But though one would expect the two writers to corroborate each other's vision at some points, Proust's dogmatic authority, reposing as it does on methods of analysis copied from science and philosophy, is foreign to Shakespeare, and its illuminations are of a quite different order to those of *Othello*. In the enclosed world of Proust the idea of freedom depends on the universality of error: people and their emotions seem endless because of the infinite number of ways one can get them wrong. As a hypothesis about love 'Proust's Law' is abstract and rigid: it admits no outlet, while Shakespeare's poetry not only indicates with extraordinary compression and subtlety comparable facts about love but also celebrates its infinite potentiality, a freedom based not on error but on the absence of definition. Confined in their separate visions, the lovers do not 'place' each other; their incomprehension is, paradoxically, a form of spaciousness, and it is this which Shakespeare manifests as a positive glory. Nothing is fixed and fated, because of the largeness of love's world, the sheer quality of room it makes available. The magnificence of Othello and his impression of physical size, the sweep of seas and continents that are built up behind him, the heroic Odysseys and adventures of his past—all are there to emphasize the unbounded possibilities of love, and they are brought to an almost Hegelian confrontation with an equally undeniable aspect of love—its confinement in the prison of separate egos.

The fact that both Othello and Desdemona cling at all costs to their own apprehension of love gives its shape and meaning to the last act of the tragedy. Their deaths are the very opposite of the romantic *Liebestod*, but the irony of this is infinitely deeper and truer to human experience, and for that reason strikes us with the greater compassion. Death confirms their separation in love, not their union. In his jealousy Othello accepted Iago's version of Desdemona.

> *I know our country disposition well.*
> *In Venice they do let heaven see the pranks*
> *They dare not show their husbands.*

He has permitted the spaciousness of his own love vision to

be enclosed in this horrible 'placing' of the loved object. For Othello has not placed Desdemona objectively at all, and into the vacuum is dropped the deadly little miniature of Iago. With a few touches Iago fills in the portrait of a Venetian deb: the promiscuity taken for granted in her set, the sexual gratification of being possessed by a real he-man, the craze for novelty which real inconvenience would soon scare back into the orthodoxy of class. It has been well said that if the villainy of Iago is impenetrable by convention, Shakespeare also makes it so in fact. His picture of Desdemona has all the more unspeakable plausibility because he really believes all women are like that. He is inventing something that comes naturally to him. And his portrait of Desdemona demoralizes Othello completely well before he begins to manufacture the actual proofs of betrayal. For Othello has apprehended Desdemona as a marvellous mirror through which to see his own experience.

She loved me for the dangers I had passed;
And I loved her that she did pity them.

Desdemona gives a meaning to all that has happened to him; the sudden revelation of the importance and splendour of his past is a dazzling thing, which he had taken for granted and never seen in this way before. This revelation is in a sense a loss of innocence: it brings self-consciousness and confers upon him the dramatic part which he can most naturally play. But it is also one of the great positive gifts of love. Desdemona has given it to him and he loves her for it, but ironically the very magnificence of the gift obscures the giver, for the gift—Othello himself—seems to both of them so much more actual than she. Desdemona's sense of Othello is so much more real to both of them than is the sense of Desdemona to either.

Without overdoing the *argumentum ad hominem* we can all recognize the generalized force of this, and we recognize the process involved in observations like 'he's been a different man since he met her'. Even Iago allows the phenomenon to exist as a kind of absurdity, grounds for the usual snigger. Just after the love-duet he says to Roderigo, 'If thou be'st valiant—as they say base men being in love have then a nobility in their natures more than is native to them—list me'. *Valiant* is the epithet so liberally applied to Othello in the early love-choruses, and Roderigo has his function as a kind of feeble echo, debased but still recognizable, of Othello—an echo and not a parody, for there is no mockery involved: he is a poor relation in love, not absolutely stripped of dignity even when his passion—like Othello's—makes him Iago's dupe. Love gives a natural rightness to some of his assumptions, as he shows when Iago asks him with a leer if he noticed Cassio take Desdemona's hand. 'Yes, that I did; but that was but courtesy.' He and Cassio, and Othello too, talk the same language, which is outside Iago's comprehension.

One reason for the relevance of the novel-like query: Would the lovers have settled down to a happy marriage?— is Othello's response to Desdemona's support of Cassio, an episode significantly distinct from Iago's initial suggestions, although Iago's betrayal of Cassio was of course the cause of it. We hear of it first from Emilia as she chats to Cassio.

> *—all will sure be well;*
> *The general and his wife are talking of it*
> *And she speaks for you stoutly: the Moor replies*
> *That he you hurt is of great fame in Cyprus*
> *And great affinity, and that in wholesome wisdom*
> *He might not but refuse you, but he protests he loves you*

And needs no other suitor but his likings
To take the safest occasion by the front
To bring you in again.

At secondhand thus the scene comes none the less clearly
before us. In her brisk artless way, which reveals a complete
lack of knowledge of Othello and his mode of love, Desdemona takes his old friend's part and brings the business up
at a moment when the lovers might suitably be concerned
with nothing but each other. The chill of this, somewhat
drolly conveyed as it is through the medium of Emilia,
might be felt by any lover as well as Othello; and the hint
that he did his best to push it outside the scope of their
mutuality would seem an equally human reaction. The next
scene contrasts with the love-duet in its slight but painful
suggestion of a discord: their mutuality is no longer perfectly synchronized, for the excellent and commonplace
reason that an outside element—neutral and not in itself
inimical—prevents the exact intermeshing of the gears.

DESDEMONA: *How now, My Lord!*
I have been talking with a suitor here,
A man that languishes in your displeasure.
OTHELLO: *Who is't you mean?*
DESDEMONA: *Why, your lieutenant, Cassio.*

Desdemona makes a rhetorical show of mystification, one of
those nearly meaningless little demonstrations which none
the less convey that the speaker knows she is not being quite
straightforward. Perhaps aware of its slight tiresomeness,
Othello deliberately ignores her gambit. His query is
brusque. It provokes her to a greater formality and a more
defensive eloquence. The whole thing, economical as it is,
catches exactly the note of connubial exchanges.

> *Why, this is not a boon!*
> *'Tis as I should entreat you wear your gloves,*
> *Or feed on nourishing dishes, or keep you warm,*
> *Or sue to you to do a peculiar profit*
> *To your own person.*

Love is no longer talking in the symbolic idiom through which Othello apprehends it. With its touchingly matter-of-fact solicitude, the speech conveys no impression of the Desdemona with whom Othello discovered his own past and personality. On the contrary it is an intrusion comparable to that of the Cassio topic, and it brings Othello's latent irritation to a head.

> *I will deny thee nothing:*
> *Whereon, I do beseech thee, grant me this,*
> *To leave me but a little to myself.*

Committed as she is, it is natural and agreeable to her to yield the point,

> *Shall I deny you? no, farewell, my lord …*
> *Emilia, come. Be as your fancies teach you;*
> *Whate'er you be, I am obedient.*

Her sweetness produces a warmer reply from him, and the parting is on a friendlier, more understanding note. They are already beginning to learn give and take in such matters. It is the more important to realize this because of a common misunderstanding arising from Othello's next words.

> *Excellent wretch! Perdition catch my soul,*
> *But I do love thee, and when I love thee not*
> *Chaos is come again.*

Some early critics, and many later ones too, have assumed
this to mean that 'the poison of jealousy has already begun
to work in Othello'. But in Elizabethan English *wretch* was
a word of total and unambiguous endearment. Collier aptly
remarks 'such words are resorted to when those implying
love, admiration, and delight, seem inadequate', and Dr
Johnson is equally emphatic. There is the further point that
'when', like the German *wenn*, has here the sense of 'if'.
What is significant about the speech is not a display of jealousy by Othello, but his sudden awareness of the nature of
his feelings and the insubstantiality of love. What is his love
exactly, and where is it to be found? Desdemona's sweetness
and domestic solicitude in the glove speech cannot at this
moment reassure him, because they are not what he means
by love: they so emphatically do not present him with the
settled and splendid figure whose reflection he once caught
in her eye. He no longer sees his visage in her mind. It dis-
turbs the unthinking and unshakeable confidence which he
once had in himself, and which he effortlessly retained at the
stormy climax of his fortunes. The armed meeting with
Brabantio epitomized this confidence.

> *Keep up your bright swords, for the dew will rust them.*
> *Good signior, you shall more command with years*
> *Than with your weapons.*

But now the vision and the harmony are in abeyance and are
replaced by the uncertainty of two people not yet accustomed to each other. In the process of settling down all
lovers become more or less aware of the difference between
their conception of their 'love', and what is actually happening to them. Most experience, too, the alarming sensation of
the loved person suddenly seeming a total stranger, through

the appearance of some unexpected though not necessarily uncongenial aspect of their identity. Any question of identity would be likely to puzzle Othello and throw him off his balance. And there is a difference of identity here which in terms of dramatic poetry is conveyed by the Desdemona of the glove speech, and the Desdemona who proclaimed her love to the senate: it is only the former that Othello knows and loves, but in time he will be able to bridge the gap between the two. Desdemona is unaware of the gap, but her love has a natural resilience which will help to overcome Othello's sense of it. Though she assumes that her lover, to whom she feels so close and with whom she identifies herself completely, will at once see her point about Cassio, she effortlessly modifies this assumption and re-identifies herself with Othello's 'fancies'. She makes the adjustment and goes off quite blithely. But Othello is profoundly shaken. And it is at this moment that Iago, the self-appointed expert in identity, makes his attack. Preoccupied as he is, Othello does not attend for a moment. 'What dost thou say, Iago?' He is not thinking of Cassio but of Desdemona, groping for his sublime image of her—'one whole, entire, and perfect chrysolite'—and painfully aware of the confusion of the image, as if a stone had scattered a clear reflection. The actor should convey this as a moment of nullity and stasis, a dead spot in love. It is negative, unmeaning, without response or coherence, the 'chaos' which Othello fears. Persons of more emotional experience would know that the mechanism does indeed become inert in this way, for trivial reasons and for short periods, but it is Othello's first taste of such a breakdown. For a man who needs decisiveness so much, the danger of this state is that any suggested cause for it will be eagerly grasped.

This obsession with cause and reason is an ironic aspect of

the incomprehension that haunts the play. The word takes
on a deep and moving significance at the moment when
Othello advances to the act of murder.

It is the cause, it is the cause, my soul,
Let me not name it to you, you chaste stars!—
It is the cause.

The word seems to hypnotize him, and it is difficult not to
feel that he clings to it almost as he once clung to his vision
of Desdemona. It gives him a vision of universal connection
and necessity, and both visions supply his nature with the
grounds for action. 'Yet she must die, else she'll betray more
men.' His attitude to the adultery is as visionary and as
romantic as his former attitude to Desdemona herself. He
needs to be certain of it, as he once needed to be certain of
his love-vision of her. 'To be once in doubt is once to be
resolved.' Doubt is not the lover's state of mind. And it is
not the doubting person who is uncomprehending, but the
person who must be sure of himself and others: it is no paradox to say that the absence of *doubt* in Othello produces its
essential atmosphere of incomprehension and unreality.
Othello is torn between his passion for causes and certainties
and his natural scope and freedom of impulse, a division that
corresponds to the nature of sexual love as at once a prison
and a liberation. Othello still voices the claims of scope and
freedom even as he demands the proofs of Desdemona's
guilt. 'Give me a *living* reason she's disloyal!' Hemmed in
as he is by the deadness of causation and analysis—(Iago's
analysis of Desdemona's character for example)—he still
struggles impossibly to apprehend this dead material in
terms of the living dynamism of love.

The attempt is sublimely unreal and a contradiction of

great pathos. Yet it manifests his nobility, a nobility quite absent in Leontes of *The Winter's Tale*, who has the same obsession with 'the cause' which has driven him into a state of almost psychopathic unreality. Leontes tries to get rid of the thing by killing his queen, regretting that he cannot kill Polixenes—the other 'part of the cause'—too.

> —*say that she were gone,*
> *Given to the fire, a moiety of my rest*
> *Might come to me again.*

His attitude is on the most elementary moral level; he wants to get rid of the horror and go back—so far as he can—to what he was. But for Othello the cause *is* Desdemona; it is on the same plane as his love for her and must be embraced as absolutely as that love. He could not push her outside himself and return to his former being. And yet he cannot say to Desdemona, like Cordelia to her father—'no cause, no cause'—because he has confounded cause and reason with the very substance of his love. Love is now dependent on a deluded reason and serves as its liturgy. Of course, reason is a part of love, as Cordelia flatly points out in the opening scene of *Lear*, and as Othello himself would have found in time in his marriage to Desdemona. Love, as Cordelia knows, comes before reason, though its path should be smoothed and controlled by reason. But Othello can neither renounce love because of reason or discount reason because of love. He must have it both ways. He must have his convictions, however dreadful they are, and his love as well.

Although love is by its nature absolute, its working out must be contingent on the relative and imperfect nature of human minds and human dealings. From Othello's refusal to recognize this the love idiom derives both its positive splendour, its firmness, colour and clarity of outline, and also its air of unreality. It does not utter or discuss the complications of reality, it only reveals them. Our sense of 'the split appraisal' is as true of the detailed texture of the love poetry as it is of the play's general effect. Its firm certainty hides issues and nuances of which the speaker is unaware, and his ignorance keeps him isolated from the other speakers and even from himself. The audience must successively respond to the heroic simplicity and discern the complex effects to which it points. The continuous and purposive use of this poetic method is unique in Shakespeare. We find a comparable idiom used for short periods, as in the first scene of *Lear*, where Lear's expression of absolute rage is magnificent but also reveals an 'undermath', as it were, of stupidity and wounded vanity unknown to the king himself.

> *Let it be so; thy truth then be thy dower,*
> *For by the sacred radiance of the sun,*
> *The mysteries of Hecate and the night,*
> *By all the operation of the orbs*
> *From whom we do exist and cease to be;*
> *Here I disclaim all my paternal care,*
> *Propinquity and property of blood,*
> *And as a stranger to my heart and me*
> *Hold thee, from this, for ever. The barbarous Scythian,*
> *Or he that makes his generation messes*
> *To gorge his appetite, shall to my bosom*
> *Be as well neighbour'd, pitied, and relieved,*
> *As thou my sometime daughter.*

We recognize in this rage idiom the same massive and simple architectonics as in the Othello love idiom, and in the hyperbole of Goneril and Regan there is a corresponding hint of Iago's mockery of it. But this kind of dramatic poetry is rare in love scenes. Shakespeare's lovers usually share their awareness of themselves and each other simultaneously with the audience: any verbal undercurrent or nuance is included in the general effect, and this applies to *Romeo and Juliet* as much as to *Troilus and Cressida* and the jealousy sequences of *Cymbeline* and *The Winter's Tale*. Niceties of emotional response appear on the surface as part of the style, rather than being concealed under the smoothness of heroic love statement and reappearing in the spectator's appraisal of the whole play. Almost any speech of Troilus will illustrate this.

> *—where injury of chance*
> *Puts back leave-taking, justles roughly by*
> *All time of pause, rudely beguiles our lips*
> *Of all rejoindure, forcibly prevents*
> *Our lock'd embrasures, strangles our dear vows*
> *Even in the birth of our own labouring breath:*
> *We two, that with so many thousand sighs*
> *Did buy each other, must poorly sell ourselves*
> *With the rude brevity and discharge of one ...*

The figures are less elaborate than in *Romeo and Juliet*, the metaphorical agility more meaningful and less insistent, but the mode of love exposition is essentially the same, the agitation and anxieties of love conveyed on the very finger-tips of style. Troilus is not a character in the full naturalistic sense but a sensitive instrument, recording and interpreting equally. A few lines further he can see with terrible clearness

> *But something may be done that we will not,*
> *And sometimes we are devils to ourselves—*

and when he sees Cressida with Diomedes he conveys his sense of what has happened with an immediate intensity.

> *This she? No, this is Diomed's Cressida:*
> *If beauty have a soul, this is not she;*
> *If souls guide vows, if vows be sanctimonies,*
> *If sanctimony be the gods' delight,*
> *If there be rule in unity itself,*
> *This is not she. O madness of discourse,*
> *That cause sets up with and against itself!*
> *Bi-fold authority, where reason can revolt*
> *Without perdition, and loss assume all reason*
> *Without revolt: this is, and is not, Cressid.*

Troilus's sense of 'the cause' is infinitely more complex than Othello's; he sees it in metaphysical terms as a revolt against nature which nature inexplicably condones. And since we must grasp it in metaphysical terms, we are not for that reason really engaged with his emotional predicament: we can share intellectually the aspect of love that moves Troilus, but in *Othello*—with its infinitely greater realistic and dramatic cohesion—we are made to *live* the experience before reflecting on it. (This is of course to say that Othello is a much more complete character than Troilus—indeed the lack of real character in *Troilus and Cressida* is the obvious reason for its contemporary taste. It is the measure of Shakespeare's scope and variety that its characters are precisely those of an 'interesting' modern play.) Because love is not discussed intellectually in *Othello* it does not follow that its poetry is simple—it reaches the complex effect by a different route. Full critical realization of *Othello* only comes when we have penetrated the apparent simplicity of the love idiom to the complex issues involved in it, issues comparable to those communicated immediately, but in a much more theoretical and partial form, by the generally recognized 'complexity' of the Troilus idiom.

As we have seen, Othello, like Troilus, suddenly has his confidence in the absolute rightness and solidity of the love-relation (as if love were a force like gravity) effectively shaken. 'When I love thee not, chaos is come again.' He is staggered by the causeless and inexplicable withdrawal of his love vision. Cassio was the seemingly neutral and impersonal occasion of this withdrawal, and it is Cassio's name which is now brought up by Iago and coupled in an unmistakably meaningful way with Othello's love.

> Did Michael Cassio, when you woo'd my lady,
> Know of your love?

Othello takes up the point immediately, for it coincides not with any suspicions he has had but with the inexplicable jar to his own state of love. He seizes eagerly, indeed almost with relief, on the suggestion that Cassio may not be merely the occasion for this but the cause.

> IAGO: I did not think he had been acquainted with her.
> OTHELLO: O yes, and went between us very oft.

The initiative is his once more; his feelings are positive again, on the offensive; he devotes himself to a powerful assault on the now apparently uncomfortable Iago. Like most people in such a situation, Othello is not aware of this deep need to reanimate his own positive feelings. Meanwhile, like a bull-fighter making his cape seem alive, Iago swiftly fashions a Cassio–identity to dangle before Othello's lowered head. He hints that his reasoned analysis of Cassio is very different from the instinctive acceptance of Othello.

IAGO: *Men should be what they seem;*
           Or those that be not, would they might seem none.
OTHELLO: *Certain, men should be what they seem.*
IAGO: *Why then I think Cassio's an honest man.*

It is Othello's first introduction to the horrible identity
game, played laughingly by Iago and Desdemona just before
his arrival in Cyprus, but now to be played in earnest. The
question of identity must always be absorbing to the lover
who reflects on it: it now becomes so for Othello, who
fatally has no experience of the problem: 'who is she, and
whom does she think I am?' Iago introduces the game with
an appropriate commonplace about such reflection.

> *Utter my thoughts! Why, say they are vile and false;*
> *As where's that palace whereinto foul things*
> *Sometimes intrude not? who has a breast so pure,*
> *But some uncleanly apprehensions*
> *Keep leets and law-days and in session sit*
> *With meditations lawful?*

All of us involuntarily find ourselves having the most
deplorable thoughts and speculations about other people,
even about people who are close to us and whom we would
not wound or harm for the world by uttering them, just as
Iago says he would not harm Cassio. That is the man of the
world assumption to which Iago casually introduces
Othello, affecting that they share it already. By giving thus
an absolutely *true* account of the origin of the Cassio-identity
which he has just supplied to Othello, Iago clinches that
identity more firmly in Othello's mind. 'Though I perchance
am vicious in my guess' ... it is a disagreeable irony that we
often accept A's impression of B the more readily if A first

assures us that it most likely arises from lack of charity on his part. In any case the labelling game is so new to Othello that this frankness is for him simply a part of the general devastating impression of understanding and 'truth'. Iago goes on to speak of the self-portrait everyone paints of themselves, the well-guarded *persona* by which they live.

> *Good name in man and woman, dear my lord,*
> *Is the immediate jewel of their souls:*
> *Who steals my purse steals trash: 'tis something, nothing—*
> *'Twas mine, 'tis his, and has been slave to thousands;*
> *But he that filches from me my good name*
> *Robs me of that which not enriches him*
> *And makes me poor indeed.*

'The immediate jewel'—in a marvellous phrase Iago sums up the self-estimation which is so powerful a factor in the making of personality. The jewel image has an irony especially applicable to Othello, who expresses his love in such metaphors, and 'immediate' conveys with a touch of derision the instinctive working of his personality and his grand confidence of status.

> *My parts, my title, and my perfect soul*
> *Shall manifest me rightly.*

as he proclaimed at the crisis of his fortunes. The loss of this self-respect is what affects Cassio after his dismissal, and he bewails it in terms which are the more moving and revealing for being a little absurd.

> *Reputation, reputation, reputation! O, I have lost my reputation! I have lost the immortal part of myself, and what remains is bestial. My reputation, Iago, my reputation.*

I have already commented in the introduction on the relation between the public and private selves of Shakespeare's characters. One might emphasize at this point the value that is placed in so many of the plays upon being in a position to think well of oneself. Equable self-depreciation is the mark of the villain or the buffoon, not of the good man or the hero. The Elizabethan boaster, like Parolles or Jonson's Bobadil, is usually a deliberate hypocrite whose behaviour conceals a just but complacent estimate of himself, in the same way that Iago's 'honesty' conceals such an estimate. The sterile complacency of being honest and cynical about oneself is drawn by Shakespeare with the greatest acuteness, in Thersites for example, or still more in the Apemantus of *Timon of Athens*, whose relation to Timon is comparable to Iago's with Othello—'magnificence' having in *Timon* the positive force of Othello's sexual love. In comedy Shakespeare dwells more on the resilience than the sterility of such a character, but though he understands and sympathizes with Parolles's triumphant—'there's place and means for every man alive'—he does not hold up, 'simply the thing I am shall make me live', as an enlightened or admirable sentiment. The indestructibility of the human creature is its lowest moral quality, and also, significantly, its least tragic quality.

The whole trend of Renaissance morality would lead us to expect this: self-regard was seen to be one of the cornerstones of a stable and prosperous society. Honestly to wear a label, earned by oneself and recognized by others, is an upright aim, its highest aspiration to be known, like Timon, as

A most incomparable man, breathed, as it were,
To an untirable and continuate goodness.

What a sneer Iago would make of those lines! Not that he

would deny the qualities involved, any more than he denies the 'daily beauty' in Cassio's life. Goodness exists all right, but the contemptible thing about it is that it makes poor fish like Cassio so helpless—he cannot escape the label of being good! Although he thinks he has lost his reputation, Iago knows that his goodness and reliability will always be there, and always vulnerable to Iago's sense of them. Iago's reputation for honesty is much more easily maintained than Cassio's reputation because it has no real foundation: it can be put on and off like a mask. Shakespeare offers us a wonderfully subtle contrast in *Othello* between two kinds of moral assumption. Othello and Cassio assume that goodness and worth are qualities which the possessor may involuntarily jeopardise by his actions, but cannot put on and take off at will; Iago assumes that they exist only to be made use of by the neutral reason and intellect. The contrast would be less subtle if—as is often taken for granted—Othello and Cassio were examples of unconscious goodness and Iago of conscious evil. As it is, all three are quite aware of themselves: Othello and Cassio *know* they are good, and that they may lose their goodness; Iago knows that goodness is only of value in so far as it serves the will and desires of the individual; otherwise it is an absurd encumbrance and a target for malicious labelling, like Cassio's 'daily beauty', or the lady's qualities in 'She that was ever fair and never proud'.

There is a vital connection between these two kinds of moral awareness and the theme of love. The attitude towards goodness of Othello and Cassio (and even Roderigo) is like their attitude to themselves as lovers; their pride in their status is an aspect of their reverence towards it—love cannot be used or manipulated for interests outside itself. Roderigo's single-minded pursuit of Desdemona, though ludicrous and pathetic, is not ignoble, and has as we have seen its touching moments, like his instinctive knowledge of Cassio's true feelings. Iago cannot understand either love or goodness for the same reason: he is sure that both exist to be made use of by the will. One of the many aspects of the theme in *Othello* is love shown as a part of social morality, its firm substance allied with the no less firm one of 'reputation'. Both are 'jewels'. And both deprive the possessor of a kind of freedom, the freedom of not being labelled. One of the fascinations, from our point of view, of the contrasting of two moral attitudes here, is that this kind of freedom plays a highly significant part in our own moral outlook. The dilemma is the perennial one between being good, and knowing that goodness exists, or rather between the social solidity of a moral position—which may or may not include knowledge—and the social freedom of mere *analysis*. The first is, roughly speaking, the classical ethic of man-in-society, the second the romantic one of man on his own. And it is interesting that Shakespeare, at least where Othello is concerned, shows love as felt and exhibited only by man-in-society, not by independent man.

> And this word 'Love' which greybeards call divine,
> Be resident in men like one another
> And not in me: I am myself alone.

It is the same with sexual love as with the *caritas* referred to by Richard. It is being 'myself alone' which cuts off Iago from it.

Our feeling for the uniqueness of the individual—and above all for the uniqueness of our personal selves—makes us all share to some extent in Iago's moral viewpoint. So do Falstaff and Oblomov. We all feel with Oblomov, though we might not proclaim it so openly, that it is intolerable to be compared with *other people*. The interest of his case, for author and audience alike, is between Oblomov-in-society and Oblomov as an end in himself; and whereas with Falstaff, society—represented by the play's plot and framework—remains firmly in control, Oblomov takes advantage of the romantic disintegration of the union of society and character to remain triumphantly himself, triumphantly and solipsistically *Oblomov*. He, much more than Falstaff, is a comic relation of Iago, and the 19th century's critical fascination with Iago as a study in 'pure evil' reflects the relationship. By 'pure evil' the critics really meant 'pure Iago', pure, that is to say, of any social motivation or control. But Iago is the malignant converse of Oblomov: for while the latter exists to avoid being labelled, the former exists to label others and so get them in his power.

We share with both of them the wish to escape ourselves, and to corner others. To elude a label we are glad to proclaim what might be thought the worst about ourselves, and we are particularly reluctant to think of ourselves in terms of some 'form or visage' that is well recognized in society. Freely to admit, and indeed to insist, that we are mean, snobbish, malicious, unreliable, etc., is to deprive others of the power of fixing these labels to us, while it is generally assumed that to be conscious of these shortcomings in some way disinfects them and makes it possible to perform the action without wearing the label. To say that one is a snob is an insurance against being labelled as one; a mean man who says he is mean can thus behave meanly without *being* mean. The fear is not so much of doing the thing as of being the sort of man who does it. In this moral terminology the deadliest terms of criticism are those which are by definition labels and which cannot therefore be used about oneself by oneself. 'I am *worthy*', or 'I am *second-rate*' is not a possible utterance, nor could it neutralize the exhibition of the qualities concerned, while 'I only pretend to be honest', or, 'I enjoy causing trouble', will not only appear to do so but are also intriguing pronouncements in themselves. As I have suggested, the goal aimed at is a kind of freedom, and a label, a 'reputation' or 'good name', carefully secured and proudly lived up to, is a moral imprisonment to be avoided. To remain detached oneself while keeping everyone else pinned down is Iago's kind of freedom: it is in fact the real object of his celebrated motive-hunting. His wish to believe that both Othello and Cassio have slept with Emilia is the wish to add to their dossiers, to have something more 'on them'.

The critic Snider[1] rather engagingly plays Iago's game here when he suggests that Othello has indeed committed adultery with Emilia, and hence—though he is high-minded and unsuspicious in all other matters—he knows that the infidelity of wives is a fact, and so is fatally inclined to listen to Iago. To hark back to our distinction between a right and a wrong kind of fictional query about the play, Snider's 'Did Othello really sleep with Emilia?' seems to me permissible, but it illustrates precisely the attitude I have been talking about—the wish to fix a label. Snider wishes to size up Othello, humanely but also accurately, as an upright and honourable general whose only failing—which is destined to cost him dear—is his inability to leave his officers' wives alone. Attempts to explain the *Othello* relationships in terms of homosexuality arise from the same kind of impulse. And one might note that in the face of all this effort to get them placed, Othello and Cassio show no wish to label others, only themselves: they would like to be known as good men.

The 'immediate jewel' and 'immortal part', then, can be seen as either noble or absurd; capable of degradation—as

[1] Snider. *The System of Shakespeare's Drama.* (St. Louis, 1877.)

when Iago degrades Cassio by making him drunk, a fore-
taste of the much greater degradation of Othello—but capable too of the unambiguously positive warmth and splendour which distinguishes Othello and Cassio in the selves
which their imaginations present to them. It is by this
imagination that they live; it is the source of their capacity
for love and goodness, and of their absurdity or barbarity as
well. And it is this absorption in their own imaginative
vision which the most acute external analysis cannot understand or portray.

Though his own analysis often strikes us as having the
relish in hidden superiority of an Iago, Proust is very much
aware that the novelist's most exalted and most difficult task
is to enter into this imaginative life. 'No one is more in
error,' he writes, 'than the social novelists who analyse
mercilessly from outside the action of a snob or supposed
snob, but never place themselves in his position at the
moment when a whole social springtime is bursting into
blossom in his imagination.' In the tortuous (and indeed
openly disingenuous) personification of his great work, in
which the author is successively himself and an 'imaginary'
being, deluded and percipient, disinterested and absorbed,
the identity of these 'social novelists' is not much in doubt:
'they' are Proust himself, and this ability to enclose and
include his own Iago-like tendencies in a greater artistic
scope is one of the measures of his greatness. A rather similar
process of inclusion might be said to take place in the world
of *Othello*, where the analytic powers of Iago are enclosed in
the imaginative life of the positive characters. Neither Proust
nor Shakespeare operate on the limited plane of experience
in which analysis of a character can produce a discovery that
is triumphantly final, as for instance Ibsen in *The Wild Duck*
discovers for our benefit what Werle is *really like*—the con-

vention in such a work being that such a discovery is wholly satisfying and cathartic.

But all Shakespeare's characters create, as it were, the sympathy by which they are to be judged; even in *Julius Caesar*, where the portraits of Caesar and Brutus are more coolly external than in any of the other plays. For instance in the remarkable scene (Act IV, Scene 3) which follows the quarrel of Brutus and Cassius, the eye of Iago (or of Ibsen) would see something finally damaging in the apparent pretence of Brutus that he has not heard of his wife's death in order that he may arouse the messenger's admiration by his display of stoicism.[1] It is often assumed that Caesar is portrayed in the same spirit, as the conventional great man with feet of clay—the alternative reading (which we can surely discount) being that the dramatic convention would have us accept quite literally what the character affirms about himself, and that Caesar is therefore a great man because he says so. This is to shrink the whole dimension of Shakespeare's effects without getting anything in return. In fact the tone of Caesar's speeches admirably conveys—as J. I. M. Stewart has observed[2]—the idea of true greatness petrifying defensively into the pose of the great man, although in addition to this overplus of psychological effect they have the more directly dramatic function of helping to balance our sympathy between him and the conspirators. In Brutus's case there seems also to be an addition, on top of his purely dramatic rôle, of what Shakespeare actually felt him to be like—an addition rather than a fusion: in both cases the discrepancy may indeed produce that impression of brilliance, rather than unassertive mastery, which the play leaves with us.

[1] It has been suggested that this odd episode is the result of textual corruption, but on no very good grounds.
[2] *Character and Motive in Shakespeare*, p. 53.

But in neither case is the definition of personality Shakespeare's recognizable aim, although in another author the scene I have mentioned might well be used as part of a technique for demonstrating that Brutus is a fraud. In the absence of such an Iago to place him Brutus eludes us in spite of his preoccupation with the idea of himself. His 'immediate jewel' does make him noble as well as priggish, movingly altruistic in his feeling for the country people who are victims of a campaign, and determined that *his* good name shall not suffer from their spoliation. His altruism ignores the logistics of warfare, and is only retained at the expense of Cassius, whose love he is capable of inspiring, but whose feelings he is as indifferent to as he is sensitive about his own. There is a wonderfully observed and wholly realistic note of childishness in the quarrel scene:

> CASSIUS: ... *You wrong me, Brutus,*
> *I said 'an elder soldier', not 'a better':*
> *Did I say 'better'?*
> BRUTUS: *If you did I care not.*

The realism reminds us of the squabbles of the English generals before Cadiz and on the Islands voyage. Yet like those leaders, whose jealousy of their own fame was accepted by their peers as an inevitable inconvenience, Brutus's faults are positive ones, the kind that are incurred in making and keeping one's good name. They are the kind that can be 'observed, set in a notebook, learn'd and conn'd by rote'. The irony of the play is that Caesar and Brutus both fall by having too much of an idea of themselves, and of what is due to them; their reputations impose upon them a fatal rigidity; none the less, in the eyes of the others and—can we doubt?—of Shakespeare himself, they are by far the most considerable and impressive persons in the play.

This digression on ideas of virtue in Shakespeare generally and *Othello* in particular is, I hope, worth turning aside to make precisely because it has so often been necessary to resort to fictional criteria in order to bring out the full riches of the play. Though the example of the novel helps us so much in considering *Othello's* ground of the play, its psychology and its exploration of love, it is no help at all—it is indeed a confusion and hindrance—when we try to estimate the nature of worth as the play gives it to us. This is because the values that are paramount in the novel are enclosed inside the total dimension of the play and subordinated to it. Those values are essentially—almost involuntarily—concerned with discernment, not with achievement. In the fictional world, dominant in literature since the middle of the 19th century, to discern—to connect as E. M. Forster would say—is to be king. Thus encouraged, the reader of the superior novel tends automatically to equate value with social and moral insight. For George Eliot, Proust, Forster, Musil etc., and their readers, discernment is bound to be valued much more highly than achievement, because it is directly a part of the impulse both to write and to read novels. The superior man, and to a novelist the unavoidably necessary one, is the *conscience*, the fine instrument who detects, records, and

> *Knows all qualities, with a learned spirit*
> *Of human dealings.*

In the *Forsyte Saga* this superiority establishes itself in a naive and almost ludicrous way in that aspect of the work which D. H. Lawrence so much despised—the perception of the *rentier* consciousness of the Forsytes by Bosinney and Irene: a perception which constitutes the evident *value* of these two characters. A much more distinguished instance is Henry James's preoccupation with getting a good *conscience* into the centre of his work, and his criticism of *Madame Bovary* on the ground that the heroine is not able to impart the dignity of insight to her situation. For James the whole scope of the subject is degraded because Emma is such a mean awareness, whereas in, say, *The Portrait of a Lady*, Ralph Touchett and Isobel Archer are twin *consciences* who complement each other, and whose interweaving successes and failures of insight make a positively dramatic harmony. Above all James admires his Lambert Strether, of *The Ambassadors*— ('a mirror of miraculous silver and quite pre-eminent, I think, for the connexion'). To take a much slighter instance, the consciousness of the speakers in *The Waves* focuses on the one person who does not speak but acts: and there is a strong impression that the absent Percival is valued by the seven ceaseless awarenesses for his remarkable *otherness*! He does not continually announce what he is experiencing, and thus lives vicariously on their behalf.

In becoming the vehicle of modern self-consciousness the novel has seemed also to grow more realistic, but this is largely because the insights of living are also the insights of the novel, while the achievements of living are not and cannot be. When we enquire into the intimate lives of our neighbours, or analyse the texture of our own, we are doing what the novelist can do in his art, but when we pass a law, make a fortune, or command a regiment, we are doing something which is beyond his powers. Moreover the novelist always enjoys what he often confers on his chosen characters—freedom from responsibility of status. True, a great novelist like Proust, by dint of deploying whole pages of dazzling etymology, can make us realize that his character Brichot has indeed achieved greatness as a philologist, as well as being the pompous ass whose little ways were so wittily depicted for us a few paragraphs earlier. Similarly Balzac convinces us that his hero Lucien de Rubempré has indeed great journalistic talent simply by writing for him, as it were, his first dramatic notice. But on the whole novelists are less concerned with establishing the effectiveness, in a worldly sense, of their characters, than of making use of their insight or employing them as a target for the author's own. And what might be called the novel-reading morality, in which insight replaces achievement and superior awareness is insensibly taken for granted as superior value, has had a wide effect on our contemporary critical outlook. So much so, that Marxist criticism seems justified in observing that this passion for insight and apathy towards action in the modern novel is the expression of a bourgeois society in decay, though the achievements of canal-builders and steel-pipe manufacturers in the Soviet novel have not yet given us any imaginative satisfactions to compare with those of bourgeois insight.

All this is not to say that the novel cannot convey real apprehensions of achievement, but to do so it has to return to something like the spirit of poetry, dramatic poetry. We believe in the dominant and imperial qualities of Antony and Octavius because we see them effortlessly displayed in the poetry and symbol of the play; we believe in the generalship of Othello and the invincible barbarity of Tamburlaine, while we do not believe—for there is no need for us to do so—that Vronsky might have been a successful general in Central Asia. The point about Vronsky lies elsewhere, and comprehensive as the scope of *Anna Karenina* is, Tolstoy does not draw us into the exclusive world of military realities. But *Wuthering Heights*, say, is not only comprehensive, it also has poetic drama's peculiar power of concentrating itself in many different worlds. The ruthless efficiency with which Heathcliff makes his fortune and buys up the local properties are as vividly realized for us as his love for Cathy. Tess similarly impresses us by the immense positiveness, the sense of activity and possible fulfilment, which the poetic vision confers on her, and which is independent of the plot by which the author shapes her fate and of the philosophy in the light of which he views her, and which he even occasionally intrudes into her own being. Activity and accomplishment are as much her medium as they are that of a wild animal.

But novels with so much of the poetic drama in them are the exception rather than the rule. Creation by selective insight is usually the novelist's method, and such creation cannot conceal from the reader how tyrannical and manipulative is the bond between the author and his creature, the bond akin to that in which Iago tries to secure the other protagonists of *Othello*. Freedom and honour are outside this bond, and Shakespeare gives them an absoluteness which isolates Iago's penetration in its own enclave of negation and futility. Othello and Cassio are not judged, are not placed: only Iago is. His mode of freedom in evil recoils upon himself; for except to the most confirmed and conditioned of novel readers for whom analysis, even of the most satanic kind, must always be the chief interest, it is love, not evil, which is not only the dominant element here but by far the more interesting element. Ironically, Iago's knowledge of the world is as predictable as that of the bourgeois whose received opinions the novelists adored to parody. With all their absurdity—even cruelty—love and honour are by contrast unpredictable and boundless, 'as broad and general as the casing air'. And they do not require an inserted *conscience* to make them visible and to interpret them to us.

For although Shakespeare's plays are full of observers, self-appointed commentators on human folly who would be invaluable to the novelist, they remain subordinate and do not show up what they survey, or determine its value and status. In the world of poetic drama they are themselves actors who have chosen a particular rôle to play, and—as in the case of Thersites and Apemantus—it is well understood by all concerned that they are playing it because they can manage no other. In the fictional world, on the other hand, the observer is by convention 'sincere' and transparent; he has not assumed a rôle which suits his purposes; his impartiality makes him truly formidable. But when Enobarbus is checked by Antony for his bluntness and remarks aside 'that truth should be silent I had almost forgot', we do not feel that his assessment of the situation is necessarily more 'true' than that of his superior. Antony's stature is undiminished, and Enobarbus does not appear more perceptive by reason of his comments but, on the contrary, a less rich and complex spirit whose limitations will not let him see the real inwardness of the Antony and Cleopatra situation: though he can admire its splendour, he imagines his own forthright view of the situation to be 'the truth'. As 'blunt soldier', Enobarbus has something in common with Iago. He does not affect our impression of the size and worth of Antony by taking us into his insight. 'No man is a hero to his valet', remarked Hegel of Napoleon's *mot*, 'not however because the hero is no hero, but because the valet is a valet'. In this kind of heroic poetry even treachery and absurdity, even the whipping of Thyreus or Cleopatra's attempt to seduce Octavius, appear—like Antony's delights—as 'dolphin-like': erected, not revealed, they show their backs above the surface of things.

The most obvious candidate in Shakespeare for the rôle of all-wise as well as all-powerful observer is of course the Duke in *Measure for Measure*. But even here we find that in the most complex and most subtle aspects of the play the Duke is, so to speak, ousted: he does not enclose these effects in his own vision but is himself enclosed by them. True, in the play's primary and almost parabolic theme he is 'power divine', and the double meaning on 'grace' fits his nature as well as his title. That theme is: 'He who the sword of heaven will bear/Should be holy as severe', and human agents of the divine ordinance 'dressed in a little brief authority'—the authority lent to Angelo by the Duke's absence—are often imperfect both in action and example. The interrelation of justice and forgiveness is straightforwardly exhibited—'lawful mercy is nothing kin to foul redemption'. It is no depreciation of Shakespeare's treatment to say that here it is comparatively unsubtle, for the nature of the theme does not require subtlety: but the play has a much more intriguing and imponderable secondary theme, which is the nature of virtue itself, as reflected in the ideas and practice of different individuals. It is here that psychological naturalism, always in Shakespeare's hands the perfect instrument of the complex effect, comes into play, and we see both Isabella and the Duke in a different light. The unconsciously ambiguous nature of Isabella's feeling for her own virtue has often been remarked.

> *The impression of keen whips I'd wear as rubies,*
> *And strip myself to death, as to a bed*
> *That longing have been sick for, ere I'd yield*
> *My body up to shame.*

The idea of martyrdom appeals to her as leagued with that of chastity. Moreover she sees right and wrong as absolutely clear-cut, and is happiest when they are schematized in formal rules. She fears liberty, which like *grace* carries a

double meaning in the play, and she equates it with the
licence of Vienna. 'I speak not as desiring more,' she assures
the nun with whom she is discussing the liberties of convent
life,

> But rather wishing a more strict restraint
> Upon the Sisterhood, the votarists of Saint Clare.

The way she lingers on the phrase reveals her almost volup-
tuous regard for the idea of abnegation and discipline, and
the point is further underlined by the strangely beautiful
words which follow, describing how the nuns must behave
towards men when they have taken their vows.

> Then, if you speak, you must not show your face,
> Or, if you show your face, you must not speak.

Contrasting with this a few lines further on is Lucio's
exaltation of sexual liberty,

> Your brother and his lover have embraced:
> As those that feed grow full, as blossoming time
> That from the seedness the bare fallow brings
> To teeming foison, even so her plenteous womb
> Expresseth his full tilth and husbandry.

The Duke's human nature and weakness appears in his
exchanges with Lucio, that most natural of men. Lucio
gives a strong impression, which can surely be quite easily
taken and conveyed, that he is aware of the Duke's disguise
as a Friar and is baiting him in consequence.

> LUCIO: *Ere he would have hanged a man for the getting a
> hundred bastards, he would have paid for the nursing a
> thousand: he had some feeling of the sport; he knew the
> service, and that instructed him to mercy.*

DUKE: *I never heard the absent duke much detected for women;*
he was not inclined that way.

LUCIO: *O sir, you are deceived.*

DUKE: *'Tis not possible.*

LUCIO: *Who, not the duke? yes, your beggar of fifty. ... He*
would be drunk too; that let me inform you.

DUKE: *You do him wrong, surely.*

LUCIO: *Sir, I was an inward of his. A sly fellow was the duke,*
and I believe I know the cause of his withdrawing.

DUKE: *What, I prithee, might be the cause?*

LUCIO: *No, pardon; 'tis a secret must be locked within the teeth*
and the lips: but this I can let you understand, the
greater file of the subject held the duke to be wise.

DUKE: *Wise! why, no question but he was.*

LUCIO: *A very superficial, ignorant, unweighing fellow.*

The Duke is compelled rather huffily to defend his real self
without giving away his disguise. 'Let him be but testi-
monied in his own bringings-forth, and he shall appear to
the envious a scholar, a statesman, and a soldier.' So he may
indeed, and the point is not so much that it is comical in the
Duke to declare his own virtues—*Othello* shows that a
declared self-respect was perfectly proper for an Elizabethan
—but that those virtues, so far from being god-like, are just
as 'human' as those failings which Lucio, on the analogy of
himself, considers virtues and imputes to the Duke. However much the play's convention may require him to be God,
the Duke cannot forbear to be human in his own defence,
and there is a tension between the complex and disparate
human virtues and the simple morality idea of God controlling the plot. The Duke is put out that Lucio should blithely
attribute to him the failings of the *homme moyen sensuel* and
should love him in consequence.

LUCIO: *Sir, I know him and I love him.*

DUKE: *Love talks with better knowledge, and knowledge with dearer love.*

LUCIO: *Come sir, I know what I know.*

Escalus, the good deputy, also imputes his own qualities to the Duke: perhaps man always attributes his own nature to God and loves Him in consequence? But the Duke as a human being has his own individuality, and not only when in the interests of comedy his morality *persona* is thrown to the groundlings, and to their complacently instinctive preference for the kinds of human decency and indecency that are embodied by Lucio and Mistress Overdone. The Duke's nature is also connected with that of Isabella, especially in the hint that self-knowledge seems simpler to them both than it really is, and the resemblance is further emphasized by the concluding suggestion of their marriage. Corresponding to the Duke's simplicity as God and his complexity as a human being, is the wonderful and entirely suitable simplicity with which Shakespeare portrays ideal forgiveness, and the richness of equivocation and density of psychological texture which he devotes to the idea of virtue.

It is tempting to see in Hamlet a composite character of a rather similar kind, dominating the convention of the play but enclosed none the less in its actual dramatic and poetic being. His position as a witty and acute observer may well be due, as Professor Empson has suggested, to Marston's introduction of the intellectual revenge hero, in whom the intelligentsia could see 'a glass of fashion and a mould of form' which both flattered them and offered them a model. Moreover Shakespeare was probably in the position of wishing to get as far away as possible from the crude revenge-type hero of Kyd's lost play on the Hamlet theme. The previous Hamlet, like Hieronimo of *The Spanish Tragedy*, may well have been an old favourite whose appearance was the signal for the laughter and mimicry of the gentry, and Shakespeare possibly took great care to make the new hero one of themselves, one who could not fail to give a lead to the *avant garde* in wit, bearing, and sensibility. The new Hamlet thus becomes almost an intermediary between the audience and the old plot, persuading the audience to laugh *with* him at certain things—such as the ghost's sepulchral tones from the cellarage, or the old style actor's declamation—rather than at the play itself, and performing the dual rôle of tragic hero and intellectual commentator.

The problem of value and insight, which may become that of value *versus* insight, has led us a long way from *Othello*; but assumptions about it are so much the background of the criticism of the play that it has seemed worth while to bring the problem out into the open and examine it in detail. And could one not tentatively conclude that value and insight are certainly never to be taken as synonymous in Shakespeare—whatever may be the case in the novel—and may even be opposed? The interrelation of heroic existence and moral judgement in Shakespeare is an exceedingly profound and intricate one, and perhaps all that can be concluded is that, like Tolstoy the novelist, he endows all his characters with the greatest possible freedom to be themselves.

We must now return to the speech of Iago which prompted this digression. As we observed, it is part of the skill of his approach that he postpones all direct reference to Desdemona. The identity question hangs in the air; Othello is distressed by the momentary disappearance of his image of

Desdemona—which has vanished in the actuality of her domestic aplomb and in her introduction of the unfortunate Cassio topic—and it is at this moment that Iago raises the question of what Cassio is *really* like. The world of speculation thus revealed is deeply distasteful to Othello, but it coincides with the disturbance of his vision of Desdemona, a vision which he took for granted with the same sureness and simplicity which he extended to everyone he met. Instead of rejecting this new world out of hand, therefore, Othello listens fascinated to Iago's version of Cassio, the more intently because—as we have seen—conviction of any sort is fatally more acceptable to him than uncertainty. He prefers 'cause' and 'reason' to the withdrawal of emotional initiative and the infliction of mere unease, nullity, emotional slack water. Moreover Iago's comments, with their man of the world air, are impressively specious.

> But he that filches from me my good name
> Robs me of that which not enriches him
> And makes me poor indeed.

That they *are* specious, even at their most sagely generalized, appears in the fact that Iago does indeed hope to be enriched by stealing Cassio's good name: he will get Cassio's job as well as influence over Othello. There is the same air of judicial dispassion in his comment on jealousy—the candid friend concealing nothing but the pleasure he obtains from the effect of his candour.

> O beware, my lord, of jealousy;
> It is the green-eyed monster which doth mock[1]
> The meat it feeds on.

[1] The suggested emendation of *mock* to *make* is quite unnecessary and weakens the force of the passage.

The definition horribly fits Iago himself and his own attitude to love, the meat that he mocks and feeds on. In view of the support given by Dr Leavis and others to the view that Iago talks excellent and down-to-earth good sense at times, it is worth restressing the actual disingenuousness of everything he says. It comes out naturalistically in these commonplaces, as it does conventionally in the two-faced oath 'By Janus', and underlines the tragic theme of misunderstanding and incomprehension. Iago equates his cynicism with understanding, but as Conrad remarks in *Chance*, to be without illusions is not the same as to be reasonable. Iago's pseudo-sage comments reflect a kind of infernal muddle between his own desires and his conviction that he alone sees the world steadily and whole.

But his pretension to omniscience is enough to bewilder and corrupt Othello, and his exhibition of the analytic habit implies that it comes naturally to most people, e.g. to Cassio and Desdemona. Othello is made to feel isolated in an idiom totally different from theirs. Yet he returns a typical and spirited reply to Iago's remarks about jealousy.

> *Think'st thou I'd make a life of jealousy*
> *To follow still the changes of the moon*
> *With fresh suspicions? No! to be once in doubt*
> *Is once to be resolved: exchange me for a goat*
> *When I shall turn the business of my soul*
> *To such exsufflicate and blown surmises*
> *Matching thy inference!*

He resists passionately the proffered entertainment which is indeed the 'business' of Iago's soul. His whole nature rises to this challenge as it has risen to every other—such a response is almost comfortingly habitual. But he is not to feel this comfort for long. His reply determines Iago to launch his boldest stroke, the climax of his attack: the placing of Desdemona as a typical Venetian girl. It is a risk but it comes off. 'Dost thou say so?' Fascinated and appalled, Othello struggles to adjust himself to this new way of looking at people, catching now at something he has heard Desdemona's father say, and applying it to his own shaken conviction.

> *I do not think but Desdemona's honest ...*
> *And yet, how nature erring from itself—*

The hesitating cliché is at once taken up, but to show Othello that he is still congenitally out of things, though he has begun to use the jargon of 'knowing', Iago deliberately misunderstands him and gives *nature* his own meaning.

> *—Ay there's the point: as—to be bold with you—*
> *Not to affect many proposed matches*
> *Of her own clime, complexion, and degree,*
> *Whereto we see all things in nature tends—*
> *Foh! one may smell in such a will most rank,*
> *Foul disproportion, thoughts unnatural.*
> *But pardon me, I do not in position*
> *Distinctly speak of her, though I may fear*
> *Her will, recoiling to her better judgement,*
> *May fail to match you with her country forms*
> *And happily repent.*

Othello assumes that it is Desdemona's nature to be honest (i.e. chaste) and that a lapse from this would be unnatural in her; Iago, echoing Brabantio's

> *For nature so preposterously to err*
> *Sans witchcraft could not—*

implies that to the worldly eye the opposite is the case:

nature determines Desdemona's position as a Venetian girl, with all that that involves. And he gives the concept a further twist by suggesting that Desdemona has shown a viciousness over and above what might be expected of 'our country disposition', by giving way to an unnatural passion for Othello.

These different senses of *nature* may remind us of *King Lear*, where the king assumes that it is on the side of royalty and lawful paternity while Edmund more logically claims its authority for the amoral outlook of the natural son. But there is an illuminating difference. Nature in *Lear* is vast and mysterious, a cloudy spirit which could only manifest itself in poetic drama. In *Othello* it is a word which discloses different attitudes to life, and the misunderstanding and incomprehension which arise from them. Once again the novel lifts its head, in fact, and we shall find that in *The Golden Bowl* the same sort of use is made of different word interpretations, both deliberate and unconscious. For although, as we have seen, Shakespeare drastically modified Cinthio's *novella* in the direction of drama—even dramatic opera—he also transformed and elaborated the implications of the *novella*, and the most notable *donnée* embedded in Cinthio is the corruption of one man's vision of life by another's. Othello is corrupted by Iago's intellectual outlook, and by the logic of knowing and placing, before he is betrayed by the logic of evidence. If he had stayed true to his own nature he would have killed Iago on the spot, as he once slew the 'turbaned Turk': as it is, horror and fascination paralyse him and seduce him into the Iago consciousness. From this moment he is a lost man.

After Iago has gone, the corrupted Othello tries to make use of his wisdom and his 'learned spirit' to rationalize his own situation.

'tis the plague of great ones.
Prerogatived are they less than the base;
'Tis destiny unshunnable, like death:
Even then this forked plague is fated to us
When we do quicken.

There is a subtle piteousness about this which is rare in the
drama, rare enough even in the novel, since the novel can
hardly command such a merging of the operatic and the
realistic. Othello is trying to see his supposed fate as something inevitable for men in his position, and to see it with
the worldly calm of an Iago whom nothing puzzles or sur-
prises. Yet he cannot help bringing to the Iago vision a
certain ghastly appearance of nobility, just as he later brings
to it the instinctive values of his old confident and assertive
days. But out of their natural setting these values look incongruous, even hypocritical—

Yet she must die, else she'll betray more men.

The world's honour, we feel, cannot be preserved so. The
muddle which resolves itself into these liturgies is very like
the one which underlies Iago's assured pronouncements—it
is indeed the same muddle. Iago has compelled Othello to
rationalize in the way that he himself does, although with
Othello concepts like truth and honour are, with a horrible
irony, used in the same way as Iago's negative convictions
about love and human nature. And Iago's triumph is the
virtual absorption of Othello that comes from getting him
wholly *placed*, for how can one place someone better than by
compelling him to act strictly inside one's own chosen field
of understanding? The fallen Othello is no mystery to Iago:
he is behaving as men should behave if they are to lend
support to Iago's view of the world. That—'she must die

else she'll betray more men'—would have given Iago pure joy if he had heard it, confirming as it does his conviction that all men call their lust, love, and their jealous fury, justice. Iago is driven by the need to make men behave as he thinks they do, and Othello, with his air of massive natural distinction, his absolute singleness of being that cannot be categorized or transfixed with a definition, provides him with a compulsive challenge. He cannot relax until he has Othello safely inside the boundaries of his own perception. Then indeed he can proclaim, reversing their relations with a joyous sarcasm that is lost upon his victim: 'I am your own for ever'.

And yet not quite for ever, except in Othello's own estimation. 'That's he that was Othello.' He indeed is convinced that the demi-devil has snared his soul and that he will be eternally damned for what he has done. The fact makes T. S. Eliot's contention that in the final speeches he is 'cheering himself up' seem a trifle uncharitable, to say the least of it. Even Dante would concede that a sinner condemned to everlasting torment is entitled to whatever crumb of comfort he can get by the way. And Othello convinces us that he means what he says, and that he is sure his suicide will cut him off from the last hope of mercy. To ignore this certainty is to ignore the convictions of religion. The past is all that he has, and it is in the past and in the bounty of his remembered self that he escapes from Iago to the freedom of his love for Desdemona, who loved him for the dangers he had passed. It is here that love triumphs—endures rather—for there is nothing unified about it and nothing ideal. As well as in Othello's recollection it has survived and gleamed forth variously and disconnectedly in Desdemona's last moments; in her 'I am very sorry that you are not well'; in the charming heroine-worship of

Whatever shall become of Michael Cassio
He's never anything but your true servant;

In the pungent common sense of Emilia's views on sex equality, and her—'Who would not make her husband a cuckold to make him a monarch?'—as well as in her passionate defence of Desdemona. All have a quality and scope that cannot be defined in terms outside themselves; and Iago, the supremely uncharitable impulse, the supreme negation of love, can never wholly succeed in bringing them within the field of his own destructive understanding.

CHAPTER FOUR

LOVE AND KNOWLEDGE:

The Golden Bowl

CHAPTER FOUR

Love and Knowledge:

THE GOLDEN BOWL

I HAVE suggested that in *Othello* the world of love is a world of freedom and uncertainty, and that the capacity to love—though it contains the desire of possession—is quite separate from the urge to dominate by knowing and placing. Definition is Iago's life, and he corrupts Othello by making him share it. It is a profound irony of the play, an irony inherent in Shakespeare's vision, that we cannot say 'Othello is a great man with feet of clay', or, 'Othello loves not Desdemona but his own idea of himself', without putting ourselves outside the world of love which the play presents. By making such definitions we lose the world which Iago cannot understand and has never experienced. But without risking these definitions, it may be objected, how can we understand the play? The answer is, of course, that the medium of dramatic poetry has already implied them for us, for it is one of the properties of the greatest dramatic poetry to suggest complexities of character which are beyond the scope of the most exacting discursive analysis, which cover the expanse of the work like ripples on water and lose their nature if caught up in the hand. In what it proclaims and what it reveals the poetry of *Othello* has a subtle and singular function, unique among Shakespeare's plays, and in its peculiar blend of effect reminds us—a reminder that I'm afraid has now become too tediously familiar—of the novel.

But what novel could have this almost unfairly unique power, the power of creating contradictory glimpses of a personality and holding them in suspension without the smallest touch of defining control, so that they offer to the imagination such a challenge and yet such a luminous completeness? Othello surrounds himself with images of storm, love, and war, and also with those of simple and exotically child-like value. Were it not for Desdemona he would not have exchanged his martial freedom 'for the sea's worth': not for 'one whole entire and perfect chrysolite': in losing her he loses a pearl richer than all his tribe. Some paradox of love swims before our eyes, some glance into the implications of commonplace endearments like *my precious, mon trésor*. ... The heroic and the domestic meet and shed light upon each other. This is the merest spoonful from the *Othello* sea, but it shows something of what is involved in its imagination of personality, and this is a kind of imagining to which the novel too has come more and more seriously to devote itself.

But how much more laboriously! Look at the effective but essentially cumbrous and showy machine which Proust wheels forward when he wishes to immerse us in the sea of contradictory impressions which make up the phenomenon of the Verdurins. There is the direct and detailed observation of their pretensions, their cruelties and hypocrisies; then the deliberate contrast of the private confabulation in which they decide to help a friend with money, and decide, too, to conceal the fact they are doing so both from him and from others; finally there is the extract from a memoir of an earlier period in which the Verdurins appear as a delightful and cultivated couple, surrounded by beautiful things and genuinely concerned with art and friendship.

We can almost see the gleam in the author's eye and the satisfaction in his voice as he bids us conclude how difficult it is to know what people are really like. Our impulse is to reply: yes, but does the difficulty really present itself in this elaborate shape? No doubt it is possible to imagine a novel in which Desdemona and Othello, on their honeymoon, pass by a jeweller's shop, and we might receive the impression—without a word spoken by the author—of something gluttonous and dangerous in Othello's response to the gems which would connect itself with his attitude to his bride. It might furnish a scene of mute but meaningful symbolism common enough in good novels, like that excellent one at the beginning of *Middlemarch* where the two sisters look over the family jewels together to decide who shall have what, and we see Dorothea tempted from her first scornful renunciation of them into a kind of disingenuousness which produces a miniature of the sort of complex muddle we shall find her in later on. Even so, George Eliot cannot resist making a knowing comment as all that is intense in her heroine responds to the colour of the gems—'her thought was trying to justify her delight in the colours by merging them in her mystic religious joy'. Such a scene cannot but emphasize how pure and economical are the means by which a great dramatic poetry can achieve psychological ends.

But outside Shakespeare where shall we find such a poetry? In the kind of novel which we agree to call poetic it is so clearly the author whose vision is at work, presenting the characters with a glow no doubt, but also with a definitive accuracy; the poetry surrounds them but has not got into them—to be a 'poetic' character in a novel is usually a fairly crude distinguishing mark. True, in *Wuthering Heights* the utterance of Catherine and Heathcliff is instinct with the poetry of the whole and even crystallizes it, but that great and strange work is hardly concerned with the domestic and social passions and arrangements. Henry James, however, was deeply concerned with these things, and was also immensely preoccupied with the problems of treating them impersonally and dramatically. His *Notebooks* record the excitement he felt at the 'exquisite truth' which came to him at the time of the conception of *The Golden Bowl*: 'I almost hold my breath with suspense as I try to formulate it; so much, so *much*, hangs radiantly there as depending on it ... the divine principle is a key that, working in the same *general* way, fits the complicated chambers of *both* the dramatic and the narrative lock.'

Now it may be that this premonitory thrill so engagingly conveyed by James is exciting only in terms of his creative impulse and not in terms of our critical understanding, that what has dawned on him with such delight will mean for us as readers just the old and reliable truism that good novels often contain dramatic scenes and devices. But 'the divine principle' here may have been much less general; it seems likely that James had suddenly realized how to turn to account the old interest in stagecraft and the long apprentice-ship at the *Comédie Française* which—(as he mentions on the same page of the *Notebooks*)—has resulted in such bitter frustration and disappointment when he attempted drama proper, but which now revealed to him a method of com-bining the most formal and artificial type of *Comédie* plot with the breadth and 'incalculability' inherent in the novel form. If this was the case no wonder James was excited, for such a combination would indeed be fantastic in its difficulty and majestic in its possibilities. It is an ideal that is nothing short of Shakespearean, except in the fact that it *is* an ideal—the theory of its effects are worked out and bargained for in a way we can scarcely imagine Shakespeare's as being. As a theory it would no more permit irrelevance than would the artificial French play, but in the vision of a great artist irrelevance often comes home to us as the very substance of both freedom and meaning: such an artist can so distil it that it seems to express the mystery of life itself. And it may be that in James's theory this higher irrelevance, as it were, is equated with, or rather replaced by, what he calls in the Preface to *The Golden Bowl* 'the appeal to incalculability'. Into a rigid symmetry of plot and form must somehow be fitted the complex measurements of good and bad, the rich uncertainties of living, and the indefinable natures of human beings.

We have seen the way in which a very definitive plot contrasts in *Othello* with the non-definitive mode in which dramatic poetry illuminates personality. *The Golden Bowl* offers much the same kind of contrast. Both stories are subjected to the rigidity of dramatic coincidence, and both triumph over their imprisonment and achieve the effect of spaciousness and freedom—of having their cake and eating it—which is one of the satisfactions of a masterpiece. James has often been criticized on the ground that the golden bowl of the story is a rather clumsy and ineffective piece of symbolism, but in fact it is not really a symbol at all, any more than is the handkerchief in *Othello*—both are pieces of dramatic machinery that serve the same function of ritual coincidence. We should not expect *Othello* to be called *The Handkerchief*, and the title of *The Golden Bowl* is a little misleading, though we should remember that James wanted to call it *The Marriages* and was sorry he had already used that title. But though there is nothing truly symbolic about them, both the handkerchief and the bowl are given a certain status as emblems. Othello affirms the handkerchief to be no ordinary one—

The worms were hallow'd that did breed the silk
And it was dyed in mummy which the skilful
Conserved of maidens' hearts ...

—and the imposing but flawed golden bowl (actually of gilt crystal and of 'a rather stupid elegance'), is seen by James's lovers in an antique shop, but is left for Maggie Verver to buy later and so discover their complicity from the shop-man.

The two works have much in common, therefore, on the level of *Comédie Française* plot, but there is also a deeper affinity between them. In both of them knowledge confronts innocence; the world of definition is met by the world of incalculability. In *The Golden Bowl* the relations between these worlds are of course much more elaborate and more fully worked out; the simplicity of Othello's world of love, and Iago's denial of it, is replaced by a far more complex situation in which the separate worlds offer their different versions of love. It is a triumph of the novel, as of the play, that the questions it raises and the characters it creates are not settled and disposed of by the action but continue freely to inhabit the mind of the reader. The 'golden mist' which James several times invokes as an image for the opacities and translucencies of human society, fades out—like the evening haze of London itself—the innumerable arcades of query and possibility, while leaving the reader with the spacious impression that they are still there, still leading away into the haze of human complication, still open and explorable. The *subject* of *The Golden Bowl* cannot be clearly stated, and the problems which it raises are of the sort which can be solved after a fashion but which can never be computed; before they can be classified they have multiplied and mutated themselves endlessly, like some elemental form of life.

This is of course a property of almost all real problems involving human relations, and according to one's mood it can be either stimulating or discouraging—James might have commented that it was the task of the artist to make it the former, whatever might be the case in life. Such problems are very different from the kind that tend to be improvised as examples by moral philosophers—'X, a penniless consumptive and a potentially great violinist, is supported by Y, who loves him, but he himself has fallen in love with Z. Should he?'—etc., etc. They are also significantly different from many of James's own subjects, particularly his earlier ones—the corruption of an artist by society in *Roderick Hudson* for instance—and he nowhere attempts, so far as I know, to give a comprehensive account of *The Golden Bowl*'s scope and purpose as he does (*Notebooks* p. 15) about *The Portrait of a Lady*. Indeed that account, with all its zest at a dramatic siezure of insight, strikes one as disconcertingly *more* intriguing, more illuminating even, than the book itself turns out to be. 'The idea of the whole thing is that the poor girl, who has dreamed of freedom and nobleness, who has done, as she believes, a generous, natural, clear-sighted thing, finds herself in reality ground in the very mill of the conventional.' There could be no such 'idea of the whole thing' where *The Golden Bowl* was concerned, and its impressiveness is closely connected with this fact. The lack of a defining theme also explains its size in relation to its immediate predecessors, *The Ambassadors* and *The Wings of a Dove*, in both of which we have the sense of a much more rudimentary and theoretical contrast in ethics and outlook. This is not to say that *The Golden Bowl* has not a great deal of plot: the story of a daughter married to the lover of her father's wife, and a father to the mistress of his son-in-law, is sufficiently explicit and contrived, even extravagantly so.

And yet, as in Shakespeare, the extravagance of plot seems compatible and even allied with the sheer size and implication of the work, the resonance in our minds after the play is over or the book laid down.

That James was well aware of the artistic desirability of this kind of resonance, and even strove consciously to produce it, is shown by the elaborately inconclusive ending of *The Portrait of a Lady*, and by his comment in the preface to Roderick Hudson: 'really, universally, relations stop nowhere, and the exquisite problem of the artist is eternally but to draw, by a geometry of his own, the circle within which they shall happily *appear* to do so'. But *The Golden Bowl* is not inconclusive, and the resonance which produces its impression of mystery and of life does not strike us as a striven-for effect but rather as the inevitable overplus of a great and wholly rounded work of art. This 'sounding on' of the theme provides the perennial controversy about the novel's intention and meaning. James—again curiously like Shakespeare in *Othello*—is credited by the critics with two quite different views of his story. One school contends that it is a moral exposure of the crimes of the Prince and Charlotte and a demonstration of the wages of sin;[1] another, that the indictment is really—and much more damningly—of Maggie and her father, who have 'collected' the Prince and Charlotte like their other possessions, and who show themselves horribly equal to the business of controlling these human assets in the same way as their material ones. Still other critics, of whom Edmund Wilson is the most authoritative, maintain that James didn't really know how he felt

---

[1] Cf. a *New Statesman* competition clerihew:
  The sins of the Prince and Charlotte
  Were as scarlet
  But Maggie and her Pop
  Knew when to stop.

about it all, and was lost in the labyrinth of his own ingenuity (an opinion rarely ventured about Shakespeare, notwithstanding T. S. Eliot's suggestion that the author of *Hamlet* could find no 'objective correlative' for his unformulated feelings).

My feeling is that these criticisms do not really measure up to the level of art on which James is attempting to work and the size of the stakes for which he proposes to play. If his rapturous discovery of 'the divine principle' means what I take it to mean, he is aiming for something like the self-sufficiency of the poetic drama. its inclusiveness, and above all its effect of incalculability within the fixed limits of a formal situation. Certainly the passions which the book arouses, and the tenacity with which the various commentators maintain their theses, show that something is present here to which every bosom returns an emphatic echo. In consequence—and again as with Shakespeare—it is not difficult in the warmth of our personal response to move right away in discussion from the text and from the actual Jamesian *donnée*, and yet still be in a sense relevant—as the critic who maintains that Falstaff is not really a coward is relevant —to the possible scope of the work. Such a response does Shakespeare, or James, the important if unintentional honour of bearing witness to the size and scope of their idea. The vital consideration, though, is that this Protean quality, the capacity to expand, and contract in the individual mind, and again expand, should in no way merit the charge of *inadvertency* which Dr Leavis—in a much more deadly emendation of Edmund Wilson's point—brings against James. The size and evident implications of a work of art must never strike us as the result of muddle. Implication must be, as it were, a built-in effect of the work, must constitute—in James's own highly suggestive words—'an ambiguity of appearance that is not at the same time an ambiguity of sense'. There would be such an 'ambiguity of sense' in *Hamlet* if he openly announced a belief in Christianity at the grave of Ophelia, or something of the sort. The audience would then 'not know what to think', a very different matter from being liberated into conflicting and stimulating lines of thought.

It is reasonable enough on the face of it that James should be analysed in terms of 'moral values', and his sense of 'where life flows'—(a favourite Leavis criterion)—because these are precisely the matters of which he is so conscious. He is preoccupied with the morally significant theme, and it is what he usually starts out with. He is not like Jane Austen, whose whole pretension as a novelist is different, and who does not commend her subject uncompromisingly to the reader's moral intelligence. Jane Austen's simpler pretension makes her a popular novelist in a way that James could never be: she satisfies her audience fully at any level. But even so, the scrutiny of James's moral values and the concentration on his sense of life are apt to be misleading and irrelevant, for he does not always approach his theme with a direct moral pretension. In *The Golden Bowl*, which seems to me his masterpiece, he certainly does not. As the entry in his *Notebooks* shows, his starting-point here is not an 'idea of the whole thing', it is much more like that of Shakespeare or Jane Austen; and the results he achieves are only ambiguous if we are determined to view them from the standpoint of 'moral values', rather than from the standpoint of personality and what James makes of it.

In *Mansfield Park*, for instance, a novel with interesting resemblances to *The Golden Bowl*, the contrast of persons and principles is shown us with so many cross-currents or sympathy and humour that it is beside the point to ask ourselves which side the author is on. With the power and breadth of curiosity which is one of the clearest signs of their genius, both James and Jane Austen feel their way into radically different kinds of consciousness, the good as well as the clever, the simple and instinctive as well as the vital and knowledgeable. Emma, 'the heroine whom no one but myself will like', succeeds and contrasts with the Fanny Price of *Mansfield Park*. One cannot emphasize too much that for Jane Austen a loving absorption in individual personalities always precedes the working out of patterns of discernment. This absorption leads us with great naturalness and simplicity into the world of *Mansfield Park*, and Professor Trilling's brilliant critique of that novel[1] is seriously weakened by his handling it against the grain of Jane Austen's creative process. He starts at the wrong end, the end of pattern and intention, as if he were appraising a novel by E. M. Forster or the young Henry James. And his discoveries about *Mansfield Park* seem chimerical, not because the novel is not indeed every bit as rich and interesting as he sees it, but because the richness starts from Jane Austen's instinct for feeling herself into the character and world of Fanny, just as in her next novel she feels herself into those of Emma. She does not begin with insights into the nature of society. How misleading it can be to ignore this is shown by Professor Trilling's comments on Mary Crawford, whom he feels to be the type of the new romantic age, with its desire to try out different rôles and be always playing a part. This is a shrewd and illuminating comment on the working of romanticism in society, but it has very little relevance to Mary Crawford. She strikes us in fact a remarkably spontaneous person. We remember her warm and instant defence of Fanny against Mrs Norris, and the instinctive and ill-timed comments on her brother's 'stupidity' in eloping, which are a

[1] See the essay on "Mansfield Park" in the collection entitled *The Opposing Self*.

final revelation to Edmund of the corrupted outlook which is second nature to her. There is certainly a moral to Mary, but it is a perfectly straightforward one which we learn during a close and fascinated attention to her personality. A good but impressionable nature has been corrupted by exposure to bad principles. Professor Trilling assumes that to Jane Austen the idea of morality was complex and intriguing in itself, but it was people whom she found complex and intriguing—morality was simple enough. On the level of moral meaning Mary Crawford is much simpler than Professor Trilling makes out, but on the level of character she is a good deal more subtle.

Henry James is at the other extreme from Professor Trilling in taking for granted the native simplicity of Jane Austen's method. 'With her light felicity she leaves us hardly more curious of her process than the brown thrush who tells his story from the garden bough.' Professor Trilling has no trouble in pointing out that this is not the case, that she is as conscious and rigorous in her approach to the form and balance of the novel as James himself, but he ignores the aspect of her which struck James so strongly—the effortless simplicity of her preliminary response to her human material. It is this 'might half slumbering on his own right arm' which impressed James, and which impresses the common reader of Jane Austen. James's phrase about her echoes what was said in the days before professional criticism about Shakespeare's 'warblings wild', and it is significant that in *The Lesson of Balzac*—the essay roughly contemporary with *The Golden Bowl* in which his comment on Jane Austen appears—James goes on to express the greatest admiration for that instinctive seizure of a character which love and curiosity make possible. It is the lesson, we might infer, not only of Balzac but of Shakespeare and Jane Austen as well, the lesson of how to embrace and inhabit a character without making it either a projection of the author's self or a vessel of moral discernment. It is a lesson which James took deeply to heart in his later years, and it is this pondering of it—(for he makes it quite clear that with him it could not be a matter of instinct)—which gives to Kate Croy and Maggie and Charlotte and the Prince so much more solidity and freedom, so much more of the gusto of creation, than we can feel in Isobel Archer of *The Portrait*, directed as the latter avowedly is by the young James's 'idea' of her fate. 'It was by loving them that he knew them', he says of Balzac's characters, 'not by knowing them that he loved', and we can see in *The Golden Bowl* his own tribute to this conception of how the novelist possesses his world.

Love in *The Golden Bowl* is at first sight a fairly simple matter, of a proclaimed mutuality among the characters concerned that might seem to verge almost on the comical. Maggie 'loves' the Prince and her father; the Prince 'loves' Charlotte and Maggie; Charlotte 'loves' Maggie and her father as well as the Prince; Fanny Assingham adores them all. The inverted commas indicate that the characters distinguish between different senses of the word in their relation to those they love, though the distinctions are not necessarily, as we shall see, the same ones that are suggested on balance by the novel itself. The two ideas that form a kind of complex antithetical pattern in the novel are those of 'loving' on the one hand, and 'knowing' on the other. Are these two activities opposed to each other, or are they closely related? Certainly it would be difficult to overestimate the importance of knowledge in *The Golden Bowl*. As so often, not only in James but in the majority of psychological novels, it is a symbol for success in life, a kind of substitute for achievement. If knowledge is power in life, it is a great deal more so in the modern novel. But in *The Golden Bowl* it is more than that: it also provides a scale of value, intimately pondered by James, against which to measure love. And in this scale it is knowledge that finally sinks and love that rises.

At the opening of the novel we discover from their mutual friend, Mrs Fanny Assingham, that Charlotte and the Prince fell in love when they first met in Rome, but as neither had any money they agreed that it was better 'to put the Apennines between them as quickly as possible'. The Prince is about to marry Maggie Verver, the heiress, when he again meets Charlotte, who has come to stay with Mrs Assingham. There follows (Vol. I, p. 42)[1] one of those descriptions of the characters which are a special feature of *The Golden Bowl*, and which help to establish its extraordinary density and firmness of texture. Through the 'golden mist' an endless variety of solid and vivid details make their appearance for a purpose which Edith Wharton so signally failed to appreciate when she asked James 'what was his idea in suspending the four principal characters in *The Golden Bowl* in the void, and why had he stripped them of the *human fringes* which we necessarily trail after us through life'. She assumed that the process was deliberate, and was surprised when James professed with some disturbance that 'he didn't know he had'. It seems likely that James's chagrin was due to his friend's not having perceived the great care he had taken over precisely this aspect of the subject. Not only are the details of personal appearance and of town and country landscape and interior selected with a vividness and subtlety unmatched in the James canon, but the physical

[1] All page references are to the 2 vol. Edition in the *Collected Works* (Macmillan).

nature of life is recorded with unique emphasis. The characters have baths, use latch-keys, get their clothes wet, smoke and drink, feel hungry, and experience sexual desire. A male gesture 'tests the growth of the beard against the back of the hand'; a female voice sounds a 'high coerced quaver'. Colonel Assingham's eye is 'attentive to the good appearance of an extremely slender foot which he kept jerking in its neat integument of fine-spun black silk and patent leather'. The grotesqueness—endearing or otherwise—of physical detail, is admirably and constantly conveyed, and this unobtrusive documentation extends to every kind of relevance. We are made very familiar with nationality and background: the exact kinds of Americanness in Maggie and her father, in Charlotte and Fanny Assingham; the quality of the Prince's Roman cosmopolitanism; the Englishness of the Colonel, who 'could deal with things perfectly, for all his needs, without getting near them', and for whom 'the thing of least mystery was his club, which he was accepted as perhaps too completely managing'. We learn that Charlotte does her best to have a child by Mr Verver but is now fairly certain she will not (2.86); that Mrs Assingham was once fiercely devoted to her mother, for whom the Colonel did not care; that Maggie at her French finishing-school had been a frightened child who longed for protection, and that Charlotte, an older girl by three years, had been there too. The reverberations back and forth of these casual but significant facts ensure that the kinds and manifestations of love will appear against the background of various activity which alone can make them completely meaningful, and which we have already noted in Chaucer and Shakespeare.

Our first introduction to the importance of knowing comes from Mrs Assingham, who remarks to her husband, 'Charlotte knows the Prince. And Maggie doesn't. No, dear thing, she doesn't.' Fanny assumes that love, sexual love, and 'knowledge' are interdependent, indeed virtually synonymous, and the view of morality that naturally proceeds from this assumption comes out at the conclusion of their dialogue. Fanny is confident that whatever happens Charlotte will do the right thing, 'the thing that will best give her the chance to be magnificent'.

> He slowly emitted his smoke. 'And best give you, by the same token, yours to be magnificent with her?'
> 'I shall be as magnificent at least as I can.'
> Bob Assingham got up. 'And you call *me* immoral?'
> It made her hesitate a moment. 'I'll call you stupid if you prefer. But stupidity pushed to a certain point, *is*, you know, immorality. Just so what is morality but high intelligence?' This he was unable to tell her; which left her more definitely to conclude. 'Besides, it's all, at the worst, great fun.'
> 'Oh if you simply put it at *that*—!'
> His implication was that in this case they had a common ground; yet even thus he couldn't catch her by it. 'Oh I don't mean,' she said from the threshold, 'the fun that you mean. Good-night.' In answer to which, as he turned out the electric light, he gave an odd short groan, almost a grunt. He *had* apparently meant some particular kind.

The irony of the passage sufficiently disposes of the view that in *The Golden Bowl* James is himself too much beguiled by the 'magnificent', by high aesthetic plausibility, to see it steadily and whole in a moral light. But 'irony' has become too much a piece of critical jargon to do justice to the calmness of James's exhibition by contrast of the two viewpoints. The full use of intelligence and knowledge ensures in Fanny's view a victory for morality; and even if something should go wrong it will then go magnificently, fascinatingly, wrong: it will be 'great fun'. The Colonel supposes that by 'fun' she means the actual pleasure of adultery, illicit emotions, and so on; his misunderstanding of it reveals the dubiousness of her moral idiom, just as his equable lack of her penetration is a comment both on its limitations and his own. The exchange is worth comparing with the one between Maggie and the Prince (2. 168), where Maggie tells him how her purchase of the bowl has revealed 'your having, and your having for a long time had, two relations with Charlotte'.

> He stared, a little at sea, as he took it up. 'Two—?'
> Something in the tone of it gave a sense, or an ambiguity, almost foolish—leaving Maggie to feel as in a flash how such a consequence, a foredoomed infelicity, partaking of the ridiculous even in one of the cleverest, might be of the very essence of the penalty of wrongdoing. 'Oh you may have had fifty— had the same relation with her fifty times! It's of the number of *kinds* of relation with her that I speak—a number that doesn't matter really so long as there wasn't only the one kind father and I supposed.'

The Prince's misunderstanding is as crude as that of the Colonel—he supposes Maggie to mean he has twice committed adultery with Charlotte—but this time the 'foredoomed infelicity' proceeds from his very knowingness about Maggie, the knowingness he accepted from Charlotte when they agreed together that Maggie and her father were innocent, inviolable, different, and to be protected from the knowledge that in their idiom is the very breath of life, intimacy, and passion. This knowledge now finds itself ludicrously in the dark, and its eclipse is also the total eclipse of the intimacy and love that had depended on it. The love of Charlotte and the Prince does not and cannot survive this moment. Was it then not really love, or not the right kind of love? Being in love originally, should they have got married, despite their impecunious state, for only thus—we receive the intimation—can real love develop, the love that parallels on a still higher plane the natural love of blood relations? Instead of the marriage bond Charlotte has tried to fasten the Prince to her by a bond of knowledge, a bond sealed the day before his marriage, when she stipulated that he should not tell Maggie of their outing together. (1. 84). The word 'sacred' which each breathes out as they 'passionately seal their pledge' at the end of Chapter Five is a blasphemous imitation of the sacred trust of the marriage tie.

The dissolution of their love is presented as both unspectacular and immediate, or rather it is not presented at all but grimly conveyed to the reader in the news that the Prince has not told Charlotte that Maggie now 'knows'. The end of their shared knowledge is the end of love, and the wretched Charlotte, who certainly excites our sympathy, is left in the limbo of a kind of absolute not-knowing—'the suspended cage, the home of eternal unrest'—not knowing whether Maggie knows, or how much her husband knows, or even if the Prince still loves her. This dreadful retribution, 'having gropingly to go on, not knowing and not knowing' is only brought to an end by her gallant and stylish recovery in the garden scene (2.271 et seq.), a recovery which Maggie—who has steadfastly refused to 'know' what has been going on—deliberately makes possible by allowing her stepmother to create a new fortification of knowledge and to state that she, Maggie, has been impeding the relations of her father and stepmother. Maggie's 'sharp successful almost primitive wail' at this, confirms Charlotte in her new superiority of knowingness, her superior wifely understanding with Verver to which his daughter cannot aspire. She 'knows' now that it would be better to take him away, 'to keep the man I've married and have him at last a little to myself'. 'She held up her head now; her lighted eyes more triumphantly rested; she was finding, she was following her way.' Nor is the triumph of this merely a question of saving herself and putting a brave face on it; so complex and subtle are the ties between behaviour, character, and feeling, as James presents them, that we really are to feel that Charlotte's new establishment of knowledge involves a kind of love—her kind—and that through her successful assumption of this rôle and of 'an accepted finality of relationship', her being 'a genial wife', and more, will now be a reality.

As for the Prince, his conduct, closely considered, will be found to be not specially bad—indeed by his own code he is all but blameless. His moral outlook is fully and not unsympathetically disclosed in the early pages of the book, and the precision with which it is differentiated from the English or American sorts is a part of the accuracy of James's scene and the absence of anything approximated. James is not beglamoured by the Prince, and the emphasis on him as a valuable possession is combined with a presentation that shows his attractiveness to be of a very human kind, even of a convincingly lovable kind.

This is an important point because of the assumption that seems to get itself made not only in studies of James but in the criticism of any novelist who explores moral situations, that the character who lives in an aesthetic way—that is, makes himself as attractive as he can by means of his appearance, tastes, or status—must necessarily be an inhuman character. It is the kind of convention that would end by making the whole fictional world of moral enquiry quite arbitrary and meaningless, and it is certainly not observed by James, though the character of Gilbert Osmond in *The Portrait of a*

Lady is of so clear and straightforward an intention that it has added a lot of weight to the general acceptance of the aesthetic as the automatic adversary in any novel which concerns moral values. In the modern idiom, Osmond is not 'on the side of life', and this is accepted as a characteristic of his aestheticism; but in fact this aestheticism is not necessarily of a piece with the reptilian will and the lack of any sort of generosity which make him such a repellent figure. Grand-court, in *Daniel Deronda*, is a villain with much the same functions—indeed James avows his relation to George Eliot here—and his nastiness is embodied in his status as a rich aristocrat. In both cases aristocracy or aestheticism is a contingent and not a necessary part of turpitude; it is more in the nature of local colour to make it clearly visible: all seedy bourgeois are not devils, though Dostoevsky portrayed the devil as a seedy bourgeois. So we are not to condemn *a priori* the Prince for having an aesthetic appreciation of himself, or Mr Verver for having an aesthetic appreciation of the Prince. Bad they may turn out to be, but it will not be for this reason. James is not prejudiced beforehand by people's status and mode of life. He did not think that a rich man could not enter the kingdom of heaven: indeed he seems inclined to conclude, from experience and reflection, that other things being equal the rich man is more likely to get in than the poor one. And this is not a prejudice but the fruit of empirical enquiry; people with advantages are more likely to develop a fine moral awareness.

In any case, nobility in the true Jamesian sense, the sense in which Isobel and Ralph Touchett and even Merton Densher for all their errors are noble, is not of course imputed to the Prince. In his exotic and good-natured way he is a bit of a philistine. His life is 'deliciously dull'; he joins in the high English activities, 'shooting, golfing, walking

over the fine diagonals of meadow paths or round the pocketed corners of billiard tables' ... 'and if he didn't enjoy
them madly he enjoyed them at any rate as much as the
good people who had in the night of time unanimously
invented them, and who still, in the prolonged afternoon of
their good faith, unanimously, even if a trifle automatically,
practised them'. He doesn't 'drink', but enjoys 'the nightly
climax over the *bottigliera*, as he called it, the bristling tray'.
His rueful sense of fun doesn't prevent him from feeling at
sea 'in the fathomless depth of English equivocation'.

The Colonel, with that brutal brevity which so often
ambushes us among the pages of *The Golden Bowl*, declares
to his wife of the presumed love-affair: 'what in the world
did you ever suppose was going to happen? The man's in a
position in which he has nothing in life to do'. Certainly his
existence is principally decorative, and it is apt that the
attractiveness of this, its legitimate value even, should be
coupled with the *conscience* claimed for herself by Charlotte.
Living and knowing complement each other and make a
team whose appearance—as it manifests itself to Maggie and
her father on the balcony for instance—is certainly admirable. But though the Prince—like Stiva—in a most hearten-
ing manner *is*, his bond in intimacy with Charlotte's knowledge makes it also necessary for him to act and to pretend.
James does not tell us for nothing that he has been described
as a 'refined Irishman', a phrase that among other implications suggests the heroic tenor and the repertory melodrama.
But though it is a sign of corruption, this acting—in contrast
to the 'naturalness' of Maggie and her father—is also something to be sympathized with. James shows that it has its own
splendour and pathos; and the vision of the two in harness
and going through their exigent social rôle for the benefit of
father and daughter will make us want to be more than fair

to them. But it remains true that their love is an act; the Italian language which they share (we learn that the Prince is amazed and gratified by Charlotte's fluency in it), is a symbol of their mutual passion and knowledge, and gives a deliberately operatic effect to the moment after the country-house weekend at Castledean when the Prince calls to her to come down and she replies *'Vengo, Vengo'*.

The nature of their love is of the greatest importance to the novel's perspective, and the critical judgement that theirs is a 'decent passion', and that 'in a stale sickly and oppressive atmosphere they represent life'[1], is even more misleading than critical assertions based on a militant concept of 'life' usually are. In fact their love is based on the successful carry-ing off of the tricky mutual act which circumstances—in their view—have conspired to expect of them. It cannot come to good, and the logic that makes us feel this has no trace of *parti pris*. Their 'decent passion' would, we feel, be extinguished by the removal of Maggie and her father, just as it is by the removal of that mutuality in knowledge which enabled them to synchronize every moment of their act. For it depends so completely on the kinds of 'fun' which James so wonderfully suggests in that exchange of the Assinghams. As well as the Colonel's simpler kind, the 'fun' is knowing-ness and playing an exhilarating part—(the pleasures, we may remember, which the love-impotent Iago admits in himself, as he assumes the simpler kind on behalf of all human beings). The outburst which is imagined as trembling on Charlotte's lips—'ours was everything a relationship could be, filled to the brim with the wine of consciousness'— has the emphasis of someone determined to exploit that con-sciousness to the full by playing the passionate part. Iago's 'pleasure and action make the hours seem short' is also an

[1] F. R. Leavis, *The Great Tradition*, p. 160.

appropriate cry from this sort of consciousness. The part comes easily to them both of course, and indeed the Prince feels a comical exasperation that the 'abject innocence' of Maggie and her father in throwing him always together with Charlotte, should have the appearance of assuming that he can play a tamer and less exacting one.

The theory of it seemed to publish one as idiotic or incapable— this was a predicament of which the dignity depended all on one's own handling. What was supremely grotesque in fact was the essential opposition of theories—as if a *galantuomo*, as *he* at least constitutionally conceived *galantuomini*, could do anything *but* blush to 'go about' at such a rate with such a person as Mrs Verver in a state of childlike innocence, the state of our primitive parents before the Fall. The grotesque theory, as he would have called it, was perhaps an odd one to resent with violence, and he did it—also as a man of the world—all merciful justice; but none the less assuredly there was but one way *really* to mark, and for his companion as much as for himself, the commiseration in which they held it. Adequate comment on it could only be private, but it could also at least be active, and of rich and effectual comment Charlotte and he were fortunately alike capable. Wasn't this consensus literally their only way not to be ungracious? It was positively as if the measure of their escape from that danger were given by the growth between them of an exquisite sense of complicity.

Wasn't this consensus too, we feel, their only way of being in love? Love is a part of their sense of fitness and complicity unites them: they have no other mutual topic or point of rest. A hint of this emerges in the conversation before their 'passionate pledge', which is a climax that grows out of their getting the Ververs finally placed. The Prince emphasizes how different he feels from them.

'Yet you're not'—Charlotte made the important point —'too different from *me*.'

'I don't know—as we're not married. That brings things out. Perhaps if we were,' he said, 'you *would* find some abyss of divergence.'

'Since it depends on that then,' she smiled, 'I'm safe—as you are anyhow. Moreover, as one has so often had occasion to feel, and even to remark, they're very, very simple. That makes,' she added, 'a difficulty for belief; but when once one has taken it in it makes less difficult for action. I *have* at last, for myself I think, taken it in. I'm not afraid.'

He wondered a moment. 'Not afraid of what?'

'Well, generally of some beastly mistake. Especially of any mistake founded on one's idea of their difference. For that idea,' Charlotte developed, 'positively makes one so tender.'

'Ah but rather! ... It represents for us a conscious care'— —'Of every hour, literally,' said Charlotte. She could rise to the highest measure of the facts. 'And for which we must trust each other—'

'Oh as we trust the saints in glory. Fortunately,' the Prince hastened to add, 'we can'. With which, as for the full assurance and the pledge it involved, each hand instinctively found the other.

It is the thought of the Ververs' difference from themselves that makes them 'tender', and their 'sacred bond' is also the bond of their responsibility to the Ververs. When the latter is broken by Maggie's discovery about the bowl, the Prince logically accepts at once that the former is broken too. Mrs Assingham has already opined (1. 349), that he does not really love Charlotte, and though we need not suppose her to be right, it is quite clear that his readiness to play in the drama of love is absolutely dependent on Charlotte's knowingness. To that extent his claim about himself—'if ever a man acted in good faith'—is quite justified: he put his faith in Charlotte's having correctly *placed* Maggie and her father, and acted accordingly. Even the act of telling Charlotte that Maggie now knows what has happened would be to continue not only his bond of knowingness with Charlotte but also the placing of Maggie. The Prince comes back to Maggie from the moment he declines to go on having her placed for him, and his relation with Charlotte ends with their mutual knowingness. But though the Prince returns to Maggie, seeing her now with fascination through his own eyes instead of Charlotte's, he does not—so great is her distrust of the knowing and revealing process—learn much from her. Indeed in Maggie's attitude here we see some resemblance, curiously enough, to the point often implied in D. H. Lawrence's novels, that a love affair brings human beings unnaturally together while marriage keeps them the right and dignified distance apart. Maggie makes no attempt to know exactly what has happened, or to secure the Prince to her in an orgy of shared information and confession. She accepts his and her own isolation as a natural and commonplace thing which is recognized and rewarded in the purpose of marriage; and it is this steadfast acceptance, together with her refusal to make an all too human and violent muddle of the business, that gives her for many readers an inhuman quality. We must return to this later, but for the moment the thing to notice is its effect on the Prince. Behind her new and tormenting mysteriousness—tormenting because it reveals the possibility of a different intimacy—looms the still greater enigma of her father. How much does he know? The punishment of the knowers, as Fanny points out, including herself in the category, is this terrible indifference to knowledge which confounds and controls them, holding them in a state of uneasy speculation.

'He [Verver] may be sublime: sublimer even than Maggie herself. He may in fact have already been. But we shall never know.' With which perhaps her tone betrayed a shade of soreness for the single exception she didn't yearningly welcome. '*That* I can see.'

'Oh I say!—' It came to affect the Colonel himself with a sense of privation.

'I'm not sure even that Charlotte will.'

'Oh my dear, what Charlotte doesn't know—!'

But she brooded and brooded. 'I'm not sure even that the Prince will.' It seemed privation in short for them all. 'They'll be mystified, confounded, tormented. But they won't *know*—and all their possible putting their heads together won't make them. That,' said Fanny Assingham, 'will be their punishment.' And she ended, ever, when she had come so far, at the same pitch. 'It will probably also, if I get off with so little,—be mine.'

Again we are reminded that although this lust in knowing is at the back of so much human damage, its devotees are none the less of a high intelligence and feeling whose regard for the social forms—forms which in spite of all appearances are rooted in humanity and scrupulousness—is always rigorous. 'The forms,' says Fanny, 'are two-thirds of conduct'; and she proceeds with a zeal which is not quite casuistical and a point which is not quite specious to blame Maggie and her father for having enclosed the lovers in the wrong forms, thereby pushing them in the direction they have gone. It is at such moments that we see the complex moral situation distributing itself with a remarkable equilibrium.

It is poor Charlotte who is most trapped by her ignorance, 'afraid to ask just as she's afraid of not asking', and whose predicament is described in a terrible metaphor as having a loose silken cord round her neck with her husband holding

the other end in his pocketed hand. Equally terrible is the
metaphor of her tapping vainly from within on the glass of
her closed relationship with the Prince, tapping to attract
Maggie's attention and establish some kind of certainty from
her. It is this signal which moves Maggie to break her
determination of 'not knowing' and plead for Charlotte with
the Prince, a plea which ironically confirms their new
intimacy by defining Charlotte's predicament and confining
her more certainly in her glass cage. The Prince makes his
point at once.

'She ought to have *known* you. That's what's present to me.
She ought to have understood you better.'

'Better than you did?'

'Yes,' he gravely maintained, 'better than I did. And
she didn't really know you at all. She doesn't know you
now.'

'Ah yes she does!' said Maggie.

But he shook his head—he knew what he meant. 'She not
only doesn't understand you more than I, she understands you
ever so much less. Though even I—'

'Well even you?' Maggie pressed as he paused.

...'Even I, even I even yet'—again he paused and the silence
held them.

But Maggie at last broke it. 'If Charlotte doesn't understand me its because I've prevented her. I've chosen to deceive
her and to lie to her.'

The Prince kept his eyes on her. 'I know what you've chosen
to do. But I've chosen to do the same.'

'Yes,' said Maggie after an instant, 'my choice was made
when I had guessed yours. But you mean,' she asked, 'that she
understands *you*?'

'It presents small difficulty.'

'Are you so sure?' Maggie went on.

'Sure enough. But it doesn't matter.' He waited an instant;

then, looking up through the fumes of his smoke, 'she's stupid,' he abruptly opined.

His sense of outrage, and our sense of the relation which it has so abruptly dissipated, comes to a climax with this devastating pronouncement. In such a society it is the gravest and most comprehensive charge that can be preferred, and we have already caught the suggestion that 'wrongdoing' is fatally connected with it. And yet its crude abruptness does not strike Charlotte alone: once the fatal word is uttered it spreads like a stain over the Prince himself, and—since they are all connected by the thread of the situation—over Maggie and her father and Mrs Assingham as well. We remember Mrs Assingham's accusation against Maggie and her father, and we remember—as part of the thread of imagery 'the rather stupid elegance' of the bowl itself, to say nothing of the Assinghams' unfortunate surname. But stupidity is least excusable in those who put so high a moral premium on cleverness: innocent stupidity is excusable because it does not think worse of anybody who gets things wrong. This is important in the light of the Prince's next remark about Charlotte—'Why is she unhappy if she doesn't *know*?'—i.e., doesn't know that Maggie has at last perceived what's up. This seems breathtaking in its callous insensibility, until we reflect that the Prince is honestly giving words to his total incomprehension of Charlotte. He no longer has any inkling about her state of mind, and shows a detachment and an indifferent curiosity which might seem barbarous to anyone who did not appreciate to what extent his feelings here were dependent on knowledge, and began and ended with it. So strange to him is she now that he hardly even knows if she would be likely to 'mind' the ending of their relationship. All he can see is that she must be a different person, with different intentions and a different knowingness—that of the need to take her husband away. The unknowers, Maggie and her father, have 'so shuffled away every link between consequence and cause that the intention remained, like some famous poetic line in a dead language, subject to varieties of interpretation'. (2. 304.) After the lovers' 'exquisite sense of complicity' such an incomprehension is terrifying, and we feel that it is not only the nemesis of the relation but—in a larger sense—that it demonstrates an insight into the kind of human intercourse in which understanding too easily becomes an act of self-regard, and ignorance and 'not knowing' are a kind of charity as well as a kind of safety.

None the less, in the full imaginative equilibrium of the story, the Prince and Charlotte are in some way tragic in their fate and their endeavour; for though they achieve only 'fun' we never lose sight of her ambiguous ideal, the idea of 'a relation filled to the brim with the wine of consciousness.' It is a brave idea, and the tragic discrepancy is between what they aim for—what Charlotte in particular aims for—and what they can get. It gives us an almost Augustan—(or, in modern terms, an Auden-like)—picture of the gap between morality and the cravings of the imagination, for the imagination is represented here by the daring challenge and the difficult game. In the tragic context, too, even their acting has its high and good side, in opposition to the wholesome lowness of Maggie, who, as the couple sit for the last time magnificently side by side, 'their impersonal smile cleared of any betrayal, any slightest value, of consciousness', pays her tribute—'Charlotte's incomparable, Charlotte's great!' So they play their parts to the end, Charlotte gallantly, irrecoverably immersed in her new 'knowingness' with her husband; the Prince necessarily pursuing what

233

seems his cruel logic of total withdrawal from her consciousness. Only once does he waver—in his colloquy with Maggie before the Ververs arrive for their final visit—and we think the more of him for it.

'I shall tell her I lied to her.'
'Ah no!' Maggie returned.
'And I shall tell her you did.'
She shook her head again. 'Oh still less.'
With which therefore they stood at difference, he with his head erect and his happy idea perched in eagerness on his crest. 'And how then is she to know?'
'She isn't to know.'
'She's only still to think *you* don't—?'
'And therefore that I'm always a fool? She may think,' said Maggie, 'what she likes.'
'Think it without my protest?'—
'The Princess made a movement. 'What business is it of yours?'
'Isn't it my right to correct her'?—
Maggie let his question ring—ring long enough for him to hear it himself; only then she took it up. ' "Correct" her?'— and it was her own now that really rang. 'Aren't you rather forgetting who she is?' (2. 313.)

Convinced of the marvellous reality, as it were, of Charlotte's acting, Maggie shows how cruel it would be to strike at that act now, even from the best of motives—(and we receive the subtle intimation that hers are probably not so good as his). Moreover, as she, with her dumpy and somehow Victorian majesty, reminds him, his suggestion ignores the fact of Charlotte's present identity: she is no longer his mistress but plainly and completely Mrs Verver. To let her 'know' would be an actual impertinence. And so we come to the last scene, the scene that most shows 'the possible hero-ism of perfunctory things'. Passion is spent, harmony is achieved, and there is a thankful sinking into not knowing, 'into that strange accepted finality of relation, as from couple to couple, which almost escaped an awkwardness only by not attempting a gloss.' In other words, to risk a lame expansion of a superlatively Jamesian velleity, this needful and homely finality would be ludicrous if it attempted a fine acted consciousness of its state. It is supremely undramatic and unselfregarding; it succeeds by taking for granted. And, homely or ludicrous or not, we receive the intimation that it is in this kind of relationship that love as a permanence must do its work.

So the tragedy ends, 'the four of them ... united through the firmest abstention from pressure'. It is, to put it baldly, a victory for anti-romanticism, an abolition of Paterian intens-ities. And it is a victory for Maggie and her father. Do they deserve it? For many readers and critics they do not: they appear as monsters, even as monsters whom James did not recognize to be such, or did not realize that we might think them so. Certainly the victors in such a contest are not likely to appear in an agreeable light, and especially when the economic scales are weighted so overwhelmingly in their favour. I think, though, that James, the least sentimental of writers, would not feel himself bound to defer to the tend-ency to side with penniless passion and wrongdoing in defeat. If one had suggested to him that Maggie and her father were intolerable, particularly in their financial over-lordship of Charlotte and the Prince, he might have been disturbed—just as Mrs Wharton disturbed him—by an undue emphasis on something initially pondered by him as a given premise and allotted its due weight. None the less, as the book progresses, there is no doubt that he does become more and more beguiled by his vision of the power that father and daughter hold—the power that may be exercised by *not knowing*, by the refusal to perform acts of visibly analytic consciousness. But again we must remember that James is not, like some humanist authors, E. M. Forster for instance, thrown into a panic at the very idea of power. Far from it: power and authority fascinate him, and his treatment of them are singularly without prejudice. Especially the type of power fascinates him which has no natural *brio* about it: it is not the people born to command who intrigue him but those who have command thrust upon them— usually in the shape of money—the sheep who become wolves despite themselves. We can see here, if we wish, an unconscious preoccupation pretty common in the novelist; and in *A Small Boy and Others* James relates a nightmare, which he connected with his first revelation of the power of art, in which 'an awful agent' is trying to get in at him, and which he sallies out upon 'full of straight aggression and dire intention' and pursues down the whole length of the *Galerie des Glaces* at Versailles. The circumstance may remind us of Maggie's vision of evil as 'a bad-faced stranger in the house' —(had one appeared in fact we may be sure that Maggie would have hustled him out of the tradesman's entrance in short order)—and it is impossible to deny that James appears to ally himself with Maggie in repelling the unutterable, and repelling it—very significantly—by the technique of making it unsure of itself.

For what is so alarming about the knowledge act of the others is its confidence—the confidence that Charlotte and the Prince had in themselves and their theory—and it is this confidence that 'our young woman', under James's enchanted supervision, so effectively undermines. His collusion with her appears most vividly in the scene (2. 45) when the Castledeans come to dinner. Lady Castledean is the finest flower of the principle of knowing and placing, with an infinite assurance that she cannot herself be placed.

Her ladyship's assumption was that she kept, at every moment of her life, every advantage—it made her beautifully soft, very nearly generous; so that she didn't distinguish the little protuberant eyes of smaller social insects, often endowed with such a range, from the other decorative spots on their bodies and wings.

Maggie has to submit to their confident curiosity, to being 'passed about, all tenderly and expertly, like a dressed doll held in the right manner, by its firmly stuffed middle, for the account she could give. She might have been made to give it by pressure of her stomach' ... Surely our sympathies are with Maggie here, even though we may not join in her retaliatory dream of power, when 'it glimmers before her' à propos of the diners, 'that she might yet live to drive them about like a flock of sheep'. It is not an agreeable reaction, but it is a natural and human one which we should hasten to condone if Maggie, like Jane Eyre, were a governess at the festive board. We know too well that money gives Maggie an excellent chance of turning the tables on the guests; it means that she will never know the worst ignominies of patronage. Yet the scene shows that James is not at all sentimental about her, merely quite fair, for why should not the privileged be allowed their moments of vindictiveness like everyone else? Maggie's resentment is muffled and yet attentive; she does not glory in it, as she does not glory in any of the emotions; her lack of their kind of immediacy and spontaneity is the chief cause of her repelling so many readers. Yet it is an effect on which the author insists, and he will not temper her goodness with aesthetic vitality or with a tendency to muddle. She *is* good, but her goodness is subject to the author's deliberate 'appeal to incalculability'; like that of the observed person in life it remains both incomplete and open to question.

Her goodness is a matter of the results she gets, not of her character, for that is open, as James remarks of her handling of the whole business, 'to varieties of interpretation'. It is perhaps a part of her goodness that she accepts this dubiety willingly. Moreover it makes her exceedingly human, not necessarily in the sense that is the opposite of 'inhuman', but in the sense in which we are actually surrounded in society by such human beings, the sense—oddly enough—in which to be human is to be virtually unknown. In this important sense she strikes me as far more human than Isobel Archer, whose ideals and limitations are so adroitly suggested by James that this sort of humanness has no place; Isobel, indeed, is very nearly in the position that James blamed Thackeray for putting Blanche Amory in—the position of being too much subject to the author's intention or prejudice. James has such a vision of Isobel and her fate that he cannot resist making it all spectacularly but inhumanly clear; even the deliberate uncertainty of the ending is a flourish too pre-determined to have the air of life. Maggie is far more artfully composed. And James is helped, in her case, to combine the clarity of a 'situation' with the muffled incalculability of living, by the fact that she moves in exactly the opposite direction to Isobel (and, one might add, to most fictional heroes and heroines). Isobel yearns for the ideal and finds herself in the conventional: her only solace is the acquisition of knowledge about herself and the world: she gets things clear. Maggie, on the other hand, rejects both her immediate impulses and the desire for knowledge, and finds in the refuge of convention and deliberate 'ignorance' salvation both for herself and for the others. She burrows back into the hallowed darkness of 'the forms', like an animal seeking shelter, and the ambiguity of appearance may make us wonder if there isn't resentment and cruelty in her action, or if she is not at least repressive, priggish and narrow-minded. But however that may be, there is no ambiguity in the sense which James conveys to us that to support convention intelligently and savingly is at least as remarkable as to defy it. Both call for gifts which James does not hesitate to compare, for style and difficulty, with art itself. Maggie in her way is as much of an artist as Charlotte.

Moreover James impressively suggests the paradox that the conventional and the mysterious are closely allied, are indeed one and the same thing. It is the conventional act which challenges the imagination and produces mystery, not the daring and emancipated act: and mystery—as James sees and presents it—is the very stuff of life. The nemesis of wrong-doing is the final stupidity of clarity and definition; the Prince and Charlotte are as visible to our gaze as if they were indeed in a glass cage—we can see all round them. But goodness, embodied here in Maggie's dependence on conventional values, not only gets better results than wrong-doing but is also more interesting. It retains its mystery, which will offer an unending avenue of exploration to the finer faculties, where wrong-doing ends in a blank wall of the obvious. It would so end, that is, if it were able to declare itself for what it is, but convention and Maggie save it from that fate by drawing it under the cloak of respectable incalculability! Charlotte and the Prince are positively not allowed to appear in the stupidity of their true colours; it is one of the triumphs of Maggie that she compels them to be not only good but interesting: by 'not knowing' about them she forces them to retain the aura of mystery and convention. She protects, as it were, their higher selves, and this will not sound priggish when we have grasped the fantastic richness and humour of James's mode of appeal.

For his final effect of incalculability is to protect them in a similar way from us—just as life and the conventions might well do—by never actually disclosing if they have committed adultery or not. Though their relationship puts them in the glass cage for our benefit they are protected from the final indignity of knowledge. And though a splendid cartoon of Max Beerbohm depicts James listening intently outside a door beside which are a pair of gentleman's and a pair of lady's shoes, it seems likely that James himself did not really want to know either. As in the case of the story which became *The Spoils of Poynton*—when he hastened to cut short his informant before she could tell him what had actually happened—he preferred his own imagination, with all it could suggest of probability and interest, to the insignificance of fact. And in *The Golden Bowl* he seizes unerringly on that truth about life which is not like its facts. For the convention of not-knowing, (a charitable one in Maggie's case), is allied with the moral impossibility of knowing completely —an impossibility which he emphasizes in the novel by innumerable touches, so that art achieves on its own scale and with its own shape an effect which is shapeless in life, the effect of queries unanswered and problems unresolved.

None the less, James does appear to me to make one grave error in his delineation of Maggie. He permits her to know, and to say, what she understands by love. 'I can bear anything,' she says to Fanny.

'Oh "bear"!' Mrs Assingham fluted.
'For love,' said the Princess.
Fanny hesitated. 'Of your father?'
'For love,' Maggie repeated.
It kept her friend watching. 'Of your husband?'
'For love,' Maggie said again.   (2. 102.)

This is disastrous, and precisely the kind of 'pretended
exhibitory prose' that James by his own token was so anxious
to avoid. That the *idea* of love involved sounds morally
rather grand doesn't help at all, in fact it hinders, it is an
embarrassment—especially as Maggie herself formulates it.
A similar misfortune is her account (2. 231) of the three
kinds of love, the deepest being untouched by jealousy. But
in most contexts we get a true dramatic sense of what is so
uncomfortably on record in these exchanges—the quality of
Maggie's love is of a piece with her refusal to exercise her
critical judgement. Her unquestioning feeling for her husband and father is quite clear of any 'interest' in them; they
do not represent for her a source of 'fun' or a method of
'being magnificent'. This quality of Maggie's strikes Mrs
Assingham with 'a strange barely credible relief' when that
arch-knower is trying to wriggle out of her difficult
situation.

> She drew in, as if it had been the warm summer scent of a
> flower, the sweet certainty of not meeting, any way she should
> turn, any consequence of judgement. She shouldn't be judged
> —save by herself; which was her own wretched business.

She is being dealt with as she would not deal herself, and she
pays Maggie in return the biggest compliment she can. 'You
may laugh at me for it, but I'm bound to confess I've never
been so awfully sure of what I may call knowing you'. Not

to be known is Maggie's triumph, and by not judging she drives Mrs Assingham before her, though the latter rallies when she is at home with the Colonel and denies that she has made a hash of things. We remember her earlier announcement to him.

> 'I don't make mistakes. But I perpetrate—in thought—crimes'. And she spoke with all intensity. 'I'm a most dreadful person. There are times when I seem not to mind a bit what I've done, or what I think or imagine or fear or accept.'

This admission—or even boast—about the anarchic interior life is very revealing. Fanny has, like most of us, a dual nature: her imagination and sexual fantasy hovers round herself and others without shame or scruple; it is the means by which she passes the time inside herself. 'I can imagine the way it works', she says of the presumed adultery, and 'it was as if I were suddenly, with a kind of horrible push, seeing through their eyes.' All this is 'fun', no doubt, and yet Fanny does not—if she can help it—make mistakes; she says the forms are two-thirds of conduct, and though she enlivens her own virtue by being in on interesting situations and even trying to arrange them, she is genuinely upset when the worst seems to be happening—even if the complex humour of the book makes it likely that her distress is partly finding herself the fifth wheel of the coach. Fanny is a most discerning portrait of a certain kind of society average, and her commonplace dualism is penetrated with lively sympathy. But Maggie's imagination is of a finer kind and it is all of a piece: it is not concerned with the difference between knowing and behaving, and it can therefore rise to a situation which leaves Fanny grotesquely and even touchingly dismayed.

Their attitudes link Fanny and Charlotte closely—the younger woman begins as virtually a *protégée*—and James conveys in the early chapters the *atmosphere* of their mutual understanding, an atmosphere often found in life but singularly difficult to represent in the novel. (It is partly achieved by one of those homely touches which are so much of the character of the book: we learn that both ladies smoke like chimneys and that the Colonel even fears his wife may take to the short pipe.) Charlotte is grander and more adventurous than her mentor; like Icarus she wants to soar, and Fanny admires her wish. Charlotte is sure that her confidence in knowing can be carried into action, that the expert dualism between knowing and behaving she has imbibed from Fanny can become one between behaviour and fact. And since she has carried knowing into the world of actions, there is a grim fitness in the point that she is never allowed to state her own case (as Fanny and the Prince variously are) but only to act it.

Extremely dramatic, too, is the absence of any kind of show-down between her and Maggie. Her desire for one creates great suspense, as in the *nocturne* at Fawns, where Maggie is aware that the cage of Charlotte's uncertainty has been opened from the inside, and that her stepmother is coming after her through the warm darkness like a liberated beast of prey. But Maggie is again protected by her refusal to know. Whether this power, the power whose examination obviously fascinated James, can really exist without an implied moral judgement, is a question which occurs to one at moments like these, and it is one of the few queries to which the book does not seem to return an echo. Does the author overlook the fact that not to play is in itself a judgement on the game, perhaps the most destructive one of all? In expecting some kind of response here, however, we are ignoring how completely dramatic are the scenes in which the splendours and diversities of the game are contrasted with the two humble powerful creatures who do not play it. In such scenes as Charlotte's arrival at Portland Place (1. 263), the lovers on the balcony (2. 87), or the night at Fawns when Charlotte 'breaks out', the fullness of the dramatic impact is a fullness of revelation.

No wonder James was excited by the conception of the story, or that he was ready to bless 'the pangs and pains and miseries' of his failure on the stage since he felt it had taught him the 'precious lesson ... of the divine principle of the Scenario'. How this 'portentous little discovery' functioned exactly was probably more clear to him than it ever will be to the reader, but it is certain that we have in *The Golden Bowl* the most significant demonstration of its 'magicality'. I have already remarked on the effect of dramatic poetry with which James's idea seems to have some analogy, and which is most present in the many moments the book gives us of a kind of *soundless* meaning. It is a recurrent image——Maggie sees herself as groping noiselessly among her problems—and it dominates the dramatic side of the book, while the sounded note is also the 'exhibitory'. James suggests in his preface that 'the poetry—in the largest sense' of the book requires to be spoken aloud for its full effect, and that its appeal to the soundless and incalculable is most 'in the conditions of life' when this is done.

'Soundlessness' has a moral as well as a dramatic point. In the nature of things most of us would feel more sympathetic to Maggie and her father if there was a real bust-up; if the emotional caravan, with its 'natural joy' and stridency, which Maggie in a famous metaphor imagines approaching her, had not been turned aside 'into other defiles' but had on the contrary engulfed her and precipitated a first-class row.

At least then the air would have been cleared and life have come rushing in. But perhaps our idea of life is too automatically connected with *peripeteia*: discoveries are the life of literary plots, and out ideas of 'life' in the abstract have more connection with literature than we are usually aware. James's most telling originality lies in his treatment of the problem of how a conception of 'life' that did not depend on *peripeteia* could none the less be worked into the shape of art, into the formal tradition that goes back to Greek Tragedy. He distrusted the short cut of the 'slice of life' method, or of the short story in which nothing particular happens; on the contrary, his plots often seem oddly old-fashioned in their conventional neatness and careful forethought. *The Story in It* is his most obvious and even artificial attempt to write a conventional tale in which nothing occurs, and in which 'romance becomes a sort of consciousness'—(a phrase which startlingly suggests the theory of a later, and to James no doubt a more uncongenial, kind of writing). But what he says about this story in the preface is very illuminating.

> For the 'story' ... I had to take [a] deep and straight dive into the deep sea of a certain general truth. The general truth had been positively phrased for me by a distinguished friend, a novelist not to *our* manner born and bred, on the occasion of his having made such answer as he could to an interlocutor bent on learning from him why the adventures he imputed to his heroines were so perversely and persistently but of a type impossible to ladies respecting themselves. My friend's reply had been ... that ladies who respected themselves took particular care never to have adventures. ... There were, certainly it was to be hoped, ladies who practised that reserve—which, however beneficial to themselves was yet fatally detrimental to literature, in the sense of promptly making any artistic harmony pitched in the same low key trivial and empty. A picture

of life founded on the mere reserves and omissions and suppressions of life, what sort of performance—for beauty, for interest, for tone—could *that* hope to be? ... Discussion [of this argument], to be really luminous, would have to rest on some such perfect definition of terms as is not of this muddled world. It is, not surprisingly, one of the rudiments of criticism that a human, a personal 'adventure' is no *a priori*, no positive and absolute and inelastic thing, but just a matter of relation and appreciation—a name we conveniently give, after the fact, to any passage, to any situation, that has added the sharp taste of uncertainty to a quickened sense of life.

In *The Golden Bowl* we certainly feel that the sharp taste of uncertainty has been added to our quickened sense of life, and it is a sense of life which comes precisely from the absence of openness and revelation. We may feel with some reason that the dilemma between writing about the respectable lady to whom nothing happens, and the adventurous one who provides plots, has come to-day to seem a little quaint and unreal; and indeed might have seemed so in 1900 to anyone who had read Tolstoy, for Dolly Oblonsky is as interesting a character as Anna Karenina, though it is true that the book would indeed drop into a lower key if she had to sustain it alone. But the real point is not so much the definition of an adventure or the emphasis on 'relation', as the significant connection between the fact that nothing happens and the moral viewpoint. Without being Pascal, James was well aware that the ills which beset human relations come from not being able 'to sit quietly in a room'. He saw, too, the artificiality for the serious moral novelist of having to urge his characters irresponsibly into adventure and action. The good and the bad may indeed be contrasted in this way, but only by an initial and wanton agitation, by a disturbance that should never have occurred. On how much stronger ground is the novelist if the complexities of morality and art coincide, if the true interest and the real virtue in both cases lies in refraining from the obvious adventure and 'fun'! The novelist is fascinated by the predicaments and dramas that arise from pushing his heroes and heroines into unsuitable marriages, arranging for them to become bankrupt or incurably ill, making elaborate plans for a Charlus to be suddenly unmasked at a salon or for an English girl to have a nasty experience in an Indian cave. Sometimes—James makes the critical point obliquely against Maupassant—the writer's excitement in this exercise of his imagination is itself a morally repellent quality; and Tolstoy, in his attack on insincerity in art, mentions the same author for much the same reasons.

No doubt James understood this excitement well and had himself given rein to it, but the signs indicate that he came to see the deepest and most valuable subject in the side of life which was necessarily and valuably uneventful, the muffled relation in which there was everything to reveal because nothing was concealed. He had written when young that the moral and the artistic sense are united in the quality of the author's mind—the finer the quality the closer the union. Of course it would be absurd to imply that fineness can be achieved *only* by close attention to uneventfulness, or that the best relation is *always* the one in which nothing happens— this would be to take a tendency to conclusions which James naturally avoids—but features of his later work which may seem perverse assume their logical significance if we realize the challenge that uneventfulness presented for him to fineness, and hence to the moral sense. And it is his achievement in *The Golden Bowl* to show that the 'great scene' need not be either a matter of revelation or of imaginative display, but can be created, in its own perspective, out of opacity, silence, 'the firmest abstention from pressure'. The concluding scene of the book is sublime in this kind, and in its sense of a wholesome solution which is none the less imaginative for being purely negative and presenting us with the very opposite of a 'significance'. It stands in contrast with such an early Jamesian set-piece as the picture of the betrayed Isobel, in *The Portrait of a Lady*, observing her husband and Madam Merle together; and its subtler and more mature satisfactions seem to me the reward of its freedom from that craftsman's glee in a good moment which informs the early example and sets the artist a little apart from our own response.

The high priest of soundlessness is of course Adam Verver, and he, even more than Maggie, embodies the idea that suffocating the facts instead of liberating them is society's sagest moral expedient. Before concluding, we should therefore perhaps examine him rather more closely. James in his *Notebooks* refers to him as 'a product', a product somehow of America, even though a very exceptional, remarkable, and striking one. He is fabulously rich, of course, and is making a collection of beautiful things which will eventually form a museum in his home town. His wealth is partly inherited but he has also increased it himself, presumably setting his teeth and somehow forcing himself through what James calls the 'livid vulgarity of getting in, or getting out, first'. He is a widower, and we are told that he and his first wife 'had loved each other so that his intelligence, on the higher line, had temporarily paid for it'. We can take it for granted that the characters in James's novels will be vividly present to us in their physical selves, and Verver is no exception, he appears before us with his mild eye and his cigar, his waistcoat, his little strolls, and his air at the head of his dinner-table of 'an innocent little boy'. Yet he remains a visionary figure, eloquent of the difference between the American millionaire as he was and as James would have liked him to be. So much the worse for the American millionaire, James might retort, as he retorted of the presumed non-existence of his American poet, Geoffrey Aspern, and of the 'super-subtle' authors in *The Figure in the Carpet*. But in the case of Verver this appeal to the artist's freedom in creation will perhaps not quite do. For one thing American millionaire collectors *did* very much exist, men who indeed saw 'acquisition of one sort as a perfect preliminary to acquisition of another', but upon whom the metaphor bestowed on Verver's career—'the years of darkness had been needed to render possible the years of light'—would be grotesquely lost. So we may feel that Verver should be the Aristotelian 'real because impossible' character, but succeeds only in being an unreal because improbable one. And it is this lack of coherence between Verver as a visionary figure and as a convincing personality that makes him strike us as a monster.

Maggie's association with her father makes her share this appearance of monstrosity, yet the association itself is surely far less sinister than is often made out. As Fanny Assingham suggests, it is basically right to divide one's affections between a blood relation and a husband, no matter what complications may ensue, while it is wrong to divide them between a husband and a lover. This is an oversimplification of course, but it corrects the opposite and equally over-simplified view that the love of Maggie and her father is an unnatural and brooding force which blights and tyrannizes over the vital affections that are trying to go on around it. However complex the issues involved, and however un-predictable their working, we shall lose sight of the main watershed of the book from which they flow if we ignore the division between love as both a formal bond and a natural blessing on the one hand, and as a game or social activity on the other.

It is true that one of James's partial failures lies in his not contriving to secure an effective contrast here between the communion of Maggie and her father, and the communion of the lovers. The contrast he *attempts* to indicate is the mutual silence of Maggie and her father as against the almost sensual mutual confidences of the lovers: Maggie and her father never get around to so much as mentioning 'them', which is implied as a part of their instinctive and unconscious goodness. But instead of a contrast we really feel an uncomfortable resemblance, for in spite of its silence the intimacy of father and daughter seems just as exclusive, just as much closed against the others, as is that of Charlotte and the Prince. Our impression of two camps is unfortunate, because the point about natural love should be that it does not constitute itself into such a camp. Sometimes a moving effect of contrast is achieved, however, especially in the interview between father and daughter at Fawns, the climax of which should be set against the lovers' sealing of their pledge. Maggie risks the point that everything round her father exists at his expense, and that she in particular 'sacrifices' him.

'But to what in the world?'
At this it hung before her that she should have had as never yet her opportunity to say, and it held her for a moment as in a vice, her impression of his now, with his strained smile, which touched her to deepest depths, sounding her in his secret unrest. This was the moment in the whole process of their mutual vigilance in which it decidedly *most* hung by a hair that their thin wall might be pierced by the slightest wrong touch. It shook between them, this transparency, with their very breath. It was an exquisite tissue, but stretched on a

frame, and would give way the next instant if either so much as breathed too hard. She held her breath, for she knew by his eyes, the light at the heart of which he couldn't blind, that he was, by his intention, making sure—sure whether or no her certainty was like his. ... She might have been, for the time, in all her conscious person, the very form of the equilibrium they were, in their different ways, equally trying to save.

The thin wall, the 'exquisite tissue', is the understanding between them, which would be ruptured by anything approaching a spoken confidence: such confidences would threaten their intimacy as much as they feed that of Charlotte and the Prince. The naturalness of their affection is imaged by its silence, and equilibrium would be disturbed if they had to admit their relationship and actually confess, each to each, what it meant to them. They can only protect themselves against the lovers by continuing to affirm their own kind of love, despite the handicaps it imposes on them. These handicaps have their lighter side, and indeed it is a part of the rich and genial comedy of the book that the highly articulate lovers have to be countered by the conscientious silence of father and daughter. The comedy also distributes more effectively in the moral iconography of love the claims of speech and of silence: the latter has no romantic glory but it has permanence. It appears in a more attractive and less ambiguous light than in the relation of father and daughter when, at the end of the book, the Prince realizes the nature of the love that Maggie offers him, an intimacy without the need of any explanation or spoken confidence. And the book ends in the sheltered hush of this *rapport*, 'the strangely accepted finality of relationship, as from couple to couple', which now embraces the united Ververs as well as Maggie and the Prince.

As Maggie comments with her partial justice, she and her father are also losing each other, and it is not their fault; but for father and daughter such a renunciation looks rather like the continuation of intimacy by other means. Their silent communion will not be interrupted. Maggie, however, has not only encouraged Charlotte to exclude her from a hastily drawn-up bond of 'knowingness' with her father, but father and daughter have silently agreed to put an artificial block between themselves, a kind of analogue to the gulf they have made between Charlotte and the Prince. This agreement is that Verver has a special awareness of Charlotte, upon which he has based his marriage, and which he cannot in the nature of things share with his daughter. Though they never have any explicit difference of opinion about Charlotte herself, this is conveyed obliquely in such exchanges as the one (2. 85) in which it emerges that Verver likes Lady Castledean while Maggie does not—Maggie is only 'fascinated' by her—and from all we hear of Lady Castledean it is plain that she is an exaggerated and vulgarized projection of Charlotte, a sort of player queen of the game which Charlotte had begun. Maggie is content to find her father different here, and to accept his difference with a sensible incuriosity, however much it goes against her own emotional prejudices.

The trouble about Verver is this difference, which is conveyed as being in some way a total rightness. It is difficult not to feel that James is carried away by his vision of Verver, by the idea of someone so ordinary and yet so effective, so *outré* and yet so gentlemanly, so apparently helpless and vulnerable that he has to be protected against designing females like Mrs Lutch, and yet so actually worldly and discerning that he is a match for Charlotte and the Prince; so shrewd that he can make millions and so full of taste and judgement that he buys up all the best pieces; and yet so un-assuming that at the head of his dinner table he looks like an innocent little boy. He is a fantasy figure, but he does at least represent, in dramatic terms, a kind of challenging opacity to whom the other figures are drawn as much by their baffled interest as by their economic dependence.

I have already mentioned the lecture on Balzac, written in 1905, in which James quotes Taine's comment on Madame Marneffe of *Les Parents Pauvres*—'Balzac aime sa Valérie'—and points out that this love of one of 'his most awful little personages' was what enabled Balzac to possess his immense material and achieve the complete 'saturation of his idea' in human actuality. 'It was by loving them that he knew them ... it was not by knowing them that he loved.' James per-ceives in Balzac a process that became very dear to his own heart, and when we feel that he is too much seduced by the idea of Mr Verver we should remember how ambiguous is this concept of an author's 'love' for his creations. Otherwise we shall fall into the error of the English reviewer of Taine who seemed to James 'to deserve the highest prize ever bestowed on critical stupidity undisguised' for remarking that if Balzac loved Valérie it just showed what very odd taste Balzac had. We must beware of Verver's leading us into a similar generalization about James's moral taste, for in this very important sense James is a great deal closer to Balzac (or even to Stevenson) than he is to George Eliot. The loving absorption by which he gets to know his characters is not directly linked with moral assessment or approbation —it comes at them by much more deep and undetectable ways; ways whose simple but effective beginnings are sug-gested by James's comment, in a much earlier essay, on the personality of Alan Breck in *Kidnapped*—'Mr Stevenson both sees through it and admires it'.

But does our possible impatience with Verver crystallize an impatience with the whole nature of the book? Does an elaborate exposition of its themes deflect the real issue—the issue of James's views on the society he is describing? For isn't this society, which limits and contains James's vision, so hopelessly corrupt and so tied to money that it is impossible for us to take seriously the problem of who is right or wrong and in what proportion? *Does* James see through it as well as admire it? Isn't the real guilt here involved not in relation to other people but in relation to money? Surely Charlotte, for example, is not so much guilty in having an affair with the Prince as in giving in to the idea that she must be rich at any cost?

These queries can only be answered by an appeal to the scale of the work. James, like Shakespeare, both accepts and reveals: the two processes are inseparable, and if—like Rymer on *Othello*—we take our stand on the premise that he had no business to accept, we cannot be put down, but equally we shall not get very far on the road of appreciation. None the less James's world does present a special problem, and one that cannot really be answered by an appeal to Shakespeare's or Jane Austen's acceptance of the conditions and conventions of their time. Their acceptance comes from their being of their world as James was not of his—he was in it but not of it, an absorbed spectator, never a true participant. And it is difficult not to feel that whatever its shortcomings, theirs was precisely a *real* world, with solid vices, virtues, graces, and taboos, resting on a solid structure of custom, religion and class, as well as money; while James's Edwardian twilight is both corrupt and anarchic, a jungle in which money alone will protect you from the musky darkness and the velvet claws. The assumptions of Jane Austen's world, in fact, are ones which could be made by a sensible and discerning person, while the assumptions of James's world are not.

This objection has of course a pretty familiar sound. It is the standard criticism not only of *The Golden Bowl* but of much of the James *oeuvre*, and as such should always be kept in view. Indeed its presence is reassuring in a sense, because it shows us that with James as with Shakespeare no consideration need be left out of the area of critical judgement: the scope is too wide for irrelevance, as it would be irrelevant, for example, to criticize Stevenson for not writing about women or Hawthorne for not writing about whales. James is nothing if not a comprehensive author, and his critical sense of his time is often exceedingly imaginative and acute, as Professor Trilling has shown in his essays on *The Bostonians* and *The Princess Casamassima*. Our problem, therefore, is whether the brilliant exposure of an aspect of Edwardian society, which forms an incidental feature of *The Golden Bowl*, is involuntary or not. Did James see as a part of his subject the valuation of human beings in his social scene as if they were stocks and shares—(we remember Verver's revolted expertise on the New York market)—or does this just emerge from his narrative, as it might have emerged from a society romance by some ancient Carthaginian author? I do not see how we can answer this question except by stating it and leaving it to stand beside our total experience of the book. Can we be sure, after all, that Shakespeare's creation of patriotism in *Henry V* really had for him the penetratingly ambivalent overtones which we find in it? In terms of what we know of the creative imagination the query must seem unreal, for here, if anywhere, is an illustration of James's own cutting of the Gordian knot of creative paradox—'he both sees through and admires'. And like his more systematic brother, James was temperamentally a pragmatist; he did not look for values in society *before* he carried it into his imagination.

And society is there, in all its prosperity and glitter and its underworld of competing impulses and 'forms', a society which is intensely of its time although it also serves the purpose of 'saturating'—as James would say—persons and themes that are timelessly alive and significant. He recognizes out of what a primeval darkness his pattern takes shape and out of what a blind and instinctive exploitation of the conditions in which his characters find themselves. It is borne upon us that even the Colonel, that upright man, holds himself upright by blind adherence to assumptions of the most unexamined kind. He deals with things 'without getting near them', and like Winnie Verloc in Conrad's *The Secret Agent*, where the jungle is more obviously and more graphically imagined, implies that 'most things in life won't bear looking into.' When they *are* looked into, a sense of shared corruption and darkness enfolds the enquiry, so that the Assinghams appear in one of James's most striking phrases as if they might have been 'a pair of specious worldly adventurers driven for relief under sudden stress to some grim midnight reckoning in an odd corner'.

We feel that the Colonel is aware of this degradation, which is produced by that unholy trinity of the social jungle —inside 'knowledge', 'fun', and 'the forms'. He takes refuge in ignorance, which is an aspect of the fact that his regard for the forms is less whole-heartedly jungle-minded than his wife's. The *forms* take the jungle for granted as our native habitat, but the *feelings* with which James brings them into such dramatic contact—and which Charlotte and Maggie demonstrate so strongly in their different ways—imply the possible existence of a finer order of society. That the forms upon which the precarious and degraded civilization of the jungle is based are broken precisely by those whose feeling is for finer things, and yet upon whom the existing forms depend for whatever they have of dignity and freedom—this is one of the larger *aperçus* of the book, and one which would not be possible if James's approach to society were less delicately pragmatic.

One would not want to overstress the element of the visionary in *The Golden Bowl*, but it is undoubtedly there, and in this context there is significance in James's portrait of the Gutermann-Seuss family at Brighton, with whom Verver is negotiating for some art treasure, and who may at first strike us as oddly irrelevant to the movement of the book. This Jewish dynasty, whose characteristics are touched in by James with characteristic liveliness and lack of inhibition, are both hierarchic and fertile, augustly rigid in form and yet glowing with the gloss of health and feeling. And there is a strangely meaningful ring in the scene in which Charlotte enters briefly into their life, takes to them and is taken to by them, so that even Verver is 'quite merged in the elated circle formed by the girl's free response to the collective caress of all the shining eyes, and by her genial acceptance of the heavy cake and port wine …' There is a kind of pathos in her response here to the idea of a wholesome and spirited respectability; it occurs just before—and is clearly related to—her decision to marry Verver; and her failure to achieve anything of this idea with Verver is suggested by her inability to have a child.

But of course this response of hers is not only one that comes and goes with all the vagary of life: it also coexists with other and more dangerous visions, like that of having both the Prince and money. And in stressing the points at which the book emancipates itself from an ordinary social acceptance we must beware of implying anything overtly 'symbolic': symbolic patterns in a novel are necessarily rigid in their ideological contrasts between life and death, sterility and fertility, and so forth; and though both D. H. Lawrence and E. M. Forster use them in a discernibly post-Jamesian manner, they have hardened in *Howard's End* and *Women in Love* into a rigidity that is dogmatic and partisan. Since *The Golden Bowl* is not based on such a symbolic pattern it would be seriously misleading to say that Charlotte is connected throughout with 'life' or Verver with 'death': both are involved in living, and handle their situations with the methods most natural to them.

Though it has its visionary moments, the vitality of Charlotte is based on the essential resilience of a comedy character; and the 'truth' of such a character—the truth in life as well as in the comedy form—lies in adaptability and the power of survival, indeed of triumphant survival. Charlotte has many failures and many disappointments, but she survives, and with a kind of magnanimity she adapts herself to a vision of harmony and equilibrium when the vision of life and excitement fail her. She has the comedy toughness of Becky Sharp in one sense, but she is conceived with more depth and spaciousness than Becky, for her power to survive has a generosity in it that is linked with her possible fineness of vision. And it is this fineness which gives tragic overtones to her survival, most poignant perhaps in the scene when she follows Maggie out into the night to try to learn what she knows, or when in her state of 'not-knowing' she continues doggedly to expatiate to visitors on the beauties of Fawns. But in spite of this grimness her survival remains a triumph, and the whole effectiveness of the ending depends on our finding it convincingly so; while it also depends on the *Comédie Française* form striking us as triumphantly compatible with the moral movement of the book and its breadth of meaning. The great negative tableau of the last scene must convey the satisfactions of an artificial *dénouement*, and we must be made to see the ending as a kind of liberation, a rounding off in which the artifice of the theatre combines with the resonances of life to form a perfect equilibrium.

It was once suggested to me that such a feeling of liberation could only be achieved if Charlotte were to 'go off' at the end, to shake herself free from both the Prince who has let her down and the Ververs who have found her out. Should she not set out, in a concluding fictional question mark, for Paris, New York, or simply for London digs? But such a rupture of the given form could only mean for James a rupture of the possible meaning as well. For him the two were not divisible but closely dependent on each other, and the incalculability of life was an effect which in art should only be secured inside a strict adherence to form. He could not have admitted a dangling ending, in which one of the threads was led off at a tangent instead of being tucked into the complete pattern. The coda of *Anna Karenina*, for instance, with its pathos of confusion and anti-climax, would no doubt have struck him as being such an ending. Vronsky, off to the wars and broken-hearted about Anna's death as he is, is more immediately plagued by—of all things—raging toothache, and his disgust and weariness with his mother's conversation; while in another carriage we are suddenly introduced to three volunteers and given a penetrating sketch of the reasons which induce people to join in such movements. All seems random and disconnected, and we see why James described the novels of Tolstoy in such elliptical phrases as 'a wonderful mass of life', 'a kind of splendid accident', and 'a reflector as vast as a natural lake'.

But if we look more closely at this 'naturalness' we realize how carefully and consciously it is in fact settled and exhibited. The sudden animation of the war and the Balkan political problem contrasts with the previous dominance of the private problem and gives us a new perspective upon it. Vronsky is seen as one of a number of men who have all some reason for wanting to escape from their former lives; and the railway station and coaches which were once the scene of their falling in love and of Anna's suicide, now not only remind Vronsky of these things but also reassume their rôle as a centre of public and impersonal unrest and activity. This impersonality is conveyed to us, too, in the talk of Vronsky's mother, who speaks of Vronsky's reaction to Anna's death, and her hard conventional tones show us from the outside what had been so inward and agonizing before.

All moves so naturally that it seems indeed to have happened of itself, but can James, with all his understanding of the novelist's task, really have thought so? One cannot help feeling him to be a little disingenuous in his attitude to the 'naturalness' of Tolstoy, as if the whole issue upset him and he did not want to look it squarely in the eye. And yet there was surely no need to be disingenuous (if James was really being so) for clearly what is absent in Tolstoy here is not *art* but *form*, as James understood it, the shape and convention, the deliberate external bonds to which James felt that the true fictional craftsman must submit himself. And, as Chekhov might have put it in his sensible way on this issue, as he did on that of art *versus* science—'we are treating here of assets only'. It is just that James does not do for us what Tolstoy can, and *vice versa*. Tolstoy's conception of art makes no allowance for the kinds of illumination which cannot be disassociated from form, the kinds of meaning which reveal themselves to us in the artifice of poetic drama or in the highly formalized entries and dialogues of *The Golden Bowl*. A meaningful scene in *Anna*, like the mushroom gathering and the proposal that was never made, gains nothing from the idea of form, whereas the scenes at Fawns between Maggie and her father and between Maggie and Charlotte gain everything. And there is nothing ambiguous about the mushroom scene: though it depends upon the silent and the unspoken, its clarity and its power to move and to amuse us are definite and complete. But in James's novel it is the form that actually permits, and as it were controls, the incalculability and 'the relation between a given appearance and a taken meaning'.

In the dialogue at Fawns between Maggie and her father we are held by the riddle of dramatic possibility. Is Maggie being gently snubbed by her father and acquiescing gladly in the reminder that he and his wife have their own understanding and their own intimacy; or are father and daughter conspiring together against Charlotte, wordlessly but with perfect understanding? And when Charlotte in her turn, 'finding and following her way', magnificently attacks Maggie for interfering with her father and stepmother's relations, to what extent does she really believe this and find in the intoxication of the initiative a new point in loving Verver and a new mode for doing so? It is their dramatic form that saves these problems from running away in those sands of mere speculative ingenuity in which *The Sacred Fount*, for example, dries up: and the reconciliation of this form with such an abundance of data and such a copiousness of meaning is the measure of *The Golden Bowl's* success and its status as a masterpiece. Through the most artificial of forms James succeeds in presenting to us, not only the extraordinary complications of human motive and appearance, but their fundamental unknowability, a mystery in which reside both the principle of art and the principle of love. The statement and *credo* with which the Colonel echoes the cry of his wife's baffled penetration might be taken as the book's epigraph. ' "We know nothing on earth!" It was the soldier's watchword at night.'

CHAPTER FIVE

EPILOGUE:

Character and Nature

Epilogue:

CHARACTER AND NATURE

THESE THREE studies have brought us no nearer to a conception of the ideal masterpiece about love. It was not to be expected that they should, and in fact it would have been a disaster if they had. For my whole argument is that no such conception is possible. Love is not a theme that can be penetratingly explored, compassionately revealed, and so forth. It cannot be revealed at all: it can only be embodied. The author cannot show us what love is like, but his characters—and only his characters, not his insight, his sensitivity, his powers of analysis or his deployment of symbols—can create it for us in the reality of their separate and unique existence. Love is the condition of personality, and *vice versa*.

To reiterate this may look like critical complacency, and it is true that the whole direction of this book may seem to be towards a rather futile kind of literary primitivism, a nostalgia for the past and for the ideal classical epoch when the author, like Moses, laid down without self-consciousness the great outlines of humanity which his audience received with joy and accepted as experience. I do indeed feel such a nostalgia, but I also think it a sentiment that can be usefully employed when we are considering the present and the future. We cannot put the clock back or attempt a

classical revival or a return to 'traditional values' that is anything but hopelessly artificial, and in fact exacerbates by its
very self-consciousness the kind of attitudes that are called in
question. The classicism invoked by T. E. Hulme and T. S.
Eliot shows this all too clearly. Yet by asserting an extremely
simple point—the supremacy of personality in the greatest
literature—we are touching what might be the principle of
continuity. 'We know that the individual is unique', says
Sartre, 'but how can we say so?' A sense of where the personal
in art is to be found might help us to take it for granted.

There are plenty of reasons for our lack of confidence in
personality and our lack of respect for it. Our awareness of
Freudian psychology is an obvious one, our awareness of
history is another. We are preoccupied with the exploration
and understanding of the individual consciousness, and with
the need to seize upon and identify the meaning of 'our
time,' as it passes: author, ideologue, and critic join hands to
egg each other on in the struggle for insights. Since the
Romantic movement the history of literature has become
the history of ideas; as Marx foresaw, our awareness of ourselves has become an awareness of change, above all of
political change. We are perpetually anxious about what we
are becoming. We have a passion for understanding what is
happening to us, or at least for coining myths and terminolo-
gies which seem to present to ourselves a picture of what is
happening. This is reflected to-day in the popularity of
works which range about the field of recent literature, describing and contrasting the worlds of Dostoevsky, Sartre,
Melville, Faulkner, and so forth. However different their
outlook these writers are important because of their insights,
because they create a way of looking at ourselves and catching at our uncertain and disappearing historical being.

This kind of critical preoccupation is not an immediately

contemporary growth of course. Years before the war Mr
E. M. Forster wrote an essay on Conrad in which he commented with some perturbation on the 'mist' at the middle
of Conrad's work, the central opacity. What else, one might
wonder, did he expect to find? Even in the hands of so
humane and appreciative a critic the instrument of appraisal
seems to have undergone a curious distortion, so that it is no
longer capable of examining the ground but only of penetrating the surface. And yet it is surely obvious that the
greatness of Conrad reposes very simply upon the person
and the fact? He has no myth with a view to insight: he has
scenes and he has people. And these are only revelatory
because they are what they are. In Conrad s greatest work—
the first part of *Lord Jim, The Shadow Line, The Secret Sharer,
Typhoon*—things and people have this simple but impenetrable reality. Ransome in *The Shadow Line* with his weak
heart; the bottle of quinine that has been filled with sand;
Captain MacWhirr and his barometer; the great flake of rust
that springs off the bulkhead of the pilgrim ship and persuades Lord Jim that she is sinking—these things have an
existence which is not to be got behind. A criticism which
looks *through* them, or which turns them into myth and
symbol, is denaturing Conrad's reality in the interest of its
own self-consciousness. Conrad is a particularly good illustration of the dangers of 'deep' criticism because he is such
a queerly portentous writer whose large intentions and
resounding irony are the least satisfactory side of him. When
he is great, it is because his characters and events are universally memorable: when he fails (as in *Victory*) it is because
they are shadowy and pseudo-meaningful. In this he is the
exact opposite of most modern novelists, whose meanings
are usually more real than their characters.

This may look like a nostalgic preference for the kind of

criticism that is content to repose lovingly upon the scene and the character. But why not? To recognize that the personality *is* the meaning may be the right approach to a novelist like Conrad. E. M. Forster's comments on him tell us a good deal about the ethos of the critic but they do not illuminate the author. Not that this matters—criticism of a modern writer may be most helpful when it suggests how he differs from the particular kind of modernity which the critic represents—but its danger lies in creating a language for reflecting on a work of the imagination which is fundamentally different from the language of the work itself. This is very noticeable in modern Shakespearean criticism. Hazlitt, for example, whatever his shortcomings as a critic, strikes us as writing about Shakespeare in the same language in which Shakespeare himself wrote about life. But when we read that the love between Lear and Cordelia is 'the condition of intellectual clarity, the energizing centre from which personality may grow unhampered by the need for self-assertion or evasive subterfuge ... the sole ground of a genuinely self-affirming life and energy'[1]—we cannot easily translate the comment into the language of the characters and the play. We do not necessarily dissent, for the comment may be a discerning one, but it is a discernment that has lost itself far below the surface of Shakespearean actuality.

Such criticism is well adapted to a discussion of the writers I referred to above, writers whose subject is 'the Human Condition'. But the greatest English literature is not about the Human Condition. We might say that it is about 'Nature', a term which has no equivalent in the Franco-American critical vocabulary which is current to-day. It is certainly a sufficiently vague term, but it has the merit of going back into the past and of doing no historical violence to the work

[1] L. C. Knights. *Some Shakespearean Themes.* (p. 118.)

which it might be used to describe. It implies, above all, an absence of purpose, of insistence, and of individual insight; the portrayal of 'Nature' suggests an almost involuntary fidelity to what is constant in human types and human affairs; to the repetition of birth and death, joy and sorrow; to the humours of men and women and the peculiarities that are at once recognized as universal. It implies a lack of pretension—the author gets no particular credit for his awareness of Nature though he may get credit for portraying it well. The Human Condition, on the other hand, implies a personal sense of where life is significant, of where humanity suffers especially or feels intensively; of unusual violence and unusual modes of feeling; of interesting development or of illuminating decay. The subject matter may even be the same, but those who write about Nature take it for granted, while those who write about the Human Condition take an attitude towards it.

The distinction I am proposing here is obviously a real one, though it is equally obviously artificial. All writers accept some things and take an attitude towards some things. Shakespeare, who accepts so much, has an obvious *attitude* towards, say, misused authority. Moreover there is of course a sense in which every epoch produces writers of every kind, the writer of ideas, and the creator of an obsessional world, as well as the recorder of characters and scenes: Langland is a contemporary of Chaucer, and the Elizabethan age had its Marlowe and its Bacon as well as its Shakespeare. We know that 'human nature' is not a constant factor, and we suspect that periods of intellectual and emotional stability are phantoms that vanish further back into history whenever we give them a nostalgic glance. None the less, there is something in the elusive idea of 'Nature' which is worth trying to analyse for the light that it may throw on the creation and the characters of a literature which has ceased to find point in the term.

We might begin by observing that there is no Nature in American literature. How could there be?—when America became a nation the word was already beginning to lose its force and authority. The processes of living which give their substance to the literary idea of Nature of course existed in America as much as anywhere else, but they were not available to the emergent American writer. Indeed, the complex kinds of traditional authority that Nature implies were specifically disowned by the American idea and left out of the American dream. For America, Nature had to become the Human Condition.

Not at all unjustly, the new civilization distrusted taking anything for granted, particularly the assumptions about hierarchy which are clearly implied in the 18th century view of Nature. But in fact Nature was connected not so much with the hierarchy of class (though that comes into it), as with the hierarchy of the feelings and responses. He who portrays Nature must have a sense of proportion and a sense of what is important, for only in a scale of proportions can things be taken for granted. In the scale, public custom and process is more important than personal habit and the world of the individual, the family more important than sex, average tranquillity more important than exceptional violence. Nature offers no 'subject' to the writer: indeed we might say that it is only fully present to those who are not interested in writing about it. The novel whose world is exceptional because it is the individual's world is not the vehicle of Nature, and it is this kind of novel which has become the dominant American literary form. To write such a novel is part of the American dream, and the idea of the American novel has conquered Europe.

Of course we need not regret this. The American achievement is not only great in itself, it also carries a greatness of
inspiration. Who would not put out in the same boat with
Melville and Hawthorne, dissimilar geniuses certainly, but
alike in that each of their worlds contains no natural social
and spiritual proportions but only the solitary conscience
and the solitary query? If we examined the American novel
by the light of the old European idea of Nature we should
have to give first place to *Little Women*. And yet it remains
true that the deepest source of Henry James's success is his
rediscovery of the European sense of Nature. In his masterpiece, *The Golden Bowl*, he contrives to take the idea of
Nature most for granted; and his characters, led by Maggie
with her position as wife and mother, draw their solid presence from it. 'Contrives' is of course the word, because
James feels his way into the English tradition of Nature from
the outside and illumines it with the full power of his alien intelligence. Although all the protagonists are foreign he makes
it a very English book: yet there is irony in the fact that the
anglicization of Charlotte, that intensely American character, is accomplished by two other Americans, and that
though poor Charlotte is anglicized in spirit—deprived of
her status in knowledge with the Prince and compelled
instead to accept the traditional status of being 'a genial wife
and more'—she is sent back to America in the flesh.

In his biography of Hawthorne, James comments on the
absence in America of all the institutions from which the
novel might be expected to draw its powers, and observes
that without them there was no evidence that Hawthorne
felt himself 'in any variety or intimacy of relations with anyone or with anything'. Hawthorne was thus compelled to
'*import*' a sense of sin into his creative consciousness, as being
the only tradition in his surroundings which it could with

any confidence work upon. What strikes us most about James's feeling sketch of the emptiness of the American scene is that it is no longer true—a mass of institutions, atmospheres, and social complexities have sprung up to fill the gap—but that the American novelist still feels bound to behave as if it were true. Faulkner, Hemingway, FitzGerald, O'Hara, Carson McCullers, etc, all *import* the needful requirement which will fill their literary consciousness: they have no confidence in Nature manifesting itself in their surroundings. And James's curiously expressive word retains its force if we apply it to the contemporary English novel: here too the notion of the author importing his imaginative requirement—existentialism, anger, violence, etc.—seems a remarkably apt one. He can only express himself in terms of something borrowed from outside, which does not well up naturally from his surroundings.

It is obvious that persons, characters, are not among the literary cargo which might be successfully imported. The American novelists mentioned all have an intensely stylized or formalized view of their characters; they seem beset by a perpetual and painful anxiety about them, an anxiety to prove that they are *real*. This lack of confidence in the reality of other people is woven into the whole texture of relationship, the continual harping on friendship, comradeship, sexual possibility, toughness and weakness. It would be possible to write a lengthy study on the theme in the modern novel of Anxiety about the Friend. All the natural relationships—parents, wives, children—are subordinated to, or seen in terms of, this devouring uncertainty. Can pals exist? The relation of the American hero to other persons is querulous, phantasmagorical. Again we might recall James's haunting words: 'there is no evidence of the writer finding himself in any variety or intimacy of relations with anyone or with anything'.

And there is no doubt that James was aware in himself of the same lack. England, one cannot help feeling, presented him for the first time with the intoxicating possibility of taking people for granted, the rapture of contemplating real, solid, and indifferent existences. Hawthorne, with all his imaginative bias towards a society he could feel at home in and could describe from the inside, had been compelled by the American solitude to conceive human nature more darkly and more romantically than came naturally to him. 'I should even say,' James observes penetratingly of his fellow-country-man 'that at bottom he does not take human nature as hard as he may seem to do.' James himself had to learn, from prolonged sojourn in England, to take human nature as it came, and he succeeded so well that his critics have been debating ever since just how he did take it. But of how many other novelists since Hawthorne—English or American—could it be said in implied compliment that they do not take human nature as hard as they seem to do? We should have to hope, on the contrary, that their anxiety about human nature, their compassion for it, their attitudes towards it, are in fact as real as they may appear to be.

Taking other people's reality for granted is, as I have persistently implied, the first requirement of love. And it is also the first requirement of character creation. The great strength of the idea of Nature, as it declares itself in the English literary tradition, is that it both assumes and makes possible the fulfilment of this requirement. I may seem now to be adding chauvinism to a general tendency to intellectual reaction; I may seem to be suggesting that English writers traditionally love their characters, as the English are said to love their dogs, more than the writers of other nations. And I believe that in practice this may well be so. But apart from this last doubtful assertion, it could be objected that I have not yet given a coherent account of what Nature actually *is*, and of the contexts in which the term has been and might again be used. To give it such a meaning we must first take a quick look back at our literary history.

When Dryden was praised for 'returning to Nature', it was understood that after the extravagance and idiosyncrasy of the Metaphysicals he wrote poetry that was sensible, general, and well-proportioned, that was above all not odd. He was the opposite of the poet 'who wished only to say what he hoped had not been said before'. In one sense this implied a complacent and rather defeatist kind of primitivism: the most universal and the most authoritative display of Nature is to be found in the Classics; Nature and Homer are the same, and 'to follow Nature is to follow him'. The sense in which Dryden and Dr Johnson use the term is concerned much more with life, in its shared and universal aspects of joy and sorrow, laughter and tears, etc., than with literary tradition. None the less the idea of a golden age is there, the moment, as Taine was later to formulate it, when genius combined with race and *milieu* to form the perfect masterpiece. For all their official homage to the Classics, Dryden and Dr Johnson both imply that Shakespeare has already done this for the English nation, much as we might now assume that Pushkin and Tolstoy have done it for the Russian. Can such a coincidence occur more than once in the life of a culture? Dryden hints that it cannot, and that the *Epigoni* must accept their less fortunate horoscope with modesty and equanimity. 'All the images of Nature were still present to him,' he says of Shakespeare, 'and he drew them not laboriously but luckily.' *Still* is here the operative word. By being there at the right moment Shakespeare caught Nature as effortlessly as one might catch a train. And

Dryden hints that he himself has the harder task of assembling the images of Nature by artificial means.

No doubt writers at every period have thought that things were easier for their predecessors, and Johnson sensibly abolishes the unreal antithesis which is created by Dryden's wistfulness about the past by pointing out that 'what is commonly called Nature by the critics cannot be properly opposed to *art*; Nature being, in this sense, only the best effect of *art*'. Yet these Humpty-Dumpty confusions weaken the currency of the term, and it is almost destroyed when the Romantics substitute for agreed authority the authority of the individual vision—the world as revealed by the writer's own peculiar insight—while continuing to speak of Nature as the world revealed. Wordsworth would have agreed with Johnson that 'nothing can please many and please long but just representations of general nature', and they would have agreed, as Wordsworth says in his Preface to the *Lyrical Ballads*, that the poet is concerned 'with the revolutions of the seasons, with cold and heat, with loss of friends and kindred, with injuries and resentments, gratitude and hope, with fear and sorrow'. Johnson's poem on Dr Levitt and Wordsworth's on Simon Lee start from the same premises, and Johnson would have considered the Old Cumberland Beggar a worthy piece of Nature to be justly represented.

But there the resemblance ends, for Wordsworth's vision of the Beggar is, of course, entirely and marvellously his own; so far from being 'what oft was thought but ne'er so well expressed' it gives us an entirely 'novel'—as Johnson would say—idea of age. Wordsworth is fascinated by the old man's continuity with his surroundings and with the absence in him of a reflecting being joined to an experiencing being. Wordsworth perceives (indeed creates) the old man as a mode of giving reality to his own preoccupation with consciousness, much as Camus, say, creates his *Etranger*. Though Wordsworth agrees with Johnson about the things which should move us all, and to which all our bosoms should return an echo, he sees them in a wholly personal way in which we have to learn to share. Wordsworth is in the typically romantic situation of claiming to represent what is universal, but in fact of exploring it in a highly idiosyncratic way.

The history of the term, then, brings us back to a point made in the first chapter, when I suggested that Tolstoy gives us life, and that Proust gives us a vision of it. Proust makes us see life in his own way, and for him it is controlled by two fundamental laws—the purely relative existence of personality, and the unbridgeable gulf between one kind of outlook and another. The moral laws which he goes on to lay down are therefore only authoritative if we accept the convention that Proust himself is not subject to the first two fundamental laws. And in practice we do accept the convention, because only by doing so can we accept what Proust has to tell us. But Nature in Proust, we might say, is fatally at war with outlook and method. In Tolstoy there is no such division, because his authority is not called in question by his method. He takes human reality and solidarity for granted: he knows himself a part of Nature. He appeals to us with something of the family ease of the 18th century, assuming a lot of common ground. Nature was then a kind of tacit agreement, 'the very bank and capital', in Burke's phrase, of civic reason; and a trifling instance of this unanimity would be Hume's point that all men agree to tread on the pavement instead of upon their fellows' toes. Does such an agreement still exist? In life obviously it does: for purposes of daily convenience we still agree not to tread on each others' toes, but is there any comparable agreement in

the world of the writer? Do we and Proust tacitly agree that
toe-treading is wrong? On the contrary, it is an article of
faith to-day that nothing shall be taken for granted between
reader and author; we must submit ourselves to the purity
of his insight and accept or reject it in the isolation of our
own responses. Tolstoy needs to *persuade* us of very little,
but we have to place upon Proust the burden of each separate and individual proof.

Painting will supply us with the concrete example that is
perhaps needed at this point. Although in a Nativity or an
Annunciation there may be any amount of variety of presentation, the variations will be of art and not of attitude. The
painter assumes the invariability of our response and need
supply no suggestions of his own: the differences between a
Tintoretto and a Crivelli Annunciation are fascinating,
but they do not reveal two different views of the subject.
How should they? Yet the modern artist attempting an
Annunciation is compelled to take a view of some sort: his
audience expect it, and he owes it to his own unavoidable
status as a man of insights. He paints a picture, say, of a girl
in an apron at the sink, with a packet of detergent beside her,
every line of which proclaims: 'you see, she was really just
an ordinary girl'. But an ordinary girl was exactly what she
was not: she was the Virgin, and in terms of Nature there is
no more to be said about her.

In *The Voices of Silence*, André Malraux remarks that every
work of art must undergo a continuous transmutation and
have a different meaning for every age. In practice this is no
doubt often the case, but as a principle it makes every painting answerable only to the contemporary viewpoint: it
ignores the possibility of our admitting—or educating ourselves into admitting—the personality of a picture, its unchanging selfhood. My idea of the Virgin and my feelings

about her may be very different from those of Tintoretto
or Crivelli, but what matters is my acknowledgement of the
Virgin *as she is*—as she exists in art and in the whole weight
of a common response. I may say: 'how charming! The
Virgin looks as if the angel had just asked her to a cocktail
party', but this *aperçu* only gives me pleasure because I know
it to be irrelevant to the plain nature of the event. What I am
asserting is not my ability to transform the picture's meaning
by my own perceptions, but the right to make my own
comment in face of the picture's given reality. It would give
me no pleasure at all if I felt that my comment *was* relevant
to the artist's view of his subject, and that the artist and I
were collaborating in a common enterprise and a common
search for a viewpoint. But I know the picture has a reality
outside my own comment on it, and I know that the artist,
like myself, took that reality for granted.

In fiction the complete character of Nature would be one
whose reality is fully assumed by author and reader, the
character who is so evidently and commonly accepted and
explicable that he can be made nothing of. Such characters
are obviously rare, and possibly dull or trivial. As I suggested
in the *Othello* chapter, fiction has become above all a mode of
insight, and from the point of view of the novelist, and the
penetration into appearances which usually makes his world,
the completely given character cannot help being a dull character. Nature is hardly a promising field for the novelist, and it
is significant that its decline as a critical term should coincide
with the rise of the novel. *Ulysses* is a moving and impressive
example of what might be called 'pseudo-nature' in the
novel—moving because Bloom and Molly are such heroic
attempts at projecting the absolute nature of mere existence.
But existence here is not the same as Nature, because it is
existence as an elaborate extension of Joyce's own mind. 'I

feel that my work is more real than reality itself,' he once said. Could Shakespeare possibly have said such a thing? Joyce's view of reality is like Mallarmé's 'toute au monde existe pour aboutir à un livre'. But the sense of proportion that produces the effect of Nature takes it for granted that the world is a great deal more real and more important than the author's work. There is a close connection between Shakespeare as the supreme 'poet of nature', and the astonishing but seldom sufficiently emphasized fact that he did not—in the Joycean sense—appear to care about his work. His indifference to the reality of his achievement is a vital part of its total reality for us: the existence for us of Falstaff and Othello as a part of Nature is a consequence of their lack of a personal and peculiar reality for Shakespeare himself.

The natural character, we might say, is the character in whom his creator need not bother to believe. Trollope's and Thackeray's refusal to take their characters seriously, which so much annoyed Henry James, has a kind of degraded kinship with Shakespeare's magnificent lack of this kind of seriousness. Becky Sharp and Mr Harding are no doubt manipulated by their creators, but they are manipulated not in the interests of vision and purpose but in the frivolous assumption that the end of a novel should be a feast of sugar-plums. They steer a course between the aesthetic seriousness of Joyce, with his credo that the artist's work is the only thing that is real to him, and the ideological seriousness of Sartre and the moderns, whose sense of external realities is indeed pressing—so pressing that their sense of the individual nature of human beings is subordinated to it. By their very lack of artistic or moral seriousness the two Victorian novelists provide one answer to Sartre's query: 'how can we say that the individual is unique?' For them the problem does not exist.

'I've known a lot of Beckys, or 'I once met an Iago', or, 'He's a bit of a Micawber'—such comments give a good indication of the character drawn from Nature. When the dying Balzac asked for Dr Bianchon, one of his own characters, he was putting himself as he slipped out of life in the position of one of his own readers. We might think it shows that Balzac, like Joyce, imagined that only his own world was real, but the difference is that Balzac was dying, his hold on the real world was loosened, and his sense of his creations had ceased to be his own. However much they may reflect their creators' romantic megalomania, we still feel that the great characters of both Balzac and Dickens are a part of Nature, because they embody not so much a personal world as their authors' robust zest for life in the real one. Vautrin and Pickwick are not 'more real than reality itself' for their creators, but they are a way of increasing their capacity to live; Dickens became more and more obsessed with the life of acting and reciting which his characters could, so to speak, most completely share with him. But for all its display of Nature the world of Dickens or of Balzac is ultimately an encapsulated world. As I suggested in Chapter One, the enclave in which most authors are confined by their personal vision does not and cannot *admit* itself to be such— it must maintain the appearance of being *the* real world. Only Shakespeare and Tolstoy, perhaps, can make us feel that 'there is a world elsewhere'; a feeling which, from the sense of space and freedom it gives us, adds to the effect of the particular fiction they are putting before us instead of subtracting from it.

The increasing complexity and self-consciousness of society tends to shrink each separate writer's enclave, the world in which he has authority and vision. The mutual incomprehension and contempt which Proust noted between Baudelaire and Merimée and their following has become the rule, and Proust's Law—as we might call it— applies to-day with greater force than ever. But the natural characters, the Iagos, Beckys, or Micawbers, are both universally recognizable as types and yet completely unique as individuals. It is on this paradox that the characters of Nature —and Shakespeare's characters above all—are solidly founded. Yet the critic's distrust of judging in terms of 'character' to-day arises from the total absence of agreement about what people are really like and how they can be portrayed. There are no minimal requirements for character drawing, and the close connection between the type and the individual, between Nature and selfhood, is no longer taken for granted. (We can see this connection in characters like Conrad's Captain MacWhirr and Captain Whalley, and in Kipling's chief engineers.)

Instead, there remains in most modern novels the much deeper and uneasier distinction between the Aristotelian or functional idea of character, and the idea of 'character for its own sake'. In the *Poetics*, character appears to be understood as a moral quantity, and its appropriateness limited to the scope of dramatic form or moral function —to-day it might be a symbolic function. The actual quiddity of an individual is irrelevant for Aristotle's purpose, whereas to 19th century sensibility it was all-important. Blake gives the original romantic view when he mocks Aristotle and maintains that goodness and badness have nothing to do with character. Shakespeare has it both ways: his persons exist both in themselves and as parts of a natural structure, either more or less: Aristotle would have understood Macbeth but would have been baffled by Falstaff and Othello. Nineteenth century sensibility, following Morgann's essay, might defend Falstaff from the charge of cowardice, his appropriate Aristotelian quality in the play, by pointing out what is certainly true—that he is too much of a *person* to appear to us simply as a coward. More-over, such a person cannot be wholly contained by a play—the play is rather an episode in his individuality.

The natural consequence of this revelling in character for its own sake is not drama, but the dramatic monologue as it is given us by Dickens and Balzac, and in poetry by Browning. Their attitude to character is like that of an animal trainer, who puts the beasts through their most characteristic paces. The romantic hankering after drama, which in the poets of the 19th century became almost obsessional, could only work through the detached and 'interesting' personality, since the moral order which made such a character nugatory, except in so far as he conformed or failed to conform with it, had lost all general authority. The persons of the dramatic monologue are beyond good and evil, and like all good romantics they are completely solitary, explaining them-selves only to themselves—indeed the most piquant aspect of the monologue is the way in which the speaker reveals him-self to us without caring that he does so or without even being aware of it.

Such a full-blooded pursuit of personality does of course insist too much. It is a possessive kind of love, and it separ-ates the relished individual from the social and moral back-ground of the old order of Nature. It can end up by produc-ing nothing but Long John Silvers. But this relish for a 'char-acter' is preferable to a conscientious affection for certain classes of person in the pursuit of a theory of what should interest and move us. George Eliot's account of the Poyser family in *Adam Bede* is a perfect example of a slightly bogus portrait from Nature. Like Wordsworth, George Eliot assures us with such earnestness that simple and entirely ordi-

nary people are worthy of our deepest attachment that she
begins to sound rather like the Victorian song.

> *I love it! I love it! Let nobody dare*
> *To chide me for loving my grandmother's chair.*

Certainly Mrs Poyser achieved universal appeal—she was
quoted in parliamentary debates—in a generation of readers
hungry for a more balanced and humane view of the simple
character that Dickens had given them: to the serious and
socially-minded reader the Poysers are much more satisfying
than the Peggottys. But for Mrs Poyser's conversation
George Eliot is surely remembering the books rather than
the farmers of her childhood: she invests her with an aura of
Chaucer and Shakespeare—a comparison with Dairyman
Crick of *Tess* shows how the Poysers' vitality is grounded in
literature rather than in life.

This would not necessarily matter, but George Eliot
makes it matter by insisting so much on their humble
actuality. I am not complaining of any lack of realism
in the Poysers—far from it. Nature and realism have little
in common, for realism ignores the individual's, or the
tribe's, sense of itself. An account of our daily lives,
however remorselessly realistic, will seem as unfamiliar
to us as our voices do on a tape recording. An account of a
miner's life which strikes us as wonderfully 'realistic' in a
documentary book or film will seem totally unreal to the
miners themselves, however much they recognize its accuracy. And it is an irritating kind of falsification, for realism is
often a peculiarly arrogant kind of romanticism, creating and
hugging to itself a dead accurate image of our external selves,
and then saying: 'this is your life'. The sailors of Nelson's day,
ruthlessly conscripted and subject to every kind of tyranny

and abuse, used to listen (so we are reliably informed) with complacent approbation to the words of the patriotic song:

> To Honour we call you, not press you like slaves,
> For who are so free as the sons of the waves?

Honour, freedom—what a gulf of irony between those words and the facts of their lives! And yet—so strangely perverse are human responses and so interrelated with atmosphere and art—they felt the words were truer than the facts. They were pleased to be thought of like that, and pleased to hear themselves described in these words—words possibly as true to the nature of the inner man as an account of squalor and brutality would be to the facts of his outward condition. The concept of Nature assumes and balances the claims of these inner and outer selves; recognizing the interpenetration of consciousness and external appearance of "realism" and the subjective feelings.

The trouble with the Poysers is that George Eliot is thrusting a kind of Chaucerian or Shakespearean 'innerness' upon them. But, granted that her handling of character is dominated by her outlook and theories, this is far better than trying to create them in terms of external reality. An attributed richness of consciousness is preferable to an imprisoning load of observation—all udders, apple-pies and earth-closets. And in her display of the Poysers she has achieved the most vital and characteristic effect of Nature in art—joyfulness.

The word may arouse distrust. Nature, it may be felt, has all along been a cover-up for every kind of sentimentalism: happy endings, silver linings, cheerful peasants and bourgeois complacency of the 'full-many-a-flower-is-born-to-blush-unseen', kind—here is the final proof of it. On the contrary, the joy which accompanies the great presentation of Nature has got nothing to do with the external circumstances described, still less with the attitude of the author towards them—I have already suggested that the wholly successful portrait from Nature does not, so far as such a thing is possible, take any attitude. The joy in Nature is a logical consequence of love, the logical consequence of the artist's feeling for the freedom of his creation: and joy is the follower and companion of freedom.

So also perhaps is humour, or at least an absence of seriousness and self-importance, and it is this lightness of touch which is lacking in the Poysers. As hard to pin down as Nature itself, lightness of touch is an essential part of it, and it is equally a quality which the critical spirit to-day does not know quite what to make of. We are apt to esteem only the kind of humour which can be taken seriously. 'A's bizarre insight', 'B's nightmare sense of fun', 'C's preoccupation with the grotesque'—these are our terms of praise for modern comedy which is certainly not remarkable for lightness of touch or lack of self-importance. But when is Shakespeare heavy? Of all modern authors, the closest to Shakespeare is certainly James Joyce, but for all its marvellous and intricate power to move us *Ulysses* is leaden with its own art, sunk in its richness like a great plum-cake. The lordship of language that makes Shakespeare's world so spacious turns Joyce's into a prison. Absurd as it may sound, we can find more of the Shakespearean buoyancy in P. G. Wodehouse, the same lightheartedness in the exercise of the muscles, joy that makes for a sense of life far greater than that of more preoccupied humorists.

And in Wodehouse as in Shakespeare we feel that the source of lightness and joy is ultimately, and quite simply, the virtue of the writer. It is curious how much we have come to take for granted to-day the opposite intimation in the novelist: we feel that his personal badness, his suppurating wound, is identified not only with his power and insight but with his need to take his art seriously, more seriously than he takes anything else. Our communion with the usual novelist is essentially a communion of earnestness and of badness, of responding to these in him and in ourselves. But Nature always has the proportions of goodness, and our communion with Nature in Shakespeare, Hardy, or Scott, is bound up with the recognition that they themselves are good.

An aspect of goodness here is a certain relation—by no means a simple one—to stability. In the first chapter I quoted Ezra Pound's view of writers as 'the antennae of the race', and what is true of the writer is also true of his characters—they are seen as always on the move. The modern idea of personality is of a state of flux, in which new attitudes are forming, and which continually requires new methods of presentation. The lack of interest which modern criticism shows in Scott's characters is presumably because they are static; they offer no significance, no moral or symbolic followthrough. Indeed to the modern sensibility they seem in some curious way *complacent*. It offends our susceptibilities that a farmer or servant should be portrayed not as an emergent or potential being but as a given one, especially when the artist is seeing them from an equally fixed viewpoint. Yet we admire Wordsworth's portrait of the leech-gatherer—who in a striking image is seen as a part of Nature, immutable as a boulder on a hill-top—perhaps because he is absorbed and carried onwards in the living flow of Wordsworth's consciousness and our own. We can *do* something with the leech-gatherer. The Poysers, too, invested as they are with the anxious geniality of George Eliot's moral sense, are seen as becoming rather than as being.

But there is no doubt that the joy—as I shall persist

in calling it—which shines in a good Scott portrait, is the result of one fixed being apprehending another. Scott and his characters revolve in their orbits like the stars, never varying in their distance from one another; and it is an aspect of this distance, and not of his lack of knowledge of them, that he does not tell us everything about his characters. His reticence, like that of Conrad, is a kind of respect for individuality. Its implication is that we do not necessarily know someone better for knowing more about them. And it is curious that though Scott's portraits—the housekeeper in *Old Mortality* for example—have been thought complacent and patronizing, no such objection is raised to the way in which Proust gives us his portrait of the old servant Françoise. Proust compels the old lady to illustrate his view of how human beings behave. Her devotion, her tyranny, her cruelty and comicality—they are all completely convincing and yet at the same time they are not really hers: Proust has extracted them from her and made them his own. By contrast, we know without Scott telling us that his Mrs Wilson could exhibit the same kind of qualities, because she really exists, and the reality of her existence obviously includes them.

The 'outer effect', of which Scott is such a master, confers this freedom upon his characters, but it has its obvious limitations. Only the very greatest authors can liberate the inner life of their characters as completely as Scott does their outer selves, and this triumph occurs—as I have suggested—in the three masterpieces which we have been examining. The 'inner effect' alone has been widely and successfully used, but it is always liable to the same fatal drawback: that the writer, like some self-devouring pelican, is really feeding his audience on his own consciousness, not on that of his characters. This attribution of consciousness takes place even when author and character are as different as possible from one another. Compare Caliban with T. S. Eliot's Sweeney or Musil's Moosbrugger. Sweeney and Moosbrugger are no more like the elemental inarticulate sex-killers they are supposed to be than Hamlet is like Hercules. They represent their creator's understanding of what it feels like to be such a character—a very different thing. Caliban, on the other hand, exists solidly and horribly in all his external uncouthness. What is he like inside? We have only hints and glimpses. He wants to eat his dinner and to rape Miranda; he enjoys drinking and joking with Stephano and Trinculo; and he derives a piercing and pathetic delight from the music in the air of the island.

> *Sometimes a thousand twangling instruments*
> *Will hum about mine ears; and sometimes voices,*
> *That, if I then had waked after long sleep,*
> *Will make me sleep again ...*

But these glimpses are enough. Caliban exists for us inside and out, and there is no more to be said about him. There is no strange riddle of his existence, no dark and subterranean mystery which the author is travailing to bring to light. Having conceived him, Shakespeare simply accepts him, as he might accept the person standing beside him in the street.

I have already quoted Edmund Wilson's dictum: 'the real elements of any work of fiction are the elements of the author's personality'. The symbolist novel does indeed rest on such an assumption, for the symbolic character cannot be other than an extension of his author's explorations and beliefs. But we must distinguish here between those symbolic meanings which are conceived in the mind of the writer, and those which may later suggest themselves to the

reader. Hardy's Sergeant Troy is not in the first sense a symbolic character, even though in the famous scene of the
sword exercise he appears almost as embodying the danger
and fascination of male sexuality, for he had a human and
independent existence before he acquired a possible symbolic
rôle. The same could not be said of E. M. Forster's two ladies
—Mrs Wilcox of *Howard's End* and Mrs Moore of *A Passage
to India*—who are remarkable examples of a beautifully and
sympathetically observed outer effect and a wholly incongruous and unconvincing inner one. Forster takes two
elderly mothers, the idea of whose existence appeals to
him, and has endowed them with a quasi-mystical significance which is all his own. Outwardly they exist, but
inwardly they merely symbolize: they have no depth of
individuality. It is Forster's triumph they grace, and we
should never meet them outside the world of his consciousness, whereas we are continually meeting persons like his
Charles Wilcox and his Aziz, whom we do not see inside
of and who have no symbolic burden to bear.

Edmund Wilson's dictum is curiously paralleled by
Forster himself when in *Aspects of the Novel* he selects Scott
as prototype of the novelist who simply 'tells us a story' and
can do little else. That he should be so unaware of Scott as a
great creator of persons—one of the greatest since Shakespeare—is an indication of how completely the modern
novel has come to take for granted the symbolist premises.
The form of the novel has always made it potentially
solipsistic, and now it openly embraces solipsism as its necessity and its creed. The novelist admits that the only way he
can explore other people is by exploring himself, that consciousness begins and ends at home. And consciousness must,
ipso facto, be of absorbing interest. The commonest and most
dangerous assumption the modern novelist can make is that

his world—just because it *is* his world—must fascinate other readers.

I think we are already beginning to see a great revulsion in the reading public against the whole idea of the writer's consciousness. Memoirs, biographies, accounts of war and travel in which other people have a real existence, are coming more and more to the fore. It is a paradox of modern society that we do not understand each other because we are always trying to be *aware* of each other. The creative imagination seems no longer able to break down the barriers between us, barriers erected by an anxious awareness that constantly increases under the pressure of psychological and sociological theory. In becoming such an awareness imagination defeats itself and can no longer take Nature for granted. The novel importunes us with awareness of how suburban families live, or negroes, or intellectuals, or men in camps and prisons, or the young, or the very old. But do we really understand anything from this? Doesn't the distance which the novelist's awareness puts between him and his material rather increase our sense of unreality, merging us in consciousness only, not in comprehension? And an indication of our real lack of understanding is our passion for knowing the worst: our awareness is appeased if it feels that nothing is being withheld from it. But because it takes things for granted Nature can remain at a true distance from them, the kind of distance which dignifies art without any suggestion that it is escaping from its material, the distance which—as Camus observed—the Dutch masters put between their paintings and the 17th century scene.

In attempting to analyse the various ideas of character and the various ways in which it can be presented I have probably done little more than pile up an assemblage of confused and confusing half-truths. The subject is an immensely involved one. And my conclusions—such as they are—must remain embedded in the conception of personality, in the fullest sense, which I have tried to build up in the course of the book. This remains to a large extent a negative conception, because in this last chapter in particular I have had much more to say about how the literary personality is *not*, as it seems to me, created, than about how such a creation might be accomplished. We rightly distrust, not only any appeal that we should be born anew, but any suggestion that we should give up any part of the consciousness which we have been accumulating in literature so laboriously over so many centuries. Perhaps the idea of personality that I have been trying to describe has been left behind and will not be seen again: perhaps that would be no great cause for lamentation. But I cannot really believe it, for as long as human beings accept one another with love their artists will try to embody that love in the representation of men and women and of the external world. And when we look back on the living persons who have been created by the great artists of our language, from Chaucer to Henry James, it is surely desirable from time to time—instead of submitting them to the solvents of our local consciousness and our immediate preoccupations with value and meaning—to emphasize and salute them for what they are and to respond to them as they deserve.

INDEX